AN ORDERED LIFE

G. H. LANG

A photograph taken in the garden room at Wiedenest when he was at work
on the translation of *The Triumph of the Crucified*.

AN
ORDERED LIFE
An Autobiography

BY
G. H. LANG

Shoals, Indiana

An Ordered Life

PUBLISHED BY KINGSLEY PRESS
PO Box 973
Shoals, IN 47581
USA
Tel. (800) 971-7985
www.kingsleypress.com
E-mail: sales@kingsleypress.com

ISBN: 978-0-9719983-6-0

Printed in the United States of America

Contents

"I have thought that an autobiographical book, giving experiences of God's supervising grace, and of definite answers to prayer similar to the few experiences given in one and another of your previous works, might prove of very great help and blessing to others.

"George Müller, Hudson Taylor and the like were of a previous generation and might not have now the hold that the life stories once had for their contemporaries."

"I have just laid down your book on E. H. Broadbent, after having read it with appreciation and I hope profit.

"The reading of this book has once again aroused in me the hope that you will see your way to write something of an autobiographical nature.

"Christian biography can be so greatly used of God, as is very evident; and a report of the Lord's dealings with you, I feel sure, would prove an illustration of God's wonderful ways in making use of His servants and of teaching them."

"You have written the life of others and these have been very helpful. I believe your own would be even more helpful."

"You have whetted our appetite by extracts from your spiritual autobiography in various of your writings, and I believe it would be to the glory of God and the blessing of souls if you gave us a fuller account of the Lord's dealings with you."

G. H. Lang: A Tribute

By Douglas W. Brealey

Having known G. H. Lang for nearly sixty years I am glad to pay tribute to his memory; in doing so I desire only to "magnify the grace of God" in him.

First, I would say that over the years I have been increasingly conscious of his deep spirituality; he was one of those rare souls who really lived in heaven; he found himself truly to be "a stranger and a pilgrim on the earth". His "city home" was in heaven from which he saw himself to be sent to this world as an ambassador for Christ. He was completely devoid of any earthly nationalism—it mattered little to him where he was down here, except that he should be in the place of Christ's choosing for the moment; so from time to time he was found in many countries on the service of his Lord, now enduring the scorching heat of the Near East, now the freezing cold of the Carpathians; he was equally content to be posted by his Sovereign in some primitive village of "the pensive East", or in some great city of the West with all its modern amenities. Thus he roamed the world, Christ's "ambassador at large", beseeching sinners to be reconciled to God.

He was essentially a man of faith, never looking to man for the means of his subsistence, but only to his heavenly Father, and faith grew with its exercise. In this school, like his great predecessor, he learned in whatsoever state he was therein to be content; he learned the secret of how to run low and how to run over. And he was such a man of faith because he was such a man of prayer; his prayers were always unusual and as inspiring as they were unique; he spoke with an intimacy to his heavenly Father as one who knew God, but whose intimacy was the very soul of reverence.

I think I may truthfully say that he was the most apostolic man I have ever met; perhaps for that very reason he was a very controversial figure; a correspondent suggested to me that he was the most controversial figure in Brethren circles since J. N. Darby; yet it would be true to say that he himself was not a controversialist. A very close student of the Word, and an independent thinker, he was not prepared to take traditional interpretations unless he were personally convinced that they were right. Though he was completely convinced of the eternal security of the believer, many of his views on prophecy led him into avenues of thought and teaching where a number of us felt unable to follow. Unfortunately this closed doors to his otherwise extremely valuable ministry. Perhaps he was one of the greatest teachers of his time, and multitudes could testify to the great help they received from him, either from his public utterances or from his numerous writings.

To be in his presence was to realize that one was in the presence of a true saint of God whose holy life gave weight and authority to all he taught.

From our midst has gone "a prince and a great man"; he has been an ensample to the flock. If we cannot follow all he taught, we may well follow his faith, and like him, come to the Scriptures with an open mind and teachable heart, ever keeping before us that day, quickly coming, when differences of judgment will have disappeared for ever and when "we shall know even as we are known".

Publisher's Foreword

The reading of this autobiography twenty or more years ago made a profound impression on me, the effects of which I still feel today. Reading it again for this reprint has been refreshing and challenging. I hope you receive eternal benefit as you ponder its pages.

To me it's a great pity that the life and writings of G. H. Lang are so little known in our day. In my view, he deserves to be recognized as a spiritual successor to such giants in the faith as George Müller, Anthony Norris Groves and Robert Cleaver Chapman. That he is lesser known than these other great men is surely more an accident of history than any failure on his part to live and teach the same Biblical principles of absolute surrender to God and total dependence on Him for everything.

The life story unfolded in these pages is full of spiritual instruction. The author traces in precise detail the dealings of God with his soul, from the day of his conversion at the tender age of seven, through the twilight years when bodily infirmity restricted most of his former activities. You will be amazed, I think, as you read these pages, to see how quickly and continually a soul can grow in grace and in the knowledge of spiritual things if they will wholly follow the Lord.

Horace Bushnell once preached that every man's life is a plan of God, and that it's our duty as human beings to find and follow that plan. As Mr. Lang looks back over his long and varied life in the pages of this book, he frequently points out the many times God prepared him in the present for some future work or role.

The author traveled all over the world as a Bible teacher and preacher with no fixed means of support other than prayer and faith. Like George Müller before him, he told his needs to no one but God. Many times his faith was tried to the limit, as funds for the next part of his journey arrived only at the last minute and from unexpected sources.

Many of Lang's other writings are equally valuable (a number are available on our website: www.kingsleypress.com). His precise thinking made him an extremely astute Bible expositor. I highly prize his *Pictures and Parables*, which is usually the first (and sometimes *only*) place I look if needing help understanding a specific parable. Some of his teachings, particularly along prophetic lines, brought him into controversy; but this should not be allowed to detract from the immense value of his writings.

In this first Kingsley Press edition we have re-typeset the entire book, but otherwise it is little changed from the first edition published by Paternoster Press in 1959. British spelling, grammar and usage have been left untouched, for which we beg indulgence of our North American readers. The main benefit of re-typesetting is the ability to make the book available for the first time in eBook format (available at Amazon.com's Kindle Store and Apple's iBook-store). Anyone encountering typographical errors may report them to me at: editor@kingsleypress.com.

May God add His rich blessing to the republishing of this wonderful book.

Edward Cook
Kingsley Press
June, 2011

CHAPTER I

Ancestry

Heeding the call of Moses (Deut. 8:2.) I have sought to remember all the way that Jehovah my God has led me these twice forty years. The review causes me to exclaim with Addison:

When all Thy mercies, O my God,
My rising soul surveys,
Transported with the view I'm lost
In wonder, love, and praise.

And with him I recognize that:

Unnumbered comforts on my soul
Thy tender care bestowed,
Before my infant heart conceived
From whom those comforts flowed.

The only authentic information concerning my family in earlier times is that its original head was tenant of a particularly attractive property on a large and well-ordered estate and was especially favoured by the noble owner. But being discovered in alliance with an implacable enemy of his landlord, detected, in fact, as lawyers would say, *in flagrante delicto,* in the very act, he was summarily ejected, together with his wife, who, in truth, had led him open-eyed into such folly. He was thus reduced to the level of a common field labourer; and the ill effects of his ingratitude and misconduct have dogged the footsteps of each and all of his descendants unto this day. Their names were, of course, Adam and Eve.

Nor have I much to say of my immediate forbears. My revered father told me that two great-aunts of my mother, Amelia Helen Hayes, were joint-heirs with their brother of certain market gardens in what is now the Clapham area of south-west London. These lands, therefore, had become in my mother's time of no small value for good residential properties. But the brother had defrauded the sisters of their share. Their lawyer said he could easily be forced to surrender, but that in the process they would get him hanged, for he had forged a signature, for which crime, even so comparatively recently, the penalty was death. So the sisters preserved love and a good conscience, and the brother kept his ill-gotten gains and a bad conscience. Incidentally, my mother, who I understood would have inherited from the aunts, was not born with a silver spoon in her mouth, and therefore my sister and I had, as John Wesley said of his brother Charles, "a fair escape from being a rich man".

My mother's circumstances were humble. I have no information concerning her mother save that her maiden name was Martin. It was thought that her father was an army officer, but I know only that he was seriously afflicted with what I think must have been rheumatic arthritis. My elder sister and I have markedly gouty constitutions, which is *all* that we inherit from our maternal grandfather, though he told my father that some very wealthy property was in Chancery, for want of proof of the death of a certain person. So perhaps this was a second "fair escape".

There are good reasons for this ignorance. I never knew my mother, or I should know more regarding her people. Her sister's husband became an ardent spiritist, on which account my father wisely discontinued intercourse with the family, before I was old enough to be interested in them. They had gone to America before I was born. At least, he was in Chicago the Sunday before the great fire on October 8, 1871, for, as my father told me, he stated publicly from the pulpit that for the sins of the city some great calamity would shortly befall it. This is not the first time that God has constrained a lying prophet to declare a coming judgment (1 Kings 13). Satan has a limited power of foretelling. If, for example, he has been commissioned to execute a certain judgment, he can announce it in advance. But in general the predictions of his servants are unreliable and lure into danger.

My parents were both acquainted with the Lord Jesus Christ as Saviour before they were acquainted with each other. They first met at a religious gathering. I believe my father was on that occasion some distinct help in her spiritual life to the then unknown lady. On his side at least it seems to have been love at first sight, and a glance at her portrait will show the reasonableness of this. My mother was a particularly sweet woman. One of their closest friends and fellow-workers was William Bailey. I remember going with my father to see him many years after my mother's death. As we parted, the dear old man turned away with tears in his eyes, and, with a break in his voice, said, "He's just like his mother." Another friend, to whom my parents were a great help in his early Christian life, was Alfred Mace. His father was the celebrated prizefighter, Jem Mace, so that the youth needed special help from outside his family. After I left home at eighteen years of age, Mr. Mace and I did not meet for many years. His greeting, at the close of a public conference, was, "You're just like your mother." It was no ordinary beauty and tenderness of character that left so indelible an impression upon strong men.

I have copies made by her, written neatly in the pointed script of her day, of two hymns, the one expressive of joyous confidence in Christ, the other descriptive of His sufferings which made possible our joys. The former is the well-known hymn commencing:

> *My God, I am Thine,*
>   *What a comfort divine;*
> *What a blessing to know*
>   *That my Jesus is mine.*
> *In the heavenly Lamb*
>   *Thrice happy I am;*
> *And my heart it doth dance*
>   *At the sound of His name.*

The other is the much-used hymn

> *O Christ, what burdens bowed Thy head*
>   *Our load was laid on Thee;*
> *Thou stoodest in the sinner's stead*
>   *Bar'st all my ill for me:*
> *A victim led, Thy blood was shed;*
>   *Now there's no load for me.*

Her copy gives this stanza not usually printed:

> *A flame was kindled in God's ire—*
>   *O Christ, it burned on Thee.*
> *It was a hot, consuming fire,*
>   *E'en in the fair green tree;*
> *There did that fire feed and expire:*
>   *Now it is quenched for me.*

In this calm assurance and strong joy my mother lived. In a poem in a school reader well known in my boyhood, a prisoner in France, a sailor lad, says,

> *"Great was the longing that I had*
>   *To see my mother."*

His heart and mine are one.

Concerning my father's relatives I know rather more than of my mother's. On August 10, 1899, being on holiday at Ilfracombe, I took train to Barnstaple and Umberleigh. The latter village lies in a lovely north Devon valley. Having climbed the long hill that leads to the ridge south of the valley, I turned east, walked through High Bickington on to Weeks Cross, turned back on the Barnstaple-Exeter high road, and presently reached the object of my search, the house where my father was born. I knew it by its standing at the corner where the High Bickington lane joins the main road. Filial sentiment could not fail to be stirred at the sight, but my strong total abstinence convictions sustained a severe and wholly unexpected shock. There could be no doubt about it, however; there was the name large enough, "The Roborough Arms"; my beloved and honoured father was born in a country inn. I resolved to prosecute no further my purposed inquiries into his ancestry. What else might I not find? Perhaps another of my forbears swung at the crossway for sheep stealing! Ancestors of sundry noble persons were hanged, drawn, and quartered on various grounds. I did, however, go into the parlour (not the bar!), and astonished the proprietress by asking for a glass of water, and interested her by inquiring if she knew aught of a family of Langs that lived there fifty years before. She had heard the name, as also my grandmother's family name, Lock, but nothing more. I reflected that *sic transit gloria mundi,* and went my way.

Nearby was a cottage, once the lodge at the entrance to the drive to Roborough House. Here lived two elderly women, who I decided must be cousins of some degree of my father. Opposite the cottage stood a small meeting-room, where my father as a tiny child amazed the village assembly by repeating a lengthy portion of Holy Writ.

After a brief time here I resumed my walk back to Barnstaple, through the glorious Devon hills and vales. Being not sure of the way I turned into a farm yard and inquired of a countryman working on a rick. He gave some directions in Devon dialect, which therefore were not very clear to the visitor. With the folly of a young gentleman from the city I remarked, "Well, I dare say I shall get there all right if I follow my nose;" to which the yokel gave the appropriate and useful reply; "O yez, if yer keeps yer nose in the right direction!" I say *useful* reply, for I believe it has ever since served as a salutary preservative from town conceit.

My grandfather, George Lang, who for a time kept the inn, was not an altogether ordinary man. The district is not so very remote from Exmoor, and he was a sort of Jan Ridd for strength. He could reap in a day twice as much as any other man around. In his days there were still in those parts Frenchmen who had been prisoners, kept on Dartmoor, during the Napoleonic wars. One of these, a bullying type of man, with the true cowardly instinct of his type, fastened upon my grandfather as the one of the group of reapers to be the butt of his nonsense, for he saw his victim was of a quiet spirit. Great bodily vigour and a gentle spirit are not a common combination. The Frenchman, a burly man, disregarded my grandfather's quietly spoken warnings, and was much astonished, as the rest were amused, when he found himself suddenly gripped by the scruff of the neck and the back of his knees, his forehead knocked against his knees, and himself carried bodily out of the field and dropped in the ditch, with the suggestion, still quietly spoken, that it would be well if he sought work elsewhere.

One evening my grandfather became heated chasing his hat on the moor. On recovering the hat he sat for a few moments to recover breath, and caught a chill. Probably a few early doses of Camphor or Aconite would have averted the consequences, but the chill developed severely. Allopathy had not yet learned to borrow clandestinely from Homoeopathy, and the fine old "heroic" treatment of strong and heavy measures was in force. The patient was cupped and leeched, and bled and blistered, purged and salinated, in a way that explains the ancient Jewish saying: "He that sinneth before his Maker, let him fall into the hand of the physician" (Ecclus. 38: 15). He made a long and brave fight against the heavy odds, but at last even his magnificent constitution succumbed to sickness and to "treatment", and death delivered him from the doctors.

But this was not before he became an instance of the way in which the wisdom and power of God subdue even things evil to serve His purposes of grace. During this sickness he was brought to a saving knowledge of Christ by that very rare saint, Robert Chapman of Barnstaple. My father became a prominent Exclusive Brother, and for him, alas, Open Brethren were, ecclesiastically, the acme of dreadful evil. But Robert Chapman was an exception, to be mentioned with respect, almost affection. It was of him, indeed, as is reported, that J. N. Darby himself, hearing him criticized, said, "Leave Robert Chapman alone: we talk about the heavenly places, but he lives in them." And because he lived there he could show many others the way there, by introducing them to Him who is the Way, the only way.

All this was long before my birth, but my father's mother Sarah Lang I remember distinctly. She came to live in one of my early homes, "Prestland", Station Road, Sidcup, Kent, and died there, when I was in my thirteenth year, aged eighty-four, on March 29, 1887, the jubilee year of the great Victoria. I remember the fearful thunderstorm of that afternoon, and of how, through the drawn venetian blinds, I watched the vivid forked lightning.

Like her husband my grandmother also was strong of body. When eighty-two years of age, taking my father's arm, she walked two and a half miles each way to the Sunday morning meeting we attended at Chislehurst. I still see her wiry form as on that walk. She was also strong in character, a dame of an old-fashioned type that modern life does not commonly develop. She might have been the elderly lady who thanked God she was born before "nerves" were invented. From trains she maintained to the last a rooted aversion. It had been only through sheer necessity that she had come by that means from Devon to London. We lived ten miles from London. Towards evening she would inquire for my father: "Is George Thomas home yet?" (She never dropped the old practice of using both Christian names.) Learning he had not come, she has been known to say: "I wish he was home. He will go in those trains. They go blundering along, not looking where they are going. The Almighty has given us legs. Why doesn't he walk to town?" She had been accustomed to walk ten miles to Barnstaple market. Why should not her son walk in her steps?

My stepmother took to her a letter from her eldest daughter, who was unwell. She had gone to bed, and said, "Put it on the drawers, my child; I will look at it in the morning." "But Grandma, would you not like to know how Caroline is?" "No, my child; if it is good news, it will keep till the morning; if it is bad news, I'd best not know it tonight."

Of these sturdy country parents two daughters died in early middle life. One of my two earliest recollections is of being lifted up to look at an aunt in her coffin, but I was so young that whether it was aunt Selina or aunt Priscilla I am not sure. My father almost completed eighty-four years; his younger brother, Hubert Henry, was also well into the eighties at death, and the elder sister, Caroline, lived to over ninety years.

About the year 1848 a small boy, of some ten years, was to be seen on a long ladder colouring the outside of the Roborough Arms. It was my father. The scene suggests steady nerves, strong arms, and a persevering, laborious usefulness of character. The boy was father to the man. The house possessed a grandfather clock, in plain wooden case, but with good brass works. The same small boy took these to pieces, which of course most small boys would do with pleasure; he cleaned it, which most boys would not take the trouble to do; he put it safely together, which few boys, or men, could do. A century later the clock was still going well.

For a few terms my father went to Chulmleigh School. Doubtless the education would now be deemed elementary. But he learned to do at least three things well—to read; and he knew the Word of God from end to end: to reckon; he became an accurate, competent accountant: to write; he was easily the finest penman I ever knew. Mr. John Tuke, who then kept the school, was himself a first class penman. How often in my own business days, when junior after junior came and went, disfiguring my books as they passed by, did I wish that they had been taught at school to write decently, instead of being able, for instance, to repeat Greek verbs. And with what joy did I welcome at last a rosy-cheeked lad from the country who wrote legibly and was clean morally.

When my father was twelve it was decided he should go to business in London, in those days a formidable migration, amounting for the busy and the not well-to-do almost to emigration. For he had first to coach twenty-five miles to Tiverton, and to spend the night there. Then getting the train at 9 a.m. he reached Paddington at 9 p.m. This whole journey is now completed in a few hours. The carriages were not comfortable. Of this wearisome day the only incident preserved is that a woman had a baby which was so fractious that a man growled the stupid question, "Why do women have babies?" and received from the distracted mother the tart response, "If your mother hadn't you wouldn't be here to complain." On tedious and disagreeable journeys let the traveller remember, and hold his peace.

The youth entered the service of Messrs. Olney and Amsden, retail drapers in the Old Kent Road. Mr. William Olney and Mr. Thomas Olney became successively Treasurers of the Metropolitan Tabernacle in the days of the great Charles Haddon Spurgeon. My father grew up with the business, which presently became wholesale only and removed to extensive premises in Falcon Street, E.C. These were bombed in the 1939-45 war. He led to a knowledge of Christ one who entered the business as a young man and later became head of the firm. It speaks volumes for the character of a servant when he can bring to the Lord an employer.

In my young boyhood my father was already the chief of the counting house. He served the firm for fifty years, till its annual turnover was some three-quarters-of-a-million pounds, and in that long period was never away a week from illness. Beginning then to feel he could not do all that his responsible and increasing duties demanded, he retired, and supported himself by accountancy work for various smaller undertakings. He continued thus for twenty more years, at last relinquishing gradually one after another of his posts, until in his eighty-second year he wrote to me, "For the first time for seventy years I find myself out of employment." He was one of numberless instances from those Victorian days of individual freedom of how grit and integrity enabled youths to reach honourable and comfortable status without Unions to "help" or the State to "father", and so to enfeeble character.

In his eighteenth year he had occasion to consult the late Dr. Morrish, a homoeopath. Disgusted with the barbarous treatment his father had received he perceived at once the immeasurable superiority of the homoeopathic system of medicine. Thus his family, and great numbers of others, had the benefit of homoeopathy. The homoeopathic principle of selecting remedies is as distinctly a law of nature as is, say, gravity, and the general rejection of it by British doctors is to their perpetual disgrace. It has been said of classical Greek that it draws a line where other languages make a blot. The same is true of Homoeopathy as compared with other systems of medicine.

But from acquaintance with Dr. Morrish my father received a vastly superior benefit: he attended Bible readings in the Doctor's house, and received from the Word of God what, as a member of the Church of England, he had lacked before, assurance of salvation by faith in the atoning sacrifice of the Son of God. From that time throughout his long life his devotion to the Redeemer was his ruling quality. An earnest disciple was invited to take a cigar. He replied, "Thank you, I do not smoke, I blaze!" My father might have said the same. One of my earliest recollections is of a tea to the poor in Caroline Street, a wretched neighbourhood, near the South Metropolitan Gas Company's works. Mr., afterwards Sir, Thomas Livesey, the Manager of that Company, built the hall privately for the benefit of their workpeople. My father was asked to help in the spiritual efforts. Many were the sinners saved.

Later he was active at a mission-room in Willowbrook Road, Bermondsey, S.E. Here too very many were converted. He was also a leader at the Willow Road Room, Bermondsey, one of the halls of the Exclusive Brethren. To this body Dr. Morrish belonged and in it my father remained until his death. In his later years his generous spirit became increasingly tolerant. Indeed, from conversations with him near the end of his life, when confinement to the house had given him long leisure for meditation in the Word of God free from distracting influences, I found that certain of his ecclesiastical views had so much changed as, quite unconsciously to himself, not to differ greatly from those of early Brethren, before unhappy divisions took place. This is a notable testimony to a beautiful simplicity, sincerity, and childlikeness of mind that was a conspicuous trait in his character, and which enabled him, even in very old age, to unlearn and re-learn, as the Holy Spirit illuminated the Holy Scripture. He was almost the last survivor of the earlier generation of that communion, and was the embodiment of the chief excellencies of its palmiest days; and now he is wholly free from its defects.

Reverting to the mission-room mentioned: only a few years ago my sister, Mrs. Skinner, met at Bexleyheath in Kent a Christian over ninety years of age, who said that when she was a young married woman a sweet-faced lady called at the door, offered a tract and invited her to that hall. After the service the preacher for the evening shook hands with those leaving and said to her, "Do you know if your sins are forgiven?" On reaching home she said to her husband, "What a strange question the gentleman asked me." But the question provoked thought and inquiry, and before long she and her husband could answer in the affirmative. The lady was my mother, the preacher my father.

It will now be seen with what endowment I entered life. From my paternal grandfather I inherited a constitution of unusual vigour. Looking back to my boyhood I do not seem to remember ever being weary, and might almost wonder why I used to go to rest. Doubtless, however, my elders saw good reasons for packing me off to bed. On Whit Monday 1893, when eighteen years of age, I walked from Clifton to Clevedon, thence to Portishead, and back to

Clifton, twenty-six miles of hilly country, and ate only a few biscuits at Clevedon and drank a bottle of lemonade at Abbots Leigh near the end of the walk.
Reaching Clifton in the evening I finished the day well at a religious meeting.

In my fortieth year I tramped seventeen miles over the deserts of Egypt,
exploring the Mokattam Hills near Cairo, under the hot March sun. In that
land I worked steadily for seventeen hours a day with a shade temperature of
115^0 for days together, and of 95^0 after sunset for months at a time. By contrast, in Poland in my fifty-first year, forty degrees of frost were not disagreeable. After my boyhood I had lived a persistently strenuous life for forty years
before nature waved a warning signal, and this in spite of perhaps a dozen
turns of influenza.

On the other hand, from my maternal grandfather I inherit gout, which
is a perpetual saviour from the spiritual peril of strength. That affliction may
be summarized in general by saying that in early manhood it can be annoy-
ing, in middle life distracting, in later years crippling. It takes many changing
forms, and thankful may the sufferer be as long as it does not locate in one
place or organ to its permanent injury. By the mitigating mercy of God, I have
been able by homoeopathic medicines to reduce its intensity and to move it
about all over the body, so preventing that dreaded fixity of residence. But I
doubt if inherited and long-established gout is curable, in the full sense of the
term, save by the direct power of God. I am not unacquainted experimentally
with that power in weakness and in sickness, and I have looked oft to Him in
respect of this constitutional condition, but I have received no assurance that
He thought good to relieve my ship of this ballast. His love and His will are
perfect, nothing less than *perfect*. Happy is he who can sing sincerely,

> *That weakness I enjoy*
> *That casts me on Thy breast;*
> *The conflicts that Thy strength employ*
> *Make me divinely blessed.*

I have called gout an affection, rather than, as is usual, a complaint. Not
that I have any affection for it, but because that only can be a complaint of
which one complains, and as the Christian is to give thanks in every thing he
is to complain of nothing.

If I have sufficient strength of character it may be attributed to my relationship to my father's mother; if any softer natural qualities temper their
opposites it is doubtless because I am my mother's son. The like fearlessness
which took that small boy up a ladder, and the caution which enabled him to
stay up safely, have kept me from foolish rashness and yet have enabled me
to do what some would have feared to undertake. It was without any sense of

danger that as a boy of ten or eleven I walked along the outward sloping parapet of the wall of a high railway bridge in Kent. The same qualities have made
it to be not so formidable for me as for some to take extensive journeys alone
in lands the language of which I did not know. A business love of order, and
a liking for sticking at a task until it is perfected, are but reproductions of the
excellent business habits of my father. Of the far richer spiritual inheritance
more must be said hereafter.

While writing thus I by no means forgot the direct enablings of the Holy
Spirit, without whose constant and effectual inworking all natural endow-
ments were insufficient, and indeed had been only abused and wasted. Nor
do I offer any apology for describing the physical and temperamental stock
in trade with which I commenced the business of life. One who inherits an
estate need not be ashamed to speak thereof. It is nought to a man's own credit
that he inherits something. But he may, and should, give thanks to his Creator
that he starts his career with certain advantages; and if events show that he
is able to use and to improve the heritage, let him give to God alone all the
glory for the capacity so to do. "And thou shalt eat and be full and shalt bless
Jehovah thy God for the good land which He hath given thee. Beware lest…
thou say in thy heart, My power and the might of my hand hath gotten me
this wealth. But thou shalt remember Jehovah thy God, for it is He that giveth
thee power to get wealth," whether those riches be material or moral, inherited
or acquired (Deut. 8:10, 17, 18).

This will suffice to show into what physical, mental, and social conditions
I was born by the ordering of God, and to introduce my forbears and myself.

CHAPTER 2

Childhood

1874-1887

Of all the gifts Thy love bestows,
Thou giver of all good,
Not heaven itself a richer knows
Than the Redeemer's blood.
Faith, too, that trusts the blood through grace,
From that same love we gain,
Or, sweetly as it suits our case,
The gift had been in vain.

(Cowper)

My elder sister, Helen Amelia (Ella), was born April 21, 1873. I was born November, 20, 1874, at 50, Trafalgar Road, Greenwich, at that time a quiet, refined suburban district of southeast London. My mother died eight days after my birth, in her thirty-second year. She gave me my names while delirious two days after my birth, saying, "Get my dear little George Henry a little loaf; buy him a little loaf."

Left with two infants, my father wisely married again. Second marriages are often disastrous: his was prospered with the abundant blessing of the Lord. He met Harriet Pettman, as he had met my mother, at a spiritual gathering. I believe it was at the wedding of her sister Fanny to Mr. Edward Musgrove, and I am told that I, perhaps a year old, took to her at once, showing this by pulling one of her side curls out to its full length. It is said that it was my happiness in her arms that made my father think she might make me a good second mother. They were married on April 13, 1876, and for forty-six years, until my father's death in 1922, they enjoyed unbroken fellowship, natural and spiritual, creating and maintaining such a godly home as enabled the Spirit of God to quicken each of seven children in early life.

Though I owe not my natural life to my stepmother, I owe to her under God everything else that a mother can give, and also my spiritual life. As she was the only mother I knew I shall henceforth write of her simply as my mother.

Her grandfather had architectural duties in Canterbury Cathedral. He fell from a high scaffold on to the Cathedral pavement near where his little son

Thomas was playing, and was killed. The boy was found to be musical; in due time he became Cathedral organist, and was a professor of the Royal Academy of Music. I have heard that Queen Victoria being in his neighbourhood submitted to him a composition of hers for correction. He was a good singer, could play any instrument, and could sleep through any amount of playing by others, until a discord was struck, when he would wake with a snap. Mischievous grandchildren sometimes tested this idiosyncrasy. But he remained long without feeling his need of the Saviour of sinners; always at the established church as organist, but far from God. Late in life he was induced to hear Sankey sing. His comment was characteristic of the finished technician: "He has a good voice, but no crotchets or quavers!" By the mercy of God there was hope in his death.

His wife, on the other hand, was a sweet saint. I remember her distinctly, for in very early days I used often to be at Ramsgate, where they lived. They had thirteen children. In those wiser days of long ago children were sent to bed early. When all were in bed Mrs. Pettman every night went to each bedside and prayed. Those prayers were of necessity answered. All her children were converted to God. The conversion of Thomas was very striking. When a young man, already a church organist but unsaved, he came under deep conviction of sin, and for a long time could find no peace of mind. One evening, as he was walking towards the cliffs, possibly with thoughts of suicide as a way of ending the inward misery, a drunkard lurched against him and he caught the words the sot was mumbling: "Why art thou cast down, O my soul? and why art thou disquieted within me? Hope thou in God: for I shall yet praise Him, who is the health of my countenance, and my God" (Ps. 42:5, 11; 43:5). By hope he was saved from despair, and before long entered into peace with God through faith in Jesus Christ our Lord. He lived to be a blessing to many others. For many years he held beach services for children at Broadstairs.

The days of divine superintendence are not passed. Who but the Almighty could use a drunken drunkard to save a soul from death? Who else caused the two to meet in a big town late at night? In his youth the drunkard had been taught to memorize Scripture, but who but God brought to the muddled brain just such words as would cheer the troubled heart?

I shall mention only one other member of this family, Stanley. He was, I think, the eldest son, and it was correspondingly a bitter disappointment to his father that he was utterly nonmusical, while the other twelve were all highly gifted. He went through deep exercises of heart in breaking from the Church of England, in which he was reared, so as to be free from its formalities, routine, and ritual, in order to worship God as the Father in spirit and in truth. All the family did so in turn, my mother included.

It was in such a circle, with such manifestations of the power of God in her loved ones, that she was reared who was deeply, eternally to influence myself. It was with such trials and at such cost that she "grew up into Christ", instead of remaining a Christian dwarf, one of the myriads of cases of arrested spiritual development which cannot but abound in every religious system crippled by the tight swaddling-bands of humanly devised forms, rules, and creeds. In due time she had five children, Emily Elizabeth, Samuel, Selina, Margaret Sophia (Daisy), Elsie Harriet. It speaks volumes for her character and home influence that we all grew together as only one family, and have continued thus in heart. And it spoke much for the physical inheritance mentioned in Chapter 1 and the training, that we seven continued an unbroken circle until the youngest died in her sixty-fourth year in 1949.

Amid the haze of the remote past one glimpse is distinct. My earliest recollection is of my sister and myself, both very young, delighting in the small garden of a small house, and picking nasturtium seeds to be used for "caper" sauce with boiled mutton.

Which is not so trifling a memory for the beginning of a human life as the superficial may think. The pleasure and the usefulness of a garden, what is it but a faded yet clear reflection of that golden beginning of all human history when "Jehovah God planted a garden. . . and there he put the man whom he had formed. And out of the ground made Jehovah God to grow every tree that is pleasant to the sight and good for food" (Gen. 2:8, 9)? "*There* he put the man": not in a barren desert, not in a hovel in a slum, not in the dreary restriction of a tenement flat, but in a garden. And the divine order is very significant; first beauty, then utility; first trees "pleasant to the sight", then those that are "good for food". The mighty worker who wrote down the narrative caught this truth, and in the prayer of Moses, the man of God, in this petition: "Let the *beauty* of Jehovah our God be upon us: and establish Thou the *work* of our hands upon us" (Ps. 90:17). First character, then service; first likeness to God, then work that God can bless. First failure in proud self-effort, then forty years of retirement in a desert to develop the beauty of meekness; then strength, activity, authority, a life-work established for evermore.

> *Take from our hearts the strain and stress,*
> *And let our ordered lives confess*
> *The beauty of Thy peace.*

The heavenly city is pictured as a garden city, and on earth "the desert shall rejoice and blossom as the rose" (Isa. 35:1).

That house was at Brockley, then a newly-planted suburb well away from London on the southeast. But the glimpse is brief. Whether it was too far from the busy city, or, which is more probable, from the evening and Sunday gospel work, I cannot say; but my next memories are of a sadly different district.

At the Jamaica Road end of St. James' Road, Bermondsey, stands a row of tall narrow houses of the type mentioned in Lord Brougham's caustic comparison of a certain tall man to those high houses of which the upper storeys are the least well-furnished. No. 11 became our home. The solitary redeeming feature was that the house being high allowed us, from the upstairs windows, to look over the houses opposite into the churchyard, then a sort of public space, of no small value to such a locality. It was said that George Whitefield preached in that church.

The whole neighbourhood is dingy and dreary at all times, but especially in the dull and wet weather of winter. Interminable rows of small and dirty brick dwellings, grimy factories, gloomy warehouses, insufferably muddy roads, heavy skies, and foggy days, are the unpleasant memories stamped indelibly on my memory. Once I fell flat on my face in that greasy black mud, and went home a grievous spectacle, especially, no doubt, to whoever had to clean my clothes. Happily at that time they were small. Southwark Park, a quarter of an hour or so from our house, is the only relief in the shaded landscape of those days. Blessed be the man that first proposed city parks.

I was now six years of age and went to my first school, in Jamaica Road. It was kept by one Loudon, as I remember the name. He was a survival—let us hope the last—of that type of schoolmaster Dickens somewhere described, whose principal, if not sole, means of training youth was a long and thick cane. I saw him give an elder boy fifty strokes on the hand at one time. A tall youth (named Robinson, if I recollect aright) fled from the desk, and was chased round the large schoolroom by the angry master, who slashed at him right and left whenever near enough to his victim. To the rest of us it was a fearsome scene of deepest fascination (who knew but it would be his turn next?) and yet of suppressed amusement and satisfaction; for Robinson, by managing to keep *two* forms away from the pursuing fury, contrived for a while to keep out of reach, and the swinging blows were wasted. But at last the quarry was run to earth, and the demoralizing incident ended, painfully enough for Robinson. My life has a few strange features difficult of explanation: one is that I never tasted that cane .

To all eternity No. 11 St. James' Road will be memorable. When I was about seven-and-a-half years of age a most momentous event took place which neither can be nor needs to be repeated. I was converted, born again from above, born of God. The experience was so real and thorough, and its effects so enduring, that it is as vivid after more than seventy years as if it had just happened.

I was recovering from an illness, scarlatina I think. My mother sat by my bed and talked with me, quietly and simply; and as she spoke the Spirit of Truth spoke by her and made the truth effective. She said nothing more than I had heard from infancy, but what new and powerful influence it exerted! She spoke of sin: I felt myself the veriest sinner under the sun. No particular sins were mentioned, but there rose before me childish falsehoods, petty pilferings, anger, disobedience. I saw these as *guilt*, as wickedness, as making me obnoxious to the holy God and His holy wrath. I had not been brought up in a morbid, prudish, restrained manner, constantly checked, reproved, restricted, but in a simple, healthy, happy atmosphere. There can be no accounting for this sudden, intelligent, overwhelming perception of the true nature of sin by a child of seven but as a fulfilment of the words of the Son of God, "When He, the Spirit of truth, is come He shall convict the world of sin, of righteousness, and of judgment" (John 16:8).

My mother spoke of God, His holiness, His anger against sin, and the coming judgment. Her words were few, but oh, the solemnity they caused to settle upon my heart. She went on to remind me of His infinite love, love so mighty that He sent into the world His only and beloved Son on purpose to save sinners, for though He hates sin He loves the sinner. And I thought and felt what a wonderful, amazing thing it is that the great and holy God, who made the stars and this great earth, loved a naughty, sinful little boy like me. If I but shut my eyes, and lean back in my chair in thought, again I feel the hot tears that trickled down my cheeks as the sense of this overwhelming love of God melted my heart.

She said a little about the cross of Christ; how the Son of God in love to me took my place and bore my sin and its divinely appointed punishment, death. I *saw* this CLEARLY. It was made spiritually plain to my mind, as by a divine illumination. In the intervening years I have reflected upon the doctrine of the atonement, have read Dale, Denny, and others, have precisionized some ideas, have theorized somewhat, and, as a consequence, can talk about the subject as on that day on my bed would naturally have been impossible: but as regards *spiritual apprehension* of the death of Christ and its value to the sinner I have learned nothing further, for I learned then all one needs to know, perhaps all a finite being can know, and it is all in this word: "Christ died for our sins, according to the Scriptures... He loved me, and gave Himself up [to justice] for me" (1 Cor. 15:3; Gal. 2:20).

My mother added that if only I was truly sorry that I had sinned God would forgive me for Christ's sake. I could not doubt this; I saw the worthiness of Christ and the sufficiency of His death, as the meritorious cause, the only cause, the adequate cause, why God should pardon me. As a little child can do, I gratefully accepted the promised pardon. I knew I was truly sorry, and

I was only too thankful to think that the dreadful doom of the sinner, which I so richly deserved, would never be my fate, for God had loved me, Christ had delivered me by dying for me, I was saved!

Yes, I was saved, and I knew it. There stole over my troubled heart a quiet, solemn, happy peace: I had "peace with God through our Lord Jesus Christ" (Rom. 5:1), my heart had been "sprinkled from a consciousness of evil" (Heb. 10: 22); that is to say, the Holy Spirit had enabled me, by faith in what God says on the matter, to see that the blood Christ shed, the life He surrendered, had met fully the claims of the law of God against me on account of my sins. God was satisfied; I was satisfied.

In the long intervening years I have met many spiritual dangers and had many spiritual vicissitudes. It was years before I learned that Christ saves His people *from* their *sins* as well as from the punishment of them. My experience of heart holiness came long after, and my moral life was long a secret sorrow to me. Also, I have faced atheistic and other doubts by meeting with infidels, higher critics, and the like, and by reading their writings, so as to master their position, and be able to help them. But not for one moment has that deep, settled peace through the blood of Christ been disturbed. I have grown in intelligence, but not in confidence. At that first moment I rested the whole weight of my salvation from wrath upon Christ, and therefore found complete rest; I am still doing this at this moment, and therefore still have that complete rest. It is in leaning the entire weight upon the bed that the body finds rest; Christ said, "Come unto Me, and I will rest you." That day, in earliest life, blessed be God,

> *I came to Jesus, as I was,*
> *Weary and worn and sad;*
> *I found in Him a resting place,*
> *And He has made me glad.*
>
> *(H. Bonar)*

Happy indeed is the grown man who still sleeps as a little child. This I do in Christ as regards my salvation, and all other concerns of time and eternity. A weary woman said, "Blessed be the man that invented beds!" The Christian says, "Blessed be the God and Father of our Lord Jesus Christ."

And it all took place in fifteen minutes! I was brought through conviction, illumination, faith, assurance; a rational, logical, indispensable process in the divine miracle of regeneration. Nor need the suddenness and completeness of the transaction be a wonder. GOD was the worker, and He does wonders; and "I know that whatsoever God doeth it shall be for ever" (Eccl. 3:14). His work endures.

I rose in due time from my bed, and went my way as a natural, healthy boy, getting into mischief, enjoying fun and games and lessons, outwardly little different from other boys. Nor for years did I say anything about that momentous hour. But I knew a real event had happened; and if it was at all true, as my fond mother used to say, that "George never gave her any trouble", this can be attributed only to that renewing of his inner man which God then commenced. A foremost agnostic of that period said that to him the doctrines which Christians believe were incomprehensible. How then came it to pass that they suddenly became comprehensible to a tiny child of seven and permanently and beneficially effective through a long life? The infidel can give no explanation. Human skill could not effect this miracle. It is a divine work wrought by the Spirit of God Himself, and every such case is an irrefutable confirmation of the Book which teaches those doctrines and promises that the Spirit shall use them in such manner.

Of course I believe whole-heartedly in the conversion of children. Thank God a thousand times for Sunday schools; but *Christian* parents should so live with God in the home, so pray, so speak with their little ones, that *these* may not need the Sunday school teacher or other worker to lead them to Christ. It is their parents' own peculiar duty and joy, and if they cannot do this blessed service, let them inquire seriously *why* they cannot.

Of these Bermondsey years but few incidents remain in my memory. But I recall an alarming interview when my elder sister and I were accosted in Southwark Park by a formidable man, a school attendance officer, who demanded to know why we were not at school. He seemed satisfied with our assurance that we had sickness in the house. On another occasion my next youngest sister, Emily, still a little child, ran after me across the road outside our house and straight in front of a large dray and two of the magnificent horses more common then than now. With commendable and desperate promptitude the driver reined them in and she escaped. I remember well the severe winter of 1881, when for weeks the streets were filled with snow so deep that the passages cut across the roads were higher than my head. But I do not remember that I felt cold.

In 1882 a memorable change took place. We moved into the country. It was no small sacrifice to our father. It severed him from the spiritual work in the slums he loved so well, and the constant intercourse with Christian friends so long valued. And it meant that he had an extra hour a day to spend in trains to and from the city. But he felt that Bermondsey was not the place to rear five young children, so he took "Priestland", a house in Station Road, Sidcup, in Kent, ten miles from town. He changed the name to "Prestlands", which led the house agent to startle someone by the information that "Mr. Lang had lost an I".

The garden was full of long grass, in which we children raced about with sheer delight. There were two plum trees. They did not bear as freely as we should have liked, nor did the plums usually get fully ripe; the reader may guess why. The district was still far from developed, and on the other side of the road were a tiny brook, a hedge, and wide fields flanked by Longlands woods. The field nearest was a strawberry field and the fruit was ripe. Mother sent one of us with sixpence and an ordinary tea basin, which was brought back full. A larger vessel was sent each day until the largest pie dish came back full for sixpence. Halcyon days! It was the summit of the Victorian era. Would that they might return to this selfish, stricken, godless land, robbed of freedom by political theorists.

On Sundays and Wednesdays we walked to the nearest Exclusive meeting, two-and-a-half miles distant at Chislehurst. Usually I went three times on Sunday. We were not required to go to the afternoon conversational Bible reading, but my sister and I chose to go. Thus I generally walked that day fifteen miles, and thought nothing of it. In those more natural times no healthy children jibbed at walking. It was that or stay at home. I remember distinctly when the low safety-bicycle appeared on the roads, and I wondered why the tyres were so big, thinking they must be heavy to push, until I learned they were filled with air. But bicycles were a luxury of the rich, so most walked, which was far healthier.

After perhaps two years, others of the Exclusive fraternity came to the district and a meeting was commenced. One of these was a cocoa merchant named Wells. He bought two small plots of building land, to put on one a hall to be let to the meeting, and on the other a house as an investment. He employed an old countryman, named Comber, to put the close oak palings around the plots. He was a quaint old fellow, with one eye that looked the wrong way. But he was a true Christian, a Baptist. The owner of the next adjoining plot watched the old man put in the boundary post and considered it was a foot over on his land. Comber said: "Well, sir, that's where Mr. Wells told me to put it." The other replied: "I am very surprised at a religious man like Mr. Wells breaking the law. Does not the law say, 'Thou shalt not remove thy neighbour's landmark'?" (Deut. 19:14; 27:17). To this, with a sly hit at a well-known tendency to an abuse of Christian liberty, Comber replied: "Ah, sir, but if you was to talk to Mr. Wells like that he'd say he wasn't under law but under grace!"

One family that moved to Sidcup, and helped to increase the meeting, was the Musgroves, the relatives before mentioned, Mrs. Musgrove being my mother's sister. Aunt Fanny had a remarkable conversion as a girl. She was one of the sweetest women I have known. There were six children, the two eldest boys, Edward and Howard, being a little my seniors. We were great chums and roamed the countryside far and wide. There were soon no lanes or woods or commons for miles around we did not know. This developed a sense of locality and an absence of fear which have been helpful in later wanderings in many lands. In those boyhood years I would often roam the woods at night. Thus did God order those early years with a view to later years.

My cousin Edward was no ordinary companion. He was quiet and unob- trusive, but able. It was forty or more years later that I learned casually that at college he had taken gold medals in Greek and German. He was a splendid swimmer, an excellent photographer, and a competent electrician, at one time an observer of thunderstorms for the Meteorological Society. One day in his room (which usually reeked with strange chemical fumes) he told me that it had occurred to him to take a photograph by the light of a Crooke's tube. There stood in position a tiny statuette, and behind it, for a background, a slab of inch board. He handed me the negative and asked me what I saw in it. I an- swered that it showed the pattern of the wall-paper behind the board. "Yes", he said, "isn't it funny?" This was a few years before Rontgen's announcement of X-rays. Had my cousin followed up the matter they might have been known as the Musgrove rays.

Though usually silent he was a rare storyteller. Our families and visitors frequently spent Saturday afternoons and Bank holidays in extensive rambles through the charming country. Passing a tumble-down cottage, Edward would hold the company fascinated by a tale of some dreadful tragedy that had taken place in that cottage years before. At the close of the narrative there would be added quietly, "Of course, it never happened." Under God I owe much to his influence, and shall illustrate this later.

The Sunday School at the hall included a class for bigger boys, in which description I was included though actually small for my age. It was thought I would never grow, though finally I reached five feet nine. I fear I was not too amenable, nor was the class leader attractive. One afternoon he was dealing with the brazen serpent, and his involved remarks led me to ask how a brazen thing was not made of brass, which was how I had understood him. Probably I had often asked perverse questions and he felt this was another such, where- upon he said testily that he would have no more of my rudeness and ordered me to leave the school. But that time I was conscious of being quite sincere and I left with a sense of injustice on his part, and never returned. Shortly the class was transferred to the house of a good man, Lieutenant Ireland, R.N., who won our love and helped us.

It was perhaps not surprising, though quite inexcusable, that one Sunday afternoon another lad and I played truant from Sunday School. One sin leads to another. A robin sang sweetly on a hedge; I seized a stone, swung round and flung it, and the pretty creature fell mangled and dead. It was a wanton,

wicked deed, which I mourn to this day. Though a believer in Christ as my
Saviour I was not yet indwelt by His Spirit. This explains why many Christians
do many things not worthy of His name, which fact does not prove that they
do not truly believe in Him. As related above I had been well taught the truth
of redemption and pardon and had received Christ as my personal Redeemer,
but no such instruction as to the Holy Spirit as Sanctifier and Indweller had
reached my heart (even if it had been taught in my hearing), and I had not
received *Him* by faith. Let Christian parents and teachers take this to heart
and be as careful to instruct children upon the latter theme as the former. For
communion with God depends upon the water of the laver as much as on
the blood at the altar; holiness requires the *Spirit* of Christ as well as Christ;
power in service calls for Pentecost after Calvary. And faith must be exercised
for benefiting by each, which requires instruction upon both, seeing that faith
cometh by hearing and one cannot believe what one had not heard, and heard
with intelligence and personal application.

There happened one day an event which might have shrouded our home
with gloom. "Prestland" was a four-storeyed house with a well staircase from
attic to basement. My sister Emily, six or seven years of age, was sliding down
the banister from the attic and fell down the well. I was at the bottom when
she arrived. Her head struck the foot of an old-fashioned wooden peram-
bulator. It was salvation that it was there or she might have struck an iron
pipe which projected from the cupboard under the stairs. After a few moments Emily rose and ran off to play, seemingly unhurt. But some seven years
later facial paralysis appeared, the effect of the blow, as was considered. By
the blessing of God, the leading homoeopath of England, Dr. J. Compton
Burnett, remedied this affection, and during the sixty-five or more intervening
years my dear sister has lived a strenuous and useful life and is still active. The
life spared in childhood has been well employed unto full age, and God, the
Preserver of all men, is glorified.

Later, the youngest of us, Elsie, still almost an infant, was found clinging
to the banister rail ready to drop down the well. She was rescued, but father
decided that such a house was not suitable for a young family and we removed
to Handen Road, Lee.

My schooling illustrates the secret superintendence of God over the development of a boy.

My first school at Sidcup was a preparatory school for boys kept by Miss
Langridge. I was eight years old. The chief item I remember was the learning
of poetry. Each term some lengthy poem had to be memorized and to be repeated at the end of the term. One such piece was the first canto of *The Lady
of the Lake*, perhaps 600 lines. This practice developed a strong and tenacious
memory, a faculty mighty for good or evil. It also fostered a love of poetry,

which a little later prompted attempts to write in verse.

When about ten or eleven years old I was sent to a school kept by a Mr. Swan at Milton Villa, Church Road, Bexleyheath, Kent. This was four miles from Sidcup. I walked there, had a midday meal at school, and walked home. One can think with sadness of what the ordinary boy of today would say were it proposed that he should walk four miles to school, but then boys in decent homes did what their parents directed, and were all the happier for the discipline.

My first day at school, the first question was whether I was to be put in class 3 or class 2. I know not whether to regard it as a Divine providence, but the test was how to ask in French the question, How do you do? It is fact that this was the one and only phrase in French that I knew. I was exalted to class 2.

That day a boy inquired where I lived, and learning it was Sidcup offered the blunt remark: "You're a fool. Coming all that way *he* would have let you get here at half-past-nine instead of nine." But the instinct of a regenerate heart told me instantly that this was bad advice. All the terms I went to Milton Villa I was never late. The virtue of punctuality had been formed by us children having to be at the breakfast table at 6.30 a.m., summer and winter, and by the example of our dear father who left at 7.10 to catch the 7.20 train to London (never without reading a Scripture and praying with us), so as to be at his office by 8.30 to open the heavy mail of the wholesale house where he was chief of the counting house. The habits of far too many young people today are deplorable. At school, at college, in one of the services, they are *compelled* to be punctual; but the moment holidays or furloughs start they lapse into complete disregard of time and of the courtesy due to others, and waste hours of the morning in bed. It shows an absence of morals in doing what is wise and right; they are in time only so long as they *must* be so, not at all because it is good and right. Yet of all the things we use time is easily the most valuable, for some of it must be expended on every other act. Some words of Gladstone to the students of St. Andrews University made in me a lasting impression. I give them from memory: "Gentlemen, let me recommend to you thrift of time. It will repay you with a usury beyond your utmost expectations."

On one occasion when walking from Bexleyheath to Bexley, I encountered a gang of rough street boys who ambushed me. Just as I was about to answer cheekily something arresting happened. There rang in my heart words I had no recollection of having heard or read, but which from their style and tone I felt must come from the Bible: A soft answer turneth away wrath, but grievous words stir up anger (Prov. 15:1).

That reverence for the Word of God which characterized my home and training caused me at once to change my tactics. I answered quietly, explaining that I came from Sidcup, not Bexley, and was allowed to go home without damage, but with the lesson indelibly fixed in my heart that it is as wise as it is right to obey the Word of God immediately.

In ancient times a lad of about fifteen years was dying of thirst under a shrub in the desert south of Palestine. We read that "God hath heard the voice of the lad where he is" and sent guidance and deliverance (Gen. 21:12-19). Three thousand and seven hundred years pass, but what is that to the Eternal? Again He looked down on a small lad in trouble and gave guidance and deliverance. I know not whether it was His own good Spirit who spoke those words into my mind or whether He spoke through an angel, as to Hagar about Ishmael that day in the desert; but I know that that experience has been a determining factor throughout the subsequent sixty years. It has been with me a ceaseless expectation, something that I have simply and without effort taken for granted, that the God of Abraham *will* work, *will* speak, *will* guide, *will* help, and that the Bible is the medium He chooses to use for His messages. Further illustrations will be given in these pages. I have met many sceptics, honest or dishonest, and have read much infidel literature, by avowed opponents of the faith or by less candid modernists posing as Christians; but their subtleties and sophistries have never deceived or troubled my soul. *I know* the God they say does not exist; *I have heard His Voice* in the Book they decry, and not once but many, many times.

For a short while I went to school in Sidcup under a clergyman who took a few private pupils. From July to September he went to Archangel, on the White Sea, as chaplain to the British who traded or called there. In consequence we had but a few days of holiday at Christmas and Easter but three months in the summer. After my cousins had returned to school the remaining six weeks dragged heavily. Idleness is wearisome as well as hurtful. My father, thinking rightly that so much waste time was harmful, took me up to the counting house of which he was chief, where I stamped letters, ran errands, and did such minor items as might be entrusted to a boy of eleven years. The discipline involved was beneficial. No doubt it was needful that legislation should prohibit children being employed in some of the arduous and hurtful work they formerly did, as in mines and chimneys. But it has been pushed to an extreme. Country boys and girls are not harmed by picking stones off fields. I was decidedly the better for learning to be respectful to seniors, to be methodical and punctual, to keep books and papers in order, to be tidy. These habits have helped me greatly in my later literary work on a considerable scale, done often under difficulties of travel and other interruptions, as well as on its business side of personally selling my books by post, with the keeping of stocks and accounts and the doing up of parcels. Thus the God I was to serve began my training betimes.

This preparation can be traced down to detail. My father could not know, what God foreknew, that I was to be a longdistance traveller and to find my way about many great and foreign cities, but he helped towards this. A daily walk in the heart of London was between Cannon Street Station and Falcon Square, near the G.P.O., Aldersgate Street. After I had several times done the journey by his side, he told me one afternoon to go ahead and find my own way. That first time he had once at a corner to call from behind and keep me on the right road, but after that I was safe though alone, and it was not long before I knew well the courts, alleys, and short cuts of that central area of the City.

When, after being in the office for six weeks, I was returning to school, William Olney told my father to give me £2 pocket money. I felt very wealthy; but my wise father did not leave me to waste all these riches on boyish fancies, but bought for me sundry useful articles, leaving me the smaller part. This early lesson in the wise use of money was invaluable. It set me on the healthy line of not indulging idle whims but of using money profitably, and this carried with it salvation from the pernicious misuse of money for self-indulgence. In consequence, I have been able without hardship to live in many lands at a minimum cost, as, for example, in Heliopolis, Egypt, where I lived alone for six months at the rate of sixteen shillings a week, excluding rent. A chief secret of healthy and happy living is *to do without*. Profoundly true and practical are Wesley's words: "We should be continually labouring to cut off all the useless things that surround us; our God usually retrenches the superfluities of our souls in the same proportion as we do those of our bodies" (*A Plain Account of Christian Perfection*). Such conditions as jealousy, bitterness, greed, bad temper, depression are "superfluities of the soul", states plainly superfluous to our true wellbeing, indeed destructive of it. Selfish indulgence of the body fosters these and must be discontinued before they can be retrenched.

At that time the Rev. Gilbert McCall, a Congregational Minister, opened a school in Longlands Road, Sidcup. His boys had the special advantage of being under a man who knew how to teach us to teach ourselves. One day he drew on the blackboard a hexagon and said: "Now boys, by putting in three lines you can turn that into a cube. I have something I want to do, so I will leave you. When one of you has seen how to do it, come and tell me." Thus he put us on our honour not to lark about in his absence; no one abused this confidence, and at the same time he left us to use our brains.

Another day he said: "When you get out into life, you will meet two sorts of men. One will chum up to you the first day, tell you his secrets, and will want you to tell him yours. Do not make friends with such; they will abuse your trust. The other fellow will stand off for a time till he is sure you are worthy of his friendship. Cultivate his acquaintance."

He once dropped a hint that often stood me in good stead in the burning heat of the tropics. On a summer day he asked for a drink from my bottle of lemonade. He took one mouthful. I begged him to take more, but he said, "No; if you take a little and do not gulp it down but let it trickle slowly over the mouth and throat it will moisten the membranes better than drinking much liquid quickly." I have often found this to be true. When the soldiers came straight from England to the deserts of Egypt in 1914, they were given a small flask of water to last for a day's route march. The new lads would use this up in the first hour or so, and they had to learn economy by hard experience; but Mr. McCall's hint saved me from this trouble, and I have made a thermos of water last over many an hour on the deserts.

Mr. McCall was an excellent mechanic in wood and metal. He had made a locomotive, perhaps three-feet-six long, which I have seen working well. He built an excellent model of a parish church, with tower, buttresses, and glass windows complete. Technical colleges were not yet known, but we boys were made at home in his workshop and he taught us to use tools. This I have found of great value in many lands, as well as in home repairs.

He took us into the playground with a looking-glass and a triangle and showed us how to take the elevation of the schoolhouse. He then repeated the workings on the blackboard and we had to reproduce them to scale on paper and colour the picture. A local builder acted as judge. Another boy took the prize for colouring, but my drawing was given first place for accuracy. This proved a determining factor in my life. I still use the book won then, *Every Man His Own Mechanic.*

Though a Christian, I was no little cherub in disguise. A Frenchman taught us French, a rather nervy little man. The class was full and I was seated on a music stool right under the teacher. The stool squeaked, of which I took full advantage by twisting about. It got on his nerves and he reproved me sharply. I demurely turned to the boy behind me and looked reprovingly at him. "No, sir, it is *you, you* I mean; you will leave the class." Another lad, one of the best-behaved in the school, was also ejected. We sauntered into the playground and saw the Head busy putting up a greenhouse. It spoke much for our confidence in him that we did not slink away but went to him. By our being there in classtime he must have known that something was amiss, yet he made no inquiry, but pleasantly asked us to help in the work. In my case at least this treatment made me regret my misconduct more than if he had chastised me.

It was of God that at this susceptible age I was under the influence of Mr. McCall, this wise Christian teacher. I owe him much. He taught but did not force his pupils. There were examinations, but he had little belief in them; he considered "cramming" for them to be injurious and the passing of examinations by this means to be fallacious as a test of knowledge and ability. He said it was like stuffing string into a box and getting it out again, if you could. There is something in this simile, for if knowledge so gained is recovered by the memory it is too often like tangled string, confused and troublesome.

We had a mathematical master of some quality. His name was Widdeson. He would work on the blackboard a long problem in algebra; when the board was full, he would rub all out and continue the working without the earlier figures. Not being myself specially good at figures I watched this feat with due reverence. But that he could teach was shown by the fact that by the time I was thirteen I had turned into algebra all the forty odd problems of Euclid's first book, and proved the geometry by the algebra. Yet as I reflect I see that, though I had learned *how* to do it, I did not really understand *what* I was doing, with the inevitable consequence that, not having occasion later to use algebra, I shortly forgot completely how to do this. It is an example of our Lord's words on vastly more important subjects, that "When anyone heareth the word of the kingdom, and *understandeth* it not, then cometh the evil one, and snatcheth away that which hath been sown in his heart" (Matt. 13:19).

This early taught me a most important lesson as a preacher, even that the truth must be made *thoroughly intelligible* to the mind of the hearer. C. G. Finney has told us that he never put any pressure on the will of his hearers to obey the call of the gospel until he felt assured that they *clearly understood* the message, with the nature and results of the step of trusting the Saviour. He would go over and under, round and through his subjects, and repeat the process, until he felt sure they were fully informed as to what he proposed they should do. Only then did he seek to persuade to action and to bow the will to obey the command of God to believe on His Son. There would have been fewer weak converts and much less backsliding had this been the regular practice of evangelists. A lawyer, an infidel, was persuaded to hear Finney because of the latter being a lawyer. Asked what he thought of his preaching he gave the illuminating reply: "The man does not preach: he *explains* what other people preach."

CHAPTER 3

Business

1887-1899

I was now rather more than thirteen years of age. A second local builder saw the drawing of the schoolhouse and at once offered to take me into his office. It had not been intended that I should leave school so young, but the family was growing, my father consented, and God was over it.

The small boy (for I was still diminutive for my age) now sat at an office desk instead of a school desk. The former experience in my father's counting house prevented any feeling of strangeness. I now made tracing copies of plans for houses, kept the prime cost ledger, gained elementary knowledge of building construction, of materials, wages, and of working men. All knowledge is useful to one who has the gumption to apply it.

In the summer work started at 6 a.m., in the winter at 7 a.m. Our regular early rising at home made these hours quite easy. The office was ten or twelve minutes away. I went home to breakfast and dinner. Work ceased at 5 p.m. Neither myself nor anyone of whom I heard in those days was hurt by working nine hours a day. Life at that time furthered habits of diligence, routine, exactness, and punctuality.

The chief purpose of God in this two and a half years of my life is clear. My sole office companion was the clerk of the yard, a gentlemanly man named Hunt, of perhaps thirty years of age. He was ever kind and considerate to his youthful junior, and did all he could to help me gain proficiency. I remember him gratefully. But he was an atheist and, for those days, a pretty advanced Socialist. Almost daily we discussed religion. He was, I think, rather interested that a boy of fourteen could face up to his arguments. It declares the soundness of my conversion, the illumination of my mind by the Spirit of truth, and the profound value of children being early saturated with the words of the Bible, that my faith was not in the least weakened by those discussions, while my knowledge was greatly extended as to the arguments of infidels and the views of Socialists. This proved invaluable when a little later I was serving in the gospel in working-class districts, and had to encounter such at open-air meetings and personally.

When the career of even a youth is ordered by God he will be safe. "The way of Jehovah is a stronghold to the upright" (Prov. 10:29). Here is a singular combination of ideas: the open road is a castle; it is as safe to the upright as a

fortress if it be the way appointed by God. He knew that His previous training had informed my mind and fortified my spirit to profit by this constant
contact with unbelief.

All through life I have marked another gracious and very exact working
of God. Without my having sought them, or even had knowledge of their
existence, books have come to me exactly suited to my needs or service. At this
time I found on my father's shelves a work by a former atheist, later a clergyman, named Thomas Ragg. It was entitled *Creation's Testimony to God,* and was
a well-written marshalling of the argument for the existence and nature of the
Creator. Its science might not be thought today to be wholly correct, but its
reasons and reasonings were convincing. By the time I was sixteen I had read
and re-read this book until I had mastered all its arguments save one, and was
pretty well primed to meet the common objections, and some of the philosophical objections, to the Christian faith.

The last I knew of Mr. Hunt was that he disagreed with our employer and
was dismissed. He and other discontented men made an effigy of the master
and gathered to burn it on Sidcup Green. But the police prevented this. It
would not surprise me if there were some substantial grievance against the
employer, though no justification for their proposed public insult. For before
this he had dismissed me without notice, with no honest reason and in no
pleasant mood. I had gained in his office what advantages were possible and
the divine Over-ruler now moved me forward on His path for me.

My next job was with wholesale jewellers in Hatton Garden, London. It
was a pretty business. Jewels are fascinating to the eye. The two partners differed greatly. One was well-built and hearty; the older man was smaller and
intense. He would go into a fierce rage about trifles and his hands tremble
with anger. Yet he never raised his voice. I have since reflected that perhaps
the poor man was really struggling to control himself and deserved to be pit-
ied. But it was unpleasant to the junior clerk. The other partner could weigh
a jewel on the tip of his finger almost exactly and could calculate its value in
his head to three places of decimals. He out-widdesoned Widdeson, and I
marvelled. But the office was dark and confined, my head began to ache, and I
stayed only a month. It contributed a little more to my knowledge of men and
their ways. It takes all sorts to make a world, and the more varieties one knows
the more one can help them.

Presently I found myself serving The Travellers Accident Insurance Company, Limited, a small and new company with its office at 9, Gracechurch
Street, London, E.C. I was the junior Clerk and ran errands and licked stamps.
But shortly the Assistant Manager hinted that if I would learn shorthand
quickly he would suggest that I take the place of the corresponding clerk who
was about to leave. This came to pass.

Here again I had a taste of how unreasonable an employer can be. The Manager told me he would require me to meet him at the office at 10 a.m. on a Bank Holiday, to deal with letters before he left for the north. I took the hour's journey to town, but by one o'clock he had not arrived and I went home. The next morning I found on my desk a furious note threatening serious consequences should I ever so act again. The Assistant Manager, a really pleasant and friendly man, showed the letter to one of the Directors and I heard no more of it. But this was the kind of treatment which in carnal men bred resentment and fostered Socialism.

One of the directors was a barrister. It frequently fell to me to take papers for his signature at his chambers in the Temple. At the head of his staircase I used to see the name W. R. Moore, B.A., barrister-at-law. Years later he was to become one of my faithful friends, as will be related.

In the year 1892 this Company was acquired by the Crown Accident Insurance Company, Limited, with its head office at Bristol. I was by now in charge of the claims department and the buying Company offered to take me to Bristol. My salary was £40 a year, which they increased to £60. I believed this to be the will of God, my father concurred, I packed a bag and a box, said goodbye to my boyhood's home, and took my first long journey by rail (long as I then felt). I reached Bristol on Saturday afternoon, April 16, 1893. I was eighteen years of age.

A new chapter in life had opened, and its first lesson was one of the gracious care and provision of God. I knew not a soul in this great city. The first necessity was to find a lodging. One who knew Bristol had given me a small map and had pointed out one or two districts where lodgings would be within my means. He specially warned me against Clifton as being the area of high class residents and very expensive. Being an Exclusive Brother I went first to one who kept their Bible and Book Depot, not far from the top of Park Street. This is on the way to Clifton, and he sent me to another of the fraternity, an assistant in a shop in the Mall, at the very heart of Clifton. He at once introduced me to Mr. Sims, another assistant in the same business, who sent me to his wife. They lived right against the Parish Church. Mrs. Sims offered me a small bedroom at the modest charge of 5 s. a week, and thus in two hours from reaching the city I found myself the occupant of a quiet room, in the most aristocratic and beautiful part of Bristol, and with kind, Christian people, members of a Baptist church. This was the first of several occasions, to be mentioned in turn, of the goodness of God in providing rooms or houses.

Whit Monday came a few weeks after my arrival. As before mentioned, I spent the day walking to Clevedon, Portishead, and back to Clifton, perhaps twenty-six miles. I ate only a biscuit or two. At Abbots Leigh, some six miles from Bristol, a pleasant woman of some sixty years told me she had never been to Bristol. In the evening I went to the prayer meeting as usual.

The "Crown" Company was older and larger than the "Travellers" and brought wider experience. We dealt with Accident, Sickness, Employer's Liability, Burglary, and Fidelity Guarantee insurances. This afforded insight into many branches of commercial life as well as into human nature. The claims department is naturally the principal spending department of an insurance company, and also the most contentious. It was not long before I was in charge of this with my new Company. It involved the drafting of legal documents, such as proposal forms, policies, claims forms, and agreements. I was often in consultation with solicitors, had to prepare for them cases that were to be taken to the Courts, and occasionally to attend the proceedings. It was my part to ascertain accurately the facts of every claim and to prepare the first summary of matters that could not be settled at once.

Grace has law as its background, for its kindly office is to mitigate the severity of law or even to deliver the culprit entirely from the action of law. Yet this must be done in full harmony with justice. Therefore he who is to be a herald of grace ought to know the essential principles of law, so as to show how grace can act without dishonour to law. My daily duties brought to me such knowledge, to serve me as a preacher of God's message of mercy.

But other real advantages accrued to further my preparation for later work. God prepares in advance the works of each servant: "good works which God hath afore prepared that we should walk in them" (Eph. 2:10). He also prepares the servant for the works. My preparation included such elements as these:

1. *Great care in collecting facts.* We lost an action in the High Court through our Liverpool agent having been aware of a single material fact which he had not communicated to us at Head Office. The rule held that the knowledge of the agent is in law the knowledge of the principal. A seemingly good exegesis of Scripture may be wrong because perhaps only one relevant passage or fact has been overlooked. It is a sound canon that any hypothesis which is true will cover all the facts of the case. Let the teacher of Divine truth be extremely careful that he has gathered all that the Bible has to say upon a subject before he ventures to teach that subject.

2. *Care in weighing facts.* All facts are important but not all are of equal importance. In presenting a case stress must be laid upon the weighty determining factors. Exposition and preaching may have little effect, or even an injurious effect, by secondary points being over-emphasized. A bigot may wreck a friendship or a church by obstinately insisting upon an opinion or usage which may be quite secondary.

3. *Accuracy in stating facts.* The statement should represent exactly both the nature and the value of each fact. It should neither misrepresent it, nor under-emphasize it, nor over-state it. The whole statement also should present a balanced view of the whole case. In preparing a case for Court, especially for the highly trained judges of the High Court, the final, if not the sole, determining factor is how the Court will view the matter. The servant of the Lord has to study to show himself approved unto God, and a severe study it is. And in presenting the gospel case to men the preacher should aim at exactness of statement of each fact and truth, and at due proportion and emphasis. Our message is neither wholly law nor wholly grace, neither mercy nor wrath should be pressed in isolation; neither salvation nor damnation is the whole message, and neither should be stressed at the expense of the other.

4. *Accuracy in reading documents.* The first point in reading is to note precisely what the document *says.* Not what I think it *means,* nor what I think the writer *wished* to say, but just exactly what it does say. One may then go on to read each statement in the light of what the same document says elsewhere, or of what the same writer says in some other document, and thus each statement may illuminate the whole and the whole may illuminate each separate statement. But each sentence, yea, each word must first be pondered to get its precise sense and force.

Were Bible students and teachers to treat thus the sacred writings much foolish and hurtful talk would cease. Too much supposed exegesis is like that of the boy in class, who being asked to name the most merciful man mentioned in the Bible, replied, "Please sir, Og, king of Bashan; for his mercy endureth for ever" (Ps. 136:20). In so large a book as the Word of God, covering such vast and varied subjects and so immense a mass of details, perfect accuracy may be unobtainable, but let it be aimed at. It is due to the Author and to the hearer or reader. And since such minute pains are taken in affairs temporal, much more should matters eternal be so treated.

My office life had other useful elements. It developed the knack of co-operating pleasantly with the varied types of men always at one's elbow. Working in a room with a dozen others fostered the power of concentration on one's own matters in disregard of surroundings. This is an invaluable preparation for serious reading in trains, or for withdrawing the mind into itself and communing with God while other people are around. Thus is gained control of the thoughts. Gladstone said that when he shut his bedroom door he shut politics outside. His mind did not remain in the House of Commons while his body was in bed. Such control of the mental machinery demands severe and ceaseless discipline. In my case some dozens of different claims might have to be dealt with each day. One gained the habit of dealing with each, putting its papers away and at the same moment putting the case wholly out of mind, so as to concentrate on the next. Desultory thinking is wasteful and inexact, the fruitful source of mistakes. Satan finds idle thoughts for idle minds.

The first fruit of the Spirit mentioned in Gal. 5:22 is love, the last is self-control. Without the latter the former may be sadly ill-balanced and impaired. Self-control should begin where all activities begin, in the thoughts. The brain should not be like an engine running away with itself because its governor is out of action. When such control has been gained the engineer can at will stop the machine and let it rest. An engine overworked becomes overheated. A mind never in repose easily induces heated feelings, anger, and other states most injurious to itself and to others. This ability to stop thinking at will is the chief secret of the priceless health-restoring boon of being able to sleep at will. One can suppose it was along this line that Tersteegen advanced to the experience described in his lines:

> *Oft comes to me a blessed hour,*
> *A wondrous hour and still:*
> *With empty hands I lay me down*
> *No more to work or will;*
> *An hour when wearied thought has ceased,*
> *The eyes are closed to rest,*
> *And hushed in heaven's untroubled peace*
> *I lie upon Thy breast.*

But self-control should extend over all activities. It is an excellent plan to stop reading a book in the middle of some fascinating or exciting passage. Not to be able to stop reading is as much and as injurious a state of slavery as not to be able to stop smoking or talking or drinking. I found that *Lorna Doone* was thus exciting my mind and hurrying it beyond control, so I closed the book in the middle of the attack on Jan Ridd's farmhouse and did not open it again for many years. Chess became so absorbing and exacting that the mind worked on problems when attention should have been on other matters, so I stopped playing. Soon after I went to Bristol I was made welcome in a house with four young children. They filled the gap caused by having left four younger sisters and a brother at home, and presently I found I could not easily pass the door of that house. I resolved not again to enter until I should be able to go by as easily as to go in.

These are instances of self-control in matters innocent and right. Whoever will practise it in *such* matters will the more readily gain the help of the Spirit of God to control the habits of mind and of body which are sinful. While self-control thus dominates the inner and outer man self does not obtrude as the object of life; this leaves the soul free to serve others, which is the life of love; thus the first and the last fruit of the Spirit conjoin to produce and encircle and vivify all other graces.

This mental and moral education went forward without any idea on my part of the work for which God was thus preparing me. I had no schemes for my future, but was simply diligent in present duties, doing the duty of the day in its day, and continually becoming more proficient. Let the many who are compelled to stick at routine tasks reflect that drudgery is a famous disciplinarian and turns out first-class pupils. The greatest master of men of whom history tells was subjected for forty years to the severe discipline needful for a prince of the reigning house, and for forty more years to the severer discipline of being a desert shepherd doing nothing spectacular. It was while Moses was thus quietly doing his daily duty that he was granted a vision of God and given a high and noble commission. And the Greater than Moses pleased His Father through thirty years of obscurity before He was sent out into publicity. Nazareth was the school in which the man Christ Jesus was prepared for Calvary and the throne of God. There He learned obedience.

My Managing Director and I were discussing a claim. He said: "We'll write so and so, Lang," and he dictated what he knew very well was a lie. What was I as a Christian to do? It was one of those tense and decisive moments when the roaring lion suddenly springs at one from a thicket; a moment when a young man makes or loses a spiritual fortune. It would have been easy to have juggled with conscience by the specious plea that he, not I, would sign the latter and be responsible, or that I was only doing the duty for which I was paid as a clerk. But my hand had been redeemed from iniquity by the precious blood of Christ and must not be prostituted to writing a lie. I found grace to be faithful. Of course I did not say, "That is a lie, sir!" That would have been rude from a younger man to his senior, from a clerk to his manager. But I said: "I think, sir, it would hardly do to say that; the case does not really stand so." For a few moments he rapped his desk with his knuckles, but he altered the letter, which was all that mattered. He was a shrewd man of affairs and knew very well that a clerk who would not tell a lie for him would not tell a lie to him. From that day he trusted me fully, left the department wholly to me, and I took to him only matters the responsibility of which I did not care to carry. For me as for him the saving of time and discussion was worth while. In the long run it is always best to do the right, though it is well to remember the principle in Whateley's remark, that it is true that honesty is the best policy, but he who is honest because it is the best policy is no better than a thief. One must do right even though he must suffer for it.

At the close of the year 1893 I received one of those inward and dominating intimations of the blessed will of God which are of priceless value if followed. From my youth I had cherished a secret and ardent attachment to a girl friend, like myself a Christian and in the same Christian circle. It had been a comfort to my heart and of moral value, for it kept me from any disposition to flirting. I had given her no conscious hint of my feelings and now it was borne in on my soul with distinct and irresistible force that I must renounce her in my heart. It was painful, but the effort greatly braced and strengthened inward self-mastery, as well as making room for the comfort of God. I now see that, amiable and good as she was, she would not have been fully the companion needed for the life that God had in view of service to His name.

If Thou shouldst call me to resign
What most I prize, it ne'er was mine;
I only give Thee what was Thine:
Thy will be done.

In November, 1893 the motherly care and skill of a Christian friend, a nurse, by name Mrs. Lindley, had saved my life during a severe illness. A little later I went to board with her. Miss Lindley, her daughter, removed to London and Mrs. Lindley and I moved to other apartments in Clifton. At one of these there occurred one of those experiences which baffle naturalists. A quite young kitten was put in a basket and driven in a trap at night over the famous suspension bridge and a few miles into the country. Three days later it arrived back at its first home.

We then hired rooms at No. 8, Merchants Road, Clifton. The landlord was an expert repairer of china. I don't know what his aristocratic customers would have felt had they known some of his methods. The horn of a beautiful unicorn had been broken off. The new horn consisted of a piece of wooden meat skewer, enamelled and glazed. A triangular piece had gone from the trellis edge of a fruit plate. A piece of lead pipe was hammered to the required thickness, cut to shape, enamelled and glazed. No flaw showed any mend. He had learned the art from his father, and the secret was to die with him. I would that my spiritual repairs of the souls of men had always been done so perfectly.

To all eternity that small house in Merchants Road will remain to me a sacred spot, for some momentous transactions took place there.

First, a vicious habit learned at school had continued to master me for ten or eleven years. I was a slave, and cruel was the slavemaster. How desperately I struggled, how dismally I failed. How bitterly I mourned, how sincerely I confessed, how sweetly was I always forgiven. I knew the unfailing grace of God in fulfilling 1 John 1:9, "If we confess our sins He is faithful and righteous to forgive our sins." But pardon so freely accorded did but make me the more ashamed of my sin. The way of pardon I knew; the way of victory I knew not. I had been well instructed and was well assured as to justification; the means of sanctification I had not been shown. I could tell the lost how to be saved, but could not tell the saved how to be holy. Calvary was a precious reality; of Pentecost I had no experience. Before God I was in Christ by faith, now Christ was to enter me by His Spirit. The hour of deliverance struck.

Kneeling at my bedside in an agony of conflict, fighting a desperate but losing battle, suudenly with overwhelming authority the Voice spoke the words: "I know that in me, that is, in my flesh, dwelleth no good thing" (Rom. 7:18). Instantly the whole situation was illuminated. The truth of the assertion had been burned into my soul by years of dismal failure. In the intensity of the moment I exclaimed: "Then, Lord, victory over sin will never come out of me, for that is a very good thing and there is no good thing in me, and you can't get blood out of a stone; *now, Lord Jesus, I will see what Thou wilt do for me.*"

At that instant I was free, completely free, free for ever. One moment I was the slave, the next moment the master. One moment I was a weakly infant in the grip of a giant, the next moment I was Samson rending the lion as a kid. Long I had laboured in vain to draw water out of a dry well; now I drank of the water of life, and knew that word in power: "the law of the Spirit of life which is in Christ Jesus made me free from the law of sin and death" (Rom. 8:2). From that great hour I have known experimentally what Charles Wesley declared in the matchless stanza:

> *Long my imprisoned spirit lay*
> *Fast bound in sin and nature's night;*
> *Thine eyes diffused a quickening ray,*
> *I woke, the dungeon flamed with light;*
> *My chains fell off, my heart was free,*
> *I rose, went forth, and followed thee.*

Along what routes He has led and I have followed these pages will show.

A second momentous event connected with that little house was that there I commenced consecutive reading of God's Word. I had been reading the Bible since I had read anything, but desultorily. It occurred to me that perhaps I had not read it all and that therefore there might be things my God and Father wished to say to me which I did not know. Obviously the simple cure for this was to read it straight through. Mrs. Lindley was often away for long periods nursing. I had breakfast and tea alone before and after office. The year may have been 1897 or 1898, in my twenty-fourth year. Without stopping to ponder the difficult passages I read straight through in five months.

The first impression was that I had gained a bird's eye view of the history of the world from God's point of view. It was observable that He said little or nothing about ancient events upon which human historians said and say much, but said much upon persons and events they ignore. Abraham and Moses were instances. Only events of importance in the purposes of God were selected and recorded. Human wisdom could not recognize the importance of these persons and doings and disregarded them.

On reaching 1 Cor. 2:12 I read: "But we received, not the spirit of the world, but the spirit which is of God; in order that we might know the things that are freely given to us by God," including, "the *deep* things of God" (ver. 10). This meant that the Author of the Book, the Spirit of truth was with me to open to me even the deep mysteries of God therein stated. It was as if a pupil should have as tutor the writer of the textbook used. Obviously the latter could explain all written in his book. It was only a question of the capacity and diligence of the pupil. From that hour I addressed myself to the minute study of the Bible with confidence and resolution.

Since the Old Testament is so much longer than the New I felt it would be inadvisable to read always from Genesis to Revelation, for one would be so long without studying the part addressed directly to Christians. The remedy for this was to read the two side by side, returning when finished to Genesis and Matthew. This practice I have maintained daily throughout these more than fifty years, nor have I felt the need or advantage of any other scheme or arrangement of Bible reading. It is both simple and comprehensive. It has this further distinct advantage, that every topic of Scripture is considered in the proportion assigned to it by the Holy Spirit, and the student thus surveys each topic as often and as long as it is found in the Book. The mind is thus preserved from one-sidedness, and the evil is averted of being a man of one subject only. Truth is one complete whole, and each separate truth needs to be understood in its relation and proportion to the whole. Thus does the child of God become a man of God, fully fitted for every good work and able to encourage and equip others (2 Tim. 3:14-17).

It was at that first consecutive reading that I first read the Revised Version. I knew at once that I had found a translation infinitely more exact and lucid than the Authorized Version. Whole ranges of truth opened up from single changes. This conviction of superiority has deepened by half-a-century of ever more exact study, especially when some years later I gained an elementary knowledge of New Testament Greek. Twenty-five years later, when I was about fifty years of age, I learned to read the Bible in German. It has been my habit to read daily the same passage, at first in English and Greek; and later in English, Greek, and German. It is illuminating and valuable, abundantly worth the time and labour.

I have no doubt that it was a gracious and preparatory ordering of God that when I left home I brought away my father's copy of the Revised Version.

The third determining event in my life connected with 8, Merchants Road was that there I met my wife. Mrs. Lindley invited a few friends to meet, one of whom was Florence Mary Brealey. In the middle of the last century her grandfather, George Brealey, was well known in some evangelical circles as one who turned many to righteousness, more especially on the remote and neglected Blackdown Hills, in Devon. His son, Walter J. H. Brealey, had continued to supervise that work while also ministering the Word at Copse Road Chapel, Clevedon, in Somerset. Florence was Walter's eldest daughter. Of them and her I knew nothing, but the first glance into her eyes told me that she must be mine. How this was fulfilled will be narrated in its place. It is enough now to say that, some fifteen years after our union, I had been preaching for some time at a town in Scotland when one asked if I was married. I said, "Yes, and I have a daughter. Why?" "Well, we never hear you mention your wife." "Oh," I replied, "that is easy to explain. If I once started talking about *her*, I should not know when to stop; so it is best not to begin."

Duties at the Crown Accident Company sometimes took me to a distance. I was sent to Northampton to investigate certain large defalcations by the Secretary of a Building Society whose fidelity we had guaranteed. I returned with proofs that my Company was not legally bound to pay. The Managing Director gave me an honorarium of £5.

In 1897 he sent me to Glasgow to close the office there. The fact that a branch was to be closed, taken with some other matters, caused me to suspect that the Company was to be sold. This proved to be the fact. The buyers were the Norwich and London Accident Insurance Company. Their Manager asked me to join their Head Office staff in Norwich, and offered to double my salary. Natural reasoning would have led me to accept the offer at once. God had used an amalgamation to bring me to Bristol, and it might readily be concluded that by the same means He would send me to Norwich. I had not sought this advantageous opening; it would surely be stupid to refuse it. Thus reasons nature; such was the voice of "common sense".

But some time before this my daily reading had been in 2 Sam. 5:17-25. Soon after David had been made king over all Israel the Philistines determined to smash the new monarchy and re-assert their supremacy. They pressed up the valley up which the railway now runs from Lydda to Jerusalem, and halted near the city in the valley of Rephaim, the name being reminiscent of the earlier days when giants held the land. Now David was a seasoned and experienced commander, yet was he too wise and devout to rely on himself, but asked counsel from his God. It was given. He made a fierce frontal attack, and the victory promised by God was secured.

But before long the enemy renewed the assault and took up the same position at the same valley. Now David might well have reasoned that this was the same military situation and he might rightly follow the former directions to meet it. But this he did not do; on the contrary, he sought fresh guidance from God and was given quite different instructions. He was to make a flank attack. The wisdom of this is evident. The Philistines would naturally have strengthened their front to meet another blow there; but the new assault succeeded and they were signally defeated.

From this I stored in my mind the lesson not to follow former guidance even though circumstances were repeated. Consequently I asked for a week to consider the proposal to go to Norwich. The whole week passed but I had no assurance of the will of God. My Managing Director arrived and went to his room. He might at any moment ring to learn my decision, so I went to an empty room and reminded the Lord that I had waited for His directions; that it was now needful that it should be given; would He graciously tell me what to say. Taking out a tiny New Testament which had been given to me by the dear girl I had first loved, I was immediately arrested by 1 Tim. 4:15: "Be diligent in these things; give thyself wholly to them; that thy progress may be manifest unto all." Seemingly remote from the matter in hand the words nevertheless gave immediate and clear light. From the former experience I knew that the first year or two after the amalgamation of two companies I must give much more time to merging the affairs of the old Company into those of the buying Company, and should have less time for the things of God. But as the Lord by the verse called me to be diligent in these things, and give myself wholly to them, it could not be His will for me to take the post offered, and I declined it.

Somewhat vaguely I wondered at the moment whether the verse might intimate that some day I might be called to leave business and give all my time to the work of God. But that notion did not persist. The time for it had not yet arrived and I sought another post.

Quite soon one offered. It was a promising appointment with the Bristol Water Works. The salary was good, the job permanent, with a pension in due time. But it carried the condition that every night of the month of January must be given to helping in the preparation of the balance sheet. In the light of the guidance recently given I was not free to devote a twelfth of my spare time to business, thus reducing the time already given to things divine.

My late Managing Director gave me this letter to the Secretary of the Water Works:

March 9, 1897.

I understand that Mr. Lang is applying to you for an appointment and I have pleasure in stating that he served under me for about four years and I found him honest and straightforward in all his work. I found him very capable in his department, which consisted of claims. Generally he is intelligent and possessed of tact and he can be thoroughly trusted to carry out anything he agrees to carry out.

This is to be viewed as coming spontaneously from the man for whom I had refused to tell a lie. God had made my righteousness to go forth as the light because I had committed my way unto Him and trusted in Him (Ps. 37:5. 6). The last sentence of the letter gives the exact meaning of the word *pistis* in Gal. 5:22, rendered ambiguously in the A. V. by "faith", but more adequately in the R. V. by "faithfulness". It is not here "the faith" as something that one believes, nor equivalent to "trust" as an attitude of heart; but it means "dependability, trustworthiness". This is a fruit of the Spirit of God's Son, upon whom the Father relies implicitly to carry out all His will and purposes. That Spirit had wrought in me so far as to produce in measure this fruit. No young Christian lives in vain if he so addresses himself to the daily duties as to develop by the Spirit this fruit of reliability.

I was now in my twenty-third year. My uncle was chief accountant in London to the Liverpool, London, and Globe Insurance Company. He kindly introduced me to their Manager in Bristol, and he to the Bristol Manager of the London and Lancashire Insurance Company, whose service I entered. The salary was a little lower than that paid latterly by the Crown Company, but for the first time I had the pleasure of a Christian employer. This was Mr. David Dundas Chrystal. He was an elder of the church at Bethesda Chapel. I was the only Christian in the office, and we were quickly on personal terms. He was a helpful teacher of the Word of God, simple, solid, weighty, though his style was anything but fiery.

Mr. Chrystal was an exemplary manager who commended his religion to his irreligious staff. He never entered the office till a few minutes after opening hour, and so gave us a little grace as to arriving. Some managers would glance over the morning letters, deal with anything really urgent, then go out seeking business, and return in the afternoon to dictate letters. This often led to the staff being late in leaving. Mr. Chrystal divided the letters to the departments, dictated all letters possible, and only then went out.

He seldom came into the general office, for he knew that if sundry books and papers came before him in due routine the work was being duly done. There was no spying upon us.

Every day he returned in good time, signed papers, and always left five minutes before the hour for closing, so that we could leave on time.

Consequently he was much respected by his staff, and when he retired they not only presented to him a token of their esteem but listened attentively to a pointed homily upon the benefits of diligence, morality, and godliness.

From the windows of that office I watched the vast funeral procession of George Müller on March 14, 1898, and on May 20, 1898, listened to Welsh miners play in the street the *Dead March* upon the death of Gladstone. They were two of the greatest men of their period, the one in the kingdom of heaven, the other in the kingdom of Great Britain: and heaven is high above earth.

In the spring of 1899 I was writing a letter to the manager of a local brewery upon their fire insurance. It was by no means the first time, but on this occasion the Voice suddenly said in my heart: "If you were to meet this gentleman outside the office, and a fair opportunity came, you would not mind telling him that if his premises were burned down and never rebuilt it would be a public benefit. Yet you are taking part of your salary for arranging to do what you think ought not to be done."

At once I realized that this was a first-class crisis. Should I leave the insurance business on this ground, what calling, for which my training had fitted me, would be open? For this ruin-spreading trade, like a giant and deadly octopus, had its cruel tentacles almost everywhere. If I went into a bank I must keep its accounts, or on a railway I must handle its traffic sheets.

The weeks that followed were full of deep thought and anxious inquiry. It was certain that few, even Christians, would be likely to sympathize. My esteemed Manager would not agree with the step. To justify what seemed like condemning better Christians than myself I must produce some better reason than my own opinion or preference, even some warrant from God for wrecking my prospects in life. This was equally necessary for my own peace and strength. The exercise of mind thus caused was at once profitable by sending me more than ever to the Lord. One evening I left my rooms in Clifton to go to a beloved friend and ask his advice. On Richmond Hill the Voice said distinctly: "*I* will instruct thee and teach thee in the way which thou shalt go: *I* will counsel thee with mine eye upon thee" (Ps. 32:8). The stress on the I was heavy. I replied: "Very well, Lord," and I went home.

After some period of self-examination and searching of the Scriptures the promised guidance was granted on May 27, 1899. Once again the Voice said distinctly: "Whatsoever ye do, in word or in deed, do all in the name of the Lord Jesus, giving thanks to God the Father through Him" (Col. 3:17). This illuminated and determined the matter. My heart said instantly: " You dare not go to that vile public house in that slum, which you surveyed three weeks ago, where men and women are helped to hurry to hell faster than they need go, and say to that poor bloated barman, *In the name of the Lord Jesus,* I am come to arrange to rebuild this place, if it be burned down, so that you may carry on this business, and *I thank God my Father* that I am able to do this."

I was also impressed by 1 Cor. 7:24: "Let every man wherein he is called, therein abide *with God.*" As I now saw that God was not with me in this part of my work I could not abide in my situation.

My duty and course were now fully warranted, indeed, demanded by the Word of God. On June 1, 1899, I wrote my letter of resignation and the ink on my signature was not yet dry when there stole softly into my heart a restful, all-pervading quietness. Not the least sense of care was left: henceforth it might have been some one else's affair and not mine, so richly was the promise fulfilled, "Thou wilt keep him in perfect peace whose mind is stayed on Thee" (Isa. 26:3). And throughout the fifty succeeding years of dependence upon my faithful God and Father for daily supplies, for my home, as well as for long foreign journeys and many emergencies, that peace has guarded the heart from anxious care. Thus are all the energies of the soul preserved from distraction as to ways and means, from being corrupted by and dissipated upon unworthy measures, and can be concentrated upon high and heavenly ends, in the power of the Holy Spirit. Later events will illustrate this.

The psychology of such an experience is quite simple. A man with legal tangles that baffle and harass him, goes to a lawyer in whose skill and integrity he has full confidence, places the matter in his care and feels relieved, believing that his affairs are now in competent hands. Peter exhorts troubled saints to commit the keeping of their lives unto a faithful Creator by doing what is right in His eyes (1 Pet. 4: 19). Having done this the heart receives the comfortable assurance that all must be well. How can it be otherwise when GOD is ordering all?

Isaiah and Paul use similar military figures to teach and to explain this. The former pictures a countryside overrun by a cruel foe and the people fleeing from their unprotected farmsteads to the fortified city. Once within its walls and gates fear gives place to peace. "We have a strong city; salvation will He appoint for walls and bulwarks. Open ye the gates that the righteous nation that keepeth truth may enter in. Thou wilt keep him in perfect peace whose mind is stayed on Thee, because he trusteth in Thee. Trust ye in Jehovah for ever; for in JAH, even Jehovah, is an everlasting rock" (Isa. 26:1-4). The word "mind" may be read "imagination". Many of our anxieties come not from actual circumstances but from what we fear may arise; they are fictions of the imagination: "I have had a great many troubles in life, but most of them never came." Faith fills the future, the morrow, not with phantoms but with GOD, and is at peace.

Paul varies the figure. He looks upon our own inner life as the city, whereinto fear and care seek to rush as raiders and work havoc, and the peace of God is the garrison that defends our hearts and thoughts. The Lord is personally at hand, that is, near by; turn to Him, tell Him your needs and trials, thank Him for ten thousand mercies, past and present; and the sense of His nearness, faithfulness, sufficiency will fill you with the peace of God (Phil. 4:5-7).

My business career was almost ended.

CHAPTER 4

Preaching—Unity Chapel
1892-1909

I turn back life's pages for seven years. In 1892 my cousins, Edward and Howard Musgrove, and I were still living at our homes in Sidcup, and in fellowship with the meeting of Exclusive Brethren. I was then seventeen. There began in our hearts an impulse to preach the gospel. We were not, as some youthful preachers have been, only newly converted and little acquainted with the truths of our holy faith. I had known Christ as Redeemer for ten years. And we had been blessed by being in homes and in a religious circle where the Word of God was habitually taught. What we knew we felt we must impart.

There seemed no opportunity at the meeting-room, so the pent-up stream overflowed the banks. Each Sunday afternoon we walked to the village of St. Mary Cray, about three miles from home, and preached under the big tree then on the green. It is worthy of note, this sight of three quite young men going forth thus, with no encouragement from their elders, with no "class" or "Union" to organize and direct, but just giving vent to the Spirit's urge to spread the good news. It was more common in England then than now. May God revive it, causing many to feel the force of that word, "Woe is me if I preach not the gospel!" (1 Cor. 9:16).

We continued this during the summer, and at its close considered what next to do. We called on the Congregational pastor and asked if we could be of any service. Doubtless he knew of our efforts and he kindly suggested that we should take some meetings in the Mission Hall at Swanley for which his church was responsible. On the nights arranged we left our offices in London, took train to Swanley, held the services, and then walked home to Sidcup, some seven miles. In those healthier days young men thought nothing of such a programme. Safety bicycles were only just seen, and were a luxury of the well-to-do.

That winter we worked in Spitalfields, in the east of London. Once the centre of the Huguenot weavers, it was then occupied largely by Jews. A converted Hebrew, Israel Isaiah Ashkenazi, hired a former Wesleyan chapel, one of Wesley's preaching halls, and held Saturday meetings for Jews. We hired it from him on Sundays, and scoured the dark streets for Jews and Gentiles and brought them to the gatherings. Nor were we without encouragement from God.

At times I was asked to speak in chapels nearer my home. My esteemed father did nothing to discourage me. Perhaps he remembered that J. N. Darby had to the last maintained his liberty to take the truth to every place to which the Lord might open the door. But when the name of "Mr. G. Lang" appeared on bills announcing meetings in chapels, he pointed out that our first initial was the same, and that people were thinking that it was *he* who was going to these chapels, and he asked that I would desist from this course so long as I lived under his roof. To this reasonable request I readily assented, and almost immediately thereafter God removed me to Bristol and the difficulty ceased. God seldom requires us to break through obstacles. He uses them for our discipline of spirit and Himself clears them away when they have served His ends.

It has been mentioned above that all through life I have observed the controlling care of God in bringing to me books just when they could further me in His service. During the period in view Edward helped me much in this matter. One book was Pember's invaluable treatise *Earth's Earliest Ages, and their connection with Modern Spiritualism, Theosophy, and Buddhism.* It set me thinking aright and inquiring concerning the vast and solemn topics indicated by the title. The reading of it gave a determining direction to my studies. He also gave me Kirkham's *Open-Air Preacher's Handbook,* a useful and stimulating book, and some volumes of Spurgeon's *Lectures to My Students.* These were very helpful to me as a young preacher. At the same time I "happened" on Rupert Garry's small treatise *Elocution, Voice, and Gesture.* Of this I made a thorough study, especially of the selected pieces annotated to teach accent, emphasis, modulation, and gesture. To this little book I owe, under God, whatever I have gained of the art of speaking pleasingly and effectively. One could wish that many other preachers had taken pains to master the art of speaking in public. The noblest of themes deserves the finest of styles, and the finest of styles is that of speaking naturally, and not artificially. This can be acquired and must be cultivated.

On going to Bristol in April 1893 my first association was naturally with the Exclusive meeting, at Orchard Street, and I joined in their outdoor testimony on College Green. It was neither inspiring nor encouraging, and before long I was in touch with the open-air work of the Y.M.C.A. It was on the Broad Quay in summer, and in winter in the Fruit Market, High Street. This drew me further into Y.M.C.A. work, and presently I was one of the Evangelistic Committee and Leader of the Sunday afternoon Bible Class. The latter was helpful to me at least, for I had to lead the thoughts and answer the questions of boys of twelve and men of sixty, being myself nineteen. Knowledge of the Word of God and care in expounding it were developed.

In addition to this I usually preached Sunday morning and evening at various country and town chapels or halls and commonly walked about ten miles in the day. There were also week evening engagements.

At this time God brought into my life a fresh and powerful influence, even the ministry of Dr. A. T. Pierson of America. Having profited by some of his books I suggested to the Secretary of the Y.M.C.A. that he be invited to give a series of addresses. This came to pass, to the profit of many and of none more than myself.

It was at the last of the meetings on July 11, 1897, that I had the one opportunity to hear that mighty man of faith George Müller. He and James Wright never went to the Bristol Y.M.C.A., but out of regard to Dr. Pierson they came to that meeting. It was to be "missionary" in character, upon which topic Dr. Pierson was a leading authority. The secretary asked him to what time for his address he should limit George Müller. He replied: "You will limit him to the whole evening." In fact, he spoke for an hour and a quarter. Though in his ninety-second year, he stood square and straight and gave in clear tones a resume of the seventy years of his service to God. Without notes he gave exact facts and figures of the work for orphans, of Bible and tract distribution, with the other branches of The Scriptural Knowledge Institution, as well as of his world-wide journeys. The number of orphans trained, of books distributed, of countries visited, the monies received, down to the last farthing on each account—all were set forth; and the great recital was enforced with the memorable words:

"God is still the living God, and now, as well as thousands of years ago, He listens to the prayers of His children, and helps those who trust in Him."

Dr. Pierson's opening words were: "We have listened to the greatest missionary address that I, or any of us, have ever heard."

He spoke for three quarters of an hour, and the audience listened with rapt attention. During the next ten years he was frequently in Bristol, and through public ministry and private intercourse I was very greatly benefited. He and G. H. Pember were the two men to whom I am indebted more than to all others; the former for instruction in the practical Christian life, the latter for insight into the deeper purposes of God.

Although by nature cautious, and by business training critical, it had pleased God to preserve in me a simplicity of spirit, susceptible of good impressions, though watchful as to yielding to these. In the hope that others of like mind may be helped I will repeat some statements I heard Dr. Pierson make.

He had been a Presbyterian minister in Detroit, U.S.A. Through a small life of George Müller he had some knowledge of him and his work, and hearing that he and Mrs. Müller were travelling in the States, he set off to overtake them. But all the time he was one stage behind them. When he reached San Francisco he learned that they were at Oakland, the other side of the bay, and then he could have overtaken them. But it was the Lord's day, and the ferry was such a source of sabbath desecration that he could not bring himself to use it. He therefore turned homeward disappointed. But when the train reached Ogden, the junction of the San Francisco and Oakland lines, Mr. and Mrs. Müller boarded the saloon where he sat, and they travelled together to Chicago. Later Mr. Müller visited Dr. Pierson at Detroit.

At that time Dr. Pierson held the view that the gospel is to effect the salvation of all our race and that only then will the Lord return to reign. This he expounded to George Müller, and one can believe that the case was ably presented. Mr. Müller listened in silence, in his usual posture, with his eyes to the ground and his hands between his knees. At the end of the argument he said: "I have listened, dear brother, to all that you have said on this subject. It has only one defect. It is not founded upon the Word of God." He then opened his Bible and for two hours he showed what the Word of God teaches, and continued the subject for ten days. It was a determining event in the ministry of Dr. Pierson.

During that first visit to Bristol he addressed the Preachers' Preparation Class, which I attended at the Y.M.C.A. Encouraging us to rest faith in God, he told that he and Mrs. Pierson were travelling on the Continent, with a return ticket to London, and six pounds in cash. In Switzerland they met some poor students studying to be preachers, and they felt led to give to these the six pounds. Reaching London without money, a friend they immediately met gave them six pounds from the Lord.

He was also asked to give to a company of Christian workers some account of his own life. He told of having been the minister of an up-town church where there was no spiritual movement. Becoming dissatisfied with this deadness, and praying concerning it, the Lord commenced to answer through the stately edifice taking fire and being burnt out. The only apartment spared was his study in the tower, where were his books and papers. This happy calamity drove them to the theatre for the Sunday services, where God worked in power, among a people now disturbed and awakened. God has His own effectual ways of ploughing with a view to reaping.

A company of Christians asked him to draft for them what he considered a New Testament constitution for a church. This he did, whereupon they requested him to become their pastor. He would have gladly gone to prove that the constitution was workable. But at that same time the Lord made clear that another church was His appointed sphere, so thither he went. In this church there were three wealthy members who were most dissatisfied on finding that the new minister was spiritually-minded and against the carnalities in the house of God in which they delighted. They set themselves unitedly to thwart him at every turn, and the situation became very difficult. Dr. Pierson did nothing, save to tell the Head of the church that it was He who had brought him there, and He must stand behind him and act. In a very short time the Lord *did* act, and drastically. In one week those three men were cleared out of the church. One was discovered in a social scandal, one in defalcations in business, and the third in a similar offence, the exact nature of which I do not recall. The Lord is still able to deal effectively with Ananias and Diotrephes.

The Rev. Neville Sherbrooke kindly invited a number of clergy, ministers, and a few others to meet Dr. Pierson at breakfast in Clifton. He commenced by saying that, though he had waited upon God for a theme it had only there and then been impressed upon him to speak upon Paul's farewell words to the elders at Ephesus, as given in Acts 20. As we walked away together afterwards he said that he thought the Lord wished to give the preachers gathered an evidence of how His Spirit will help in extemporaneous utterance.

He told of how when he left college, having taken some honours, he thought himself equipped for the ministry. He had studied logic and could convince anybody, and had studied rhetoric and could persuade anybody. But he had had to learn that it is "the demonstration of the Spirit" (1 Cor. 2:4) that is indispensable and effectual. The sentence from that address which left on me an indelible impression was this: "We have a saying *Magna est ueritas et praevalebit*, Great is the truth and it will prevail. But that is never so in this age. In this age truth is always with the minority; and so persuaded am I of this, that, if I find myself agreeing with the majority on anything, I make haste and get over to the other side, for I know I am wrong."

An American correspondent quotes this tribute by another American, Dr. J. P. Massee: "Dr. A. T. Pierson's mind was an intellectual ocean from which all streams of thought flowed out and to which all streams of thought returned." This powerful, cultivated, well-stored mind was devoted wholly to the glory of God and His Son, Jesus Christ.

During the succeeding fifty years I have never ceased to thank God that I was brought under the direct influence of such teaching and example. It is still bringing forth fruit in my old age to the glory of God.

Such a character and ministry are to be had only at high cost. Mr. G. F. Bergin of Bristol told me that Dr. Pierson, whom he knew well, was at one time a minister of a wealthy church, at a high salary (£2,000 a year), with a town and country house provided. He said to his wife that he felt that this was no style in which to train their children for the Lord. They therefore left that church, and he took a pastorate at only £600 a year and no house. The Lord responded, and all their family were a joy and devoted their lives to the work of God. And in due time he gave himself to a travelling ministry, in dependence upon the Lord for supplies, after the example of George Müller. It was this that enabled James Wright, in his preface to Dr. Pierson's *Life of Mr. Müller,* to say that he felt Dr. Pierson was the one to write the official biography of that man of faith, because he could do so with the ardour and force of conviction.

Constant co-operation with the Y.M.C.A., and frequent preaching in chapels and missions, so broadened my heart and outlook that the Exclusive Brethren decided that I was not in reality one of them and they terminated my formal connexion. I have always thanked God for benefits received in that circle, but equally that in early manhood I had this fair escape from the constricting spirit that stifles love and liberty. At that time I had not examined the history and principles of Brethren, nor the differences between Exclusive and Open Brethren. The separation was not on ecclesiastical questions, but on the practical matter of liberty to preach Christ wherever He gave an open door. It is regrettable that Exclusive brethren usually, and Open brethren too often, have forsaken the early practice of all Brethren which recognized fully that the Head of the church has the right to send His servants where He pleases and that they have the duty to serve His people wherever they can reach them. Their first preachers, including the chief Exclusive leaders, acknowledged their duty to the whole family of God and maintained the full liberty of each servant to obey the call of the only Master of them all. This is shown in the life of Anthony Norris Groves.

But my connexion with the Young Men's Christian Association came to an early and sorrowful conclusion. The first Y.M.C.A. was originally an Association seeking only spiritual ends, having been formed in a London business house for that distinct purpose. Later, as the sphere of activities enlarged, it widened its operations to include educational, social, and physical activities. The result was what might have been expected, even that the three departments almost swamped the one; and that, because they gratify the natural unregenerate nature, naturally-minded men were attracted and duly dominated. Examining the official Blue Book for one of those years of my connexion I found that of over thirty affiliated branches in the west of England only four had any conversions to record for the year.

In the year 1897 the Dean of Bristol informed the Secretary that he was arranging that the Dean of Canterbury, Dr. F. W. Farrar, should visit the Cathedral and he suggested that he should address a meeting of men in the Y.M.C.A. that Sunday afternoon. The proposal was adopted. This would be nominally an address to my Bible Class, though many more would doubtless attend that day. I therefore objected, on the ground that Dr. Farrar's doctrine of Eternal Hope was not acceptable and that he was well known as a Higher Critic of the Bible. I organized a petition and no small stir arose in the Y.M.C.A.

At the same time I wrote to Dr. Farrar, mentioning the part I had in the spiritual work of the Association, expressing appreciation of his courtesy in being willing to visit us, but intimating that divergence of opinion as to his views was creating conflict, and suggesting that he would really add to his kindness if he would withdraw the promise to speak at the meeting. He sent the letter to the Dean of Bristol, who expressed to the Secretary his mighty displeasure. A very full meeting of the General Committee passed by an over-whelming majority a vote of censure upon my action in writing to the Dean, and re-affirmed the engagement with him.

My attempt thus to provide an easy solution having been rejected, and my heart being unwilling to devote time and energy to maintaining spiritual life in the Association against the further conflicts I considered inevitable, I resigned membership on October 8, 1897, and have always been thankful for this second escape from an organization not contemplated in the New Testament. It was a step in my education in the Divine principles and practices for the church of God.

There was an early sequel. A few other members resigned. One of these was Mr. W. E. Milton, a customs and excise officer. I was often at his house, and on October 18, 1897, we had conversed, somewhat sadly, about the defeat of our stand at the Y.M.C.A. On the way to my rooms quite suddenly the Voice again spoke distinctly the words of Matt. 18:19: "If two of you shall agree on earth as touching anything that they shall ask, it shall be done for them of my Father who is in heaven"; and also the words, "Go back to Mr. and Mrs. Milton and ask them to agree with you in the prayer that Dean Farrar shall not come to Bristol." To me this was a new and startling challenge, but I returned, though the hour was 10.30 p.m., and we presented the petition directed. On November 6 there appeared in the daily paper an intimation that the Dean would not be able to keep the engagement to visit Bristol. The reason was most unusual. Typhoid was raging at Maidstone, the county town of Kent. The Assizes were due, but to avoid risk for the many who would need to come to the courts, the Judges had removed the session to Canterbury. It devolved upon the Dean to be at his cathedral to conduct the service which opens an assize; this fell upon the date of his Bristol visit, which had to be cancelled.

Here is an exact illustration of that "agreement" in prayer which secures answer. It is not a merely human agreement, but one brought about by the Spirit of God. Christians may fail to get the mind of God upon a matter and may agree to ask amiss. But the Spirit knows the will of God and what He purposes; He can lead minds into harmony with that purpose, whereupon their prayer will be according to the will of God and will certainly be granted (1 John 5:14, 15). It is the musical term "symphony" which is translated "agreement". The Spirit is the Master-musician who touches hearts perhaps far removed as to location, as are the bass and treble keys on a piano, and harmonizes their desires with each other and the will of God. Therefore it is essential to be susceptible to the touch of the Holy Spirit.

Mr. Milton was associated with the church of Open Brethren at Bethesda chapel, Great George Street, as were some others I knew at the Y.M.C.A. This brought me into touch with that church and I went frequently to the Monday evening prayer meeting, attended then by up to two hundred believers. Though not formally united with that church, I came to know and esteem the rest of its leaders and teachers, as I had done Mr. Chrystal. Occasionally I was asked to speak at the vigorous meeting of young people at Stokes Croft chapel, connected with Bethesda chapel. Of this meeting the leader was Mr. Devine. This increasing intercourse with good and large-hearted Open Brethren drew me further and further from Exclusivism, but as yet I had formed no distinct views as to church constitution and order. Thus matters went on up to the time of the resignation of my post with the London and Lancashire Insurance Company.

I have mentioned the Preachers' Preparation Class at the Y.M.C.A. This was of benefit to me as a young preacher. There was need for such a class to help the many brethren from ordinary walks of life who went to local chapels to preach. One godly and older man spoke to his congregation of David as a poem, adding that perhaps they did not know what a poem was, so he would tell them: A poem is a man who writes poetry! Had he said this at the Preachers' Class he would have been well corrected as was one little man, a shop-walker, prim and positive in style. He persisted in speaking of *Saint* Matthew, *Saint* James, *Saint* Peter. His name was Coopey. He was challenged as to this title and someone remarked that we might as justly speak of "*Saint* Coopey".

There were some *real* saints among local preachers. I am sorry I did not know the one who proved his saintship in the following way. After he had preached at a country chapel some ill-mannered person said to him: "Well, Mr. So-and-so, you may be a very holy man but you are the very worst preacher I ever heard!" To which rudeness he replied: "Well, dear brother, someone must be the worst preacher, and it might as well be me as anybody else." Thus was humility victorious.

The leader of this Class was Mr. W. J. Morgan, the minister of Unity Chapel, a large building in the vast slum area of St. Philip's. That work had a history. In the 1850's one of the Bethesda fellowship, named Victor, had started in that district a meeting for women. He left this to build up a lately-commenced cause at Clevedon, Somerset, and a Major Tireman, also of the Bethesda church, took up the work. It was the period of grace which culminated in the mighty revival of 1859 and 1860 and the Major saw many converted from very sinful ways. A small hall was put up in Unity Street and became a centre of blessing.

Going one evening to his home in Clifton the Major was tempted with the suggestion that it was absurd for a gentleman of his position to squander time and strength and means in such a wretched district on so low a class of people. But victory came when he remembered (or, perhaps, was reminded) that there was one whole street where the inhabitants of every house had been saved through his preaching and labours, not to speak of many others.

The work still growing, and a larger hall being needed, Major Tireman, as I was told, pondered whether he should go to the expense of marrying and setting up an establishment of his own, or should invest his money in providing the larger premises. He decided upon the latter, and Unity Chapel was built to accommodate 1,500 persons.

In the course of time Mr. W. J. Morgan, then Secretary of the Y.M.C.A., in the days when it was spiritually pure and vigorous, became associated with Major Tireman in the leadership, and succeeded him after his death. The work retained some features of a Brethren assembly, but the preaching fell to Mr. Morgan, who became the recognized "pastor", with in due time a stated salary. At a ministers' fraternal to which he belonged he was asked how he should be described in the register. As he hesitated, a leading Congregational minister, Urijah Thomas, said, "Call him an Independent Baptist Brother." This humorous suggestion was pretty accurate; for, like Open assemblies, the church was administratively distinct from any other congregation, as are the Independents; they practised the immersion of believers only, as do the Baptists; and yet retained such items of Brethren practice as the guidance by the Holy Spirit of worship at the Lord's Supper.

At the end of September 1899, I was to leave the office. Some months before this Mr. Morgan died, and the church was seeking another pastor. I had known Mr. Morgan but nothing of his church, not even its situation in Bristol, for my lodgings and interests had lain at the other side of the great city. One day in September a friend came to the office and said that the preacher appointed at Unity Chapel for the next Sunday morning wished to find a substitute: would I go? He added that he thought that Unity Chapel was just the place for me, meaning the pastorate.

There had of late recurred to my mind the question that had arisen there when leaving the Crown Accident Company, whether I might some day be "separated unto the gospel of God", but clearly this was not for me to settle, but for the Head of the church, and I, for my part, was quite prepared for Him to direct me further into business life. As yet I had no distinct views against a formal pastorate, but only a general sense that it was not fully Scriptural; yet was this feeling not so well formed or informed as to lead me promptly to reject the idea. At the same time it was vital not to be guided by anyone but the Lord, and this friend was not one of whose spiritual judgment I felt sure. I was therefore glad to be able to answer that I was already booked for a certain place. After some hours he came back to say that he had arranged for another to take my previous appointment so that I should be free for Unity Chapel.

The human mind is liable to conflicting emotions. On the one hand I felt it impertinent of him to have interfered in my affairs; on the other hand, the very fact that he had taken so unusual a step made me wonder whether perhaps the hand of the Lord was in it. After brief consideration I said I would go. The sequel showed that it was of God.

It was Sunday morning, September 3, 1899. The subject was the new birth. Later I learned of three persons who had said that their new pastor had preached that morning. This was followed by an invitation to take some other services during October.

At the end of September I left the office facing an unknown future with a month's salary, £5, in hand. But that deep untroubled peace preserved from all anxiety. The sum lasted as usual for the month. The last Sunday evening in October I attended at Brunswick Chapel, a Methodist church. I think this was in order to get someone else to hear the gospel. A few pence due for laundry I had put by at my rooms; the balance of my funds was two-pence. When the collection was taken, without particular thought I put these coins in the bag, whereupon there flashed across my mind the sweet thought that, for the first time in my life, I had given the "widow's mite", my all, an act which assured the approval of the Lord. This was followed by the comforting reflection that, as regards money, I was now as poor as I ever could be, and knew the worst. It was gracious of the Lord to bring me thus early to a complete end of my resources, and so to a complete dependence upon Himself, for this situation was to recur a hundred times.

Not a great while after I had come to Bristol my cousin Edward secured a transfer to the Bristol branch of the Bank of England. He had rooms first at Clevedon and then at Westonsuper-Mare, where I sometimes spent weekends with him. It was our custom to lunch together daily at a restaurant, and this I continued after having left business. This particular Monday I should not be able to pay for the meal. Edward, one of the most generous persons I have known, would right willingly have paid for me that day and for however many days might have been necessary, but I resolved to make this a test period of the faithfulness of God and therefore not to tell any person of my financial circumstances. For this reason I had not told even my father of my step of leaving business, lest he should send money. But as I waited upon God that Monday morning I felt clear as to going to meet my cousin and was ready to leave my rooms when the second post brought a letter from the Treasurer of Unity Chapel with a cheque for £5 in recognition of my visits there.

This was a fourth experience of profound importance which makes No.8, Merchants Road, Clifton, a spot dear to my heart.

Divine peace not only nullifies worry but also prevents excitement of spirit. He who knows the God who doeth wonders is not surprised when He works a wonder (Ps. 77:11, 14). Yet my heart, while tranquil, was exalted, though humbled by being the subject of such grace.

The Lord prepares souls for special tasks. My preparation for this entry upon a life of trust in God alone as to temporal supplies had been largely through books. In the years immediately preceding I had "happened" upon, first, the two volumes of *The Story of the China Inland Mission*. This had quoted from Fleming Stephenson's *Praying and Working,* an account of certain German Home Missions conducted by faith and prayer, which soon after came into my hands. And, thirdly, I had found in a second-hand bookshop a set of *A Narrative of Some of the Lord's dealings with George Müller,* and had read it all through, without being deterred by the much repetition of similar incidents. Indeed, to the diligent reader these volumes are a support of the statement that repetition is the only figure of speech worth much; for the almost countless number of cases given is deeply impressive, and fixes on the heart the truth of the faithfulness of God to His promises.

This faithfulness being the chief lesson of all these books, I had been encouraged to expect that the same faithful Creator would be true to me also, when I should give Him opportunity to show what He could and would do to honour faith and to answer prayer offered in the name of Jesus His Son.

Not a word had passed between the friends at Unity Chapel and myself as to money, and that God had used them to supply in this first hour of need made me to ponder further whether it might be His plan that a closer association should follow. But he who would walk with God must desist from operations of his own hands and pay regard to the operation of God's hands, otherwise he will be broken down by God and not built up (Ps. 25:4, 5; Isa. 5: 12). I therefore did nothing at all in the matter save preach there as requested during the next month or two. Before the end of the year the Secretary of the church, Mr. Alfred Dennes, made, on behalf of the church, the proposal that I should take up the pastorate for the ensuing year, to which I agreed.

This active servant of Christ was an able man of business, constantly about the city and well known in circles in which I moved, yet he had never heard my name nor I his. But during the interval after the death of Mr. Morgan, and before my first visit to Unity Chapel, no less than three persons had mentioned me to him as being the man for their sphere. He was thus prepared by God to view my coming favourably.

It may be felt that my "call" to the "ministry" was more clearly of God than the measures by which clergy and ministers in general reach their posts. Yet in later years, with increasing acquaintance with the mind of the Head of the church, I came to see that a formal "pastorate", a single "minister" to preach and guide, is not His chosen method for ordering His house. But as yet I was walking by what light I had and He graciously ordered my steps and owned my labours. Thus His acceptance and working have preserved me from that general and severe condemnation of other servants of Christ which narrow-minded Christians not seldom utter. I was in due time led out of and beyond the position as "pastor" I now had entered in good faith, and I have had the joy to lead others beyond it; but one may recognize God at work in other of His servants as He worked in me, and can leave them to His further leading, meanwhile strengthening their hands in any present sphere which they occupy according to His present will for them.

Mr. Dennes intimated that the church proposed to pay a stipend of £120 per annum. Thus my income was to be doubled. But this did not attract me. I had long seen in Scripture that the apostles, evangelists, and teachers received no agreed salary, but trusted their Lord to meet their daily needs. Without such a working faith in Him how could they have gone forth to regions where there were no Christians to help and where they were to take no help from the heathen? (3 John 7). Under public conditions then gifts from churches at a distance were infrequent and precarious (Phil. 2:29, 30; 4:15, 16). Moreover, a regular income could not but mean a suspension of that life of faith as to means, the sweets of which I had just begun to taste. But thinking it over I felt it of grace to yield the point, and said that, as I might remain with them only a year, I would not disarrange their fiscal methods; but that if, as had been hinted, our association should prove longer, the stipend would have to yield to a plan of voluntary offerings for my support.

In thus yielding I now see that I acted from a truer spiritual instinct as to the mind of the Lord than I could then have justified from His Word; for there is a principle in the ways of God upon which He bears with, or even sanctions, suspension of His rules and even of definite laws. This is a topic deserving full treatment, yet see Num. 9:9-11, with 2 Chron. 30:17-20, for an example. The law as to eating the passover was strict, but exceptions were tolerated.

Such toleration exhibits, first, the majesty of law, by its strict requirement being difficult to honour; second, the complexity of human affairs, so that no precept can provide for all possible contingencies; third, the weakness of even the dutiful subject, sometimes disenabling him from fulfilling the strict letter of the command; fourth, the grace of the sovereign in the relaxing of his just demands. Such relaxation must indeed be exercised sparingly, lest transgression, wilful or careless, be encouraged and lawlessness increase; yet without it, judicial administration would often be harsh and would defeat the true ends of all law, respect for the ruler and the well-being of the subject and of society. Thus to relax a law may more truly honour it than to enforce it, for it may better serve its true ends.

Clifton being perhaps two miles from my new sphere of service, it was necessary to find new lodgings. This offered occasion for our loving Father in heaven to display His care and superior wisdom. Mrs. Lindley and I used much time and shoe-leather hunting for rooms. An advertisement told of apartments available at Globe House, Old King Street. My experience, however, in surveying premises for fire insurance told me that in that district buildings were old and dilapidated, so "common sense" told me not to trouble to see the house. At last I said that we had spent time and strength enough on our own efforts, and that I would now leave the matter to God. Within an hour we met a lady, unknown to us, who also was house-hunting. She told us of a suite of nearly new and commodious rooms which she would have taken at once, but that they were too large. This was Globe House! On February 15, 1899, we removed thither, and they served us well.

But trams beneath the windows turned on a short and sharp curve and they ground, groaned, and almost howled, till 11.30 p.m. Mrs. Lindley was well on in age and I noticed with concern that her nerves were suffering. There was need to find quieter quarters. On this occasion I spent but little time hunting, and soon repeated the former resolve to leave the matter to the Lord. Again He graciously responded. The next day Mrs. Stanley, wife of one of the leaders at Bethesda Chapel, called, and presently mentioned a small house opposite them which she and her husband would have loved to take only it was too small. It suited us well and on June 20, 1901 we moved to 37, Kingsdown Parade, and named it "Unity Lodge". It was further from the Chapel but on high and healthy ground.

It had a sweet walled-in garden. In my boyhood at Sidcup I never could be found on Saturday afternoons when my father wanted help in the garden, but at Unity Lodge I learned the pleasure and healthfulness of gardening. It has been justly remarked that this is the only occupation for man which is not the result of the fall. Building, making clothes, even husbandry resulted from that calamity. At first I did not know the difference between a strawberry plant and a buttercup root. But God my Father provided good instructors. Fred Curtis was gardener to a large house the other side of the Downs. Only to help a younger brother, who was starting as a greengrocer not far from Unity Chapel, Fred and his wife came to live there and associated with the church. He introduced me to his brother James, also a Christian, gardener to a mansion with fine grounds, and chairman of the Bristol Gardeners' Association. James was an expert, especially with grapes. His potting shed was wall-papered with certificates from the chief horticultural shows from Shrewsbury to Exeter. These two friends soon taught me all an amateur needed to know and made the labour a delight and a means of health.

George Rogers was Spurgeon's choice as first Principal of the Pastors' College, though he was not a Baptist but a Congregationalist. I once owned the only copy I ever saw of a volume of his addresses to the annual gathering of students, and still I mourn that the book went amissing. One address was upon the words "Paul himself was minded to go afoot" (Acts 20:13). His lessons were:

1. Paul had a mind of his own. The preacher must not be a weakling yielding to every whim or opinion of men.

2. Paul was always on the go. The minister must not be indolent.

3. Paul believed in bodily exercise. He was, on this occasion, minded to go *afoot*. The preacher must not be only in his study or pulpit or visiting his people. He should not over-tax his brain and neglect his body. Let him walk or have a workshop or a garden.

4. Paul believed in solitude. "He *himself* was minded to go afoot." He had been cooped up in a crowded ship, so he walked alone across the headland while the vessel sailed round it, and thus secured a season alone with his God. I thought of this as I passed that headland (the Dardanelles) in January 1935, sailing from Istanbul to Athens.

It was the wisdom of Rogers' third lesson that I learned in my garden and in James Curtis' gardens and greenhouses. My frequent Monday relaxation, after the labours of Sunday, was to walk across the fine Downs and potter about with him, watching him work, and conversing of things heavenly; and what I then learned was most useful when many years later we had a large country garden, with glass-house and vines. God orders the present with the future in view.

About this time one of our younger brethren, Ernest C. Thompson, brought the distressing news that his sister May had just announced that she would join the Catholic Church. She and her parents were with the Church of England. She was the second hand in one of the large and stylish dressmaking establishments. One of her assistants was a Catholic and, with commendable zeal, had sought to interest her senior. Not making progress she said, "The reason why you will not meet Father Troake is that you are afraid he will convert you." The taunt stung her into consent, and in three months the priest had indoctrinated and convinced her.

I told Ernest I could see his sister at the house of Mr. Dennes the next Saturday afternoon, March 16, 1900, if he could induce her to come, but that this would be his difficulty. But we would pray. She scorned the idea, but he unwittingly prevailed by the same argument, that she would not see me lest I should persuade her. She came, and we conversed for an hour and a half, seemingly to no purpose. But God was working. I explained the grammatical and other reasons why Peter cannot be the rock of Matt. 16:18. In her heart she said, "If what he says is true Father Troake has deceived me about this."

But of this she gave no sign, and at last I said there was only one thing more I wished to say. She had been brought up in a Church where the Bible was read publicly in our own tongue and where she was encouraged to read it. She should reflect that in the Catholic Church this would not be so. With lofty scorn she answered: "You are quite mistaken! I asked Father Troake about this and he told me that theirs is the Church that insists on its children reading the Bible."

But suddenly something flashed into my mind and I said, "Well, Miss Thompson, when next you meet Father Troake ask him why it is, if his Church insists on the reading of the Bible, that only last week, in the city of Cork, a fellow-priest of his, after rioting a Y.M.C.A. open-air meeting, burnt a Bible in the open street". I told her where to find the account in print, and it was evident that a good blow had got home.

As she left, Mr. Dennes at the door courteously invited her to Unity the next evening. She came, and remained in her place after the service. A few gathered around and we prayed and spoke with her, as she knelt with her face buried in her hands on the seat in front. After some time I felt that the moment was ripe for her to decide. The discerning of this point is one of the crucial and perilous matters in winning a soul. If pressure be premature, the confession secured will be feeble and reaction be hurtful, perhaps disastrous: if left too late, the delay in deciding may prove dangerous. I said to her: "There is no reason to stay here longer. It is simply a question of whether you will or will not accept the Lord Jesus Christ as your Saviour." She lifted her head and said quietly but firmly, "I have just done so!" and the confession was unto salvation. The lines were true:

> "'Tis done! the great transaction's done!
> I am my Lord's and He is mine!"

Hers was the first conversion in which I was personally used at Unity. She was a lovely and intelligent girl, and spiritually she became a lovely and intelligent disciple, and continued so to the end of life. After some years she developed consumption. Though perplexed as to this dispensation, and though leaving a young family, her faith remained firm, her peace steady, and her joy undimmed. To recall visits to her reminds me of Spurgeon's words to ministers to the following effect: Brethren, be much at deathbeds. The dying hear wondrous things kept from other ears. The everlasting fountains cast aloft their golden showers and the spray falls this side of the narrow stream!

After forty-five years my eyes overflow from gratitude as I think of this my child after a common faith, my child by a bond eternal, stronger than any natural tie, for the heavenly transcends the earthly. Oh, what an inexpressible bliss is his who saves a soul! It is a drop from the infinite satisfaction of Him Whose travail saves us all.

The list of members of Unity had about two hundred names. Much pastoral service was needed. Being reserved and studious, I found the task of knocking at the doors of other people irksome. But the Lord called, I followed in faith, He gave access to homes and hearts, and I soon learned the benefit of teaching from house to house as well as in public (Acts 20: 20). No flock will flourish unless the sheep and lambs have personal inspection by the shepherd. Moreover, the insight thus gained into the needs and longings and dangers of souls will greatly help the preacher in making his public ministry beneficial.

In some six months I had become acquainted with all the members, everyone of whom had been a complete stranger. Though knowing nothing of the history or condition of the church, I formed the opinion, or rather perhaps I felt in my spirit, that about forty of these two hundred were in a spiritual state to prove a trouble to the fellowship. Of this I said not a word to anyone. But before long it became evident that there was a strong party dissatisfied that the new minister was on old-fashioned lines of Christian service. They had previously been working to introduce modern and unspiritual types of activities.

Before showing that I had observed this I was guided by the Lord to ask for an alteration in the method of settling business at the church meetings. Formerly this had been done by the ordinary worldly way of a majority vote. I showed from the Scriptures, Old and New, that the method approved of God is that any given number of His people, few or many, jointly concerned in service, should come to an undivided consent before a matter is considered settled. This was embodied in my paper *Unanimity, the Divine Method of Church Government.* Everybody agreed.

After a time the storm, long gathering, burst, and for eighteen months the church was in commotion as those in question pressed for changes they desired in the direction indicated. There was a body of elder men, named deacons, though actually as to their service elders and deacons. By the grace of God these stood unitedly for maintaining the spiritual character of the church. By reason of the rule of Unanimity we had only to remain firm, quietly objecting to the changes urged, so no vote in favour of them could be secured, as might well have been done had the majority been able to decide. For though those desiring change were only a fourth of the membership yet they were zealous, persistent, and attended the church meetings diligently; whereas many of the others were old and came seldom or never, or were young and easily attracted by calls for "brightness" in the meetings and such like appeals, and yet others became weary of profitless discussions and did not attend. Thus a snatch majority might easily have been secured.

At last it was suggested by the church Secretary that there had been enough of these fruitless debates and that an evening should be fixed when those discontented should meet the elder brethren separately. The leader of the opposite party was also choir leader. In how many churches have this functionary and his choir been a source of strife! They seem seldom to be spiritually-minded. He jumped at this proposal, evidently eager to come to close quarters with his adversaries. It was now that the experience of Dr. Pierson with three carnal opponents helped me. Like him I gave myself to steadfast appeal to the Head of the church, and He took an equally drastic action. The morning of the day (August 18, 1902) when the meeting was to be held an infectious sickness entered the leader's house and he could not attend. Without him the meeting was a fiasco from his point of view.

One of his fiercest attacks had been as follows. The choir practice was on Monday evenings and he had demanded that I should supply by then the hymns for the next Sunday, so that they could be practised. I pointed out the importance of the hymns being suitable to the subject of the address and that I could not command the Lord that He must give me each Monday the two themes required for the following Sunday. During a debate on this at a church meeting one of the most spiritual of the brethren urged that the contact of the pastor with the Lord in his study was holy ground where others ought not to intrude. This was reported to all and sundry as that he had said that the pastor was a holy man and the ground on which he stood was holy ground! It is sorrowful to what lengths of misrepresentation the carnal mind will go, even in a Christian.

This painful episode showed me the truth and wisdom of a remark made to me by James Wright of the Bethesda church, son-in-law to George Müller, and his successor at the Orphan Homes. Speaking of the pastoral and oversight responsibilities I was about to assume he said: "Remember that your authority is purely moral, and as soon as it is disputed it is gone." A king can enforce his authority by his soldiers, a judge by the police, but the elder of a church has no such resource against the rebellious, unless indeed, like Paul, he is able to set in motion the police of the Court of heaven (Matt. 18:18; 1 Cor. 5:3-5; 1 Tim. 1:19, 20). From this it may be seen that it is indispensable that a ruler of the house of God shall maintain that high moral character and dignity prescribed for such in 1 Tim. 3 and Tit. 1; for only such can "speak and exhort and reprove with all authority" and not be despised (Tit. 2:15), and it is only such whose decisions will be ratified by that heavenly Court.

The agitation in the church ended by the choir leader and his partisans leaving in a body and opening a hall a quarter of a mile away. They were exactly those forty-odd individuals as to whom I had privately formed an adverse opinion, though neither they nor any others ever knew of this. When some good brethren assert that the supernatural gifts of the Spirit are not now available, nor intended to be so, I differ, for it is certain that to meet this situation I was granted the gift of the "discerning of spirits" (1 Cor. 12: 10), having been led to suspect those only who proved to be troublers in Israel and no others. Merely natural insight, acquired by ordinary contacts with men, would not have accomplished this accuracy of judgment concerning so large a number of persons.

The prolonged strain of that year and a half, added to the total of life's efforts, taxed even my excellent health. It ended with six weeks of severe facial neuralgia. Neither rest nor remedies brought relief. At last I consulted my good friend Dr. J. Hervey Bodman, an expert homoeopath. He recommended a remedy which conquered this long attack in fortyeight hours, and I thanked God and took courage.

"There must be also factions among you, that they who are approved may be made manifest among you" (1 Cor. 11:19). The fire had done good by purifying the lump. We could now worship in harmony of heart and settle down to steady united work. And there was much healthy activity. A Sunday morning school of about 100 children, from 300 to 400 in the afternoon, and a different 100 at night, had some good influence on the rough district, though vastly more important was the salvation for eternity of very many scholars as the years passed. There was a Bible Class for men; Junior and Senior Christian Endeavour meetings during the week; a flourishing women's meeting; in the summer two open-air testimonies. Each week tracts were exchanged at some 1,100 houses, and singers and speakers visited a hospital all the year round. These steady activities occupied forty or fifty helpers, largely younger believers. All this good work I left entirely to those I found engaged in it, only encouraging them as far as might be.

Among these workers there were not a few estimable and eligible young women. I was now in my twenty-eighth year. It was obvious that the situation would be easier and happier if I were married. The affection felt when first I saw Miss Brealey had, if possible, deepened. Yet it was necessary to be quite sure of the approval of the Lord. I proposed to myself three tests or hindrances. If these should be removed I would go forward. First, Mrs. Lindley was to be considered. I owed her much, and she was elderly, and had no other home than mine. Should she be tried by the prospect I would wait until the

Lord should in some way remove the difficulty. In the second place I resolved to approach Mr. and Mrs. Brealey before speaking to their daughter. There was no social obligation to do this. Miss Brealey was twenty-six years of age and was not living at home. Had they demurred I should again have waited, but they did not. Lastly I spoke to the lady herself, and she agreed. This was March 13, 1902.

We saw much of each other, a more sure way of becoming inwardly one, and so of the union of heart being permanent, than a short courtship and hasty marriage. As we sat one day under the trees in the fine Promenade at Clifton, I mentioned that for a good while the word of the Lord concerning Paul had been pressed on my spirit as for myself: "I will shew him how many things he must suffer for My name's sake" (Acts 9:16). I thought it well that my beloved should face this prospect, but she was not deterred, nor has she ever shrunk from what has been involved for herself in my many and lengthy absences from home.

Indeed, the Father of mercies sent her into my life at a time of severe testing. For the neurotic condition mentioned of my kind and motherly friend Mrs. Lindley had developed acutely and was a severe and ceaseless tax. Part of the test of this was that I was under no necessity to bear it, for I could have asked her son or daughter to have carried it. But God had brought us together and it is neither dutiful nor wise to throw off a burden which He has imposed. It is healthful to the soul to learn to know God in the course of His orderings for us, especially in those which are painful. Trials are to be taken as from His hand: "Cast thy burden (Heb. that which He hath given thee) upon Jehovah, and He shall sustain thee; He shall never suffer the righteous to be moved" (Ps. 55:22).

Of this private trial no one but Miss Brealey knew, and her sympathy was a great support and knit us the more together. When the time for our marriage came Miss Lindley arranged for her mother to go to her in London. Shortly her health greatly improved.

Very quickly I saw good reason for this experience. The visiting of families which was now my service taught me how very many persons there are who are normal enough in mind except in the home and with those they really love best, but who display to these the mental disturbance hidden from others. To the relatives this is usually distressing and unnerving. I was able to explain to their relief that they must not regard the strange behaviour of their loved one as intentional, nor should they unduly reproach themselves as provoking it, for it was a well-known phase of mental disturbance. It is precious to learn that God comforts in affliction that we in turn may comfort the afflicted (2 Cor. 13-7).

At the end of my first year at Unity the financial change I desired had been made. The stipend ceased and gifts for my support were placed in boxes at the doors by such individuals as were moved to give. Humanly I took the risk; actually my income was now directly under the control of my divine Master. In the first year of the new arrangement He supplied an average of just £1 a week more than the former stipend. "It is better to trust in the Lord than to put confidence in man" (Ps. 118:8).

Of any one step of mine that helped the members of the church to trust in God this was the most important. Moreover, it opened to me the hearts of the poorest of the community; and many of them were very poor. They felt thenceforth that their pastor was dependent on God for daily supplies as were they themselves, instead of having a regular income as before, to which they had contributed part though having an uncertain income with the attendant trials. In consequence, they felt free to tell their troubles to a personally sympathetic heart, and I was the better able to comfort and strengthen them.

If faith is to grow it must be treated by trial; if it is to grow exceedingly it must be tested exceedingly. Our gracious Father saw to this in our monetary matters.

The Arab speaks of the beggar as "sitting at the gate of God." For many of those early years we sat there, having very, very often to offer literally the prayer "Give us this day our daily bread." And it was supplied. My dear wife shared helpfully in this prolonged testing and in the growth of faith it fostered. Very sweet were the detailed deliverances. There was in Easton Road a brother named Waite, a good deal restricted in body from an injury. He kept a small provision shop, and *many* were the occasions when paying pastoral visits I took home a portion of cooked meat or the like when we had nothing of the sort. In an almshouse in Old Market Street there lived an elderly sister, Miss Nott, a perfect lady by instinct and training, as well as a spiritual disciple. *Many* were the times when she slipped a half crown into my hand when we were in real need. Heavenly arithmetic is remarkable. Much affliction, abundant joy, deep poverty, when added together abound unto rich liberality (2 Cor. 8:2).

A chief advantage of these affairs being at the ordering of God is that He can educate faith by ways hindered by a regular income. Actual poverty offers circumstances for unique testimony. It was my custom to be in my room at the Chapel from seven to eight on Wednesday evenings that those might call who wished. One evening a professional tramp came in to beg. After hearing his concocted story I handed him a sixpence and asked, "How much have you now?" "Sixpence, sir, by your kindness." "Do you know that you are sixpence richer than I am?" "What do you mean, sir?" "I mean that I have given to you my last sixpence. I am now actually poorer than you are. But the difference between you and me is this. I have a rich Father in heaven. He has told me to help those who are in need; and I have only to go to Him, tell Him that I have done as He wished, then ask Him to help me as He has promised, and He will always do so. But when you are down and out you have to go round telling lies and cadging." Then followed a short appeal that he should seek God for himself. He never came again, but it will be surprising if he ever forgot that interview.

Beginning from this first period and throughout the fifty succeeding years our faith has been tested with regard to money, as well as other circumstances. All needs were met, yet not always at the time we would have liked, nor by methods we could count upon. Indeed, God takes care that the trust and expectation of His children shall be placed on Himself, not on His channels of supply. In my case, as the sequel showed, He had in view that for forty years no boxes for my benefit should be available, and so He allowed the funds thus received to be often irregular and sometimes insufficient. Then He would supply by some other channel, and thus draw faith and love towards Himself.

In October 1906 my wife's sister Ada left for gospel service in South India. Her father being minister at Copse Road Chapel, Clevedon, the friends there adopted the plan of boxes in their homes to collect money for her. G. F. Bergin, co-Director of the Bristol Orphan Homes, a man experienced in faith as to matters monetary, said to her, "That is an excellent plan for everyone except Miss Brealey." The remark was noteworthy. In due time it was proved true.

At the time when Miss Lindley gave up her business in Clifton to go to London, I had opportunity to help in this matter, and occasion to use in the process, as well as in affairs of her mother, sundry small sums totalling £20. Of this, neither of the ladies knew, but God did. When Mrs. Lindley departed a little before my marriage she kindly left with me sundry pieces of furniture, and the value of these was £20! Five Sheraton dining-room chairs were included, which she had bought at 6s. each. One by one they went out of use and were put in the store-room. A time came when I was hard pressed for nearly £5 to pay the city rates. At that very time a gentleman came to look over the house, which we were thinking to leave. He saw the chairs and gave £5 for them. Thus we were encouraged to look unto God, rather than to Unity, and not to be surprised when He used means we could in no wise foresee.

Bristol had been a great centre of interest in the work of spreading the gospel in other lands. Many had gone forth from the Bethesda church. Unity shared in this interest. Money had been raised by means of a sale of work. Garments had been made, and other articles supplied, and were sold annually. When I entered the sphere I said that I did not ask that the sale be discontinued but neither must they ask me to co-operate. I pointed out that it was no attraction to the tradespeople around that once a year trade was diverted from them by a church sale. How could they think that the church was there for their benefit? I showed further that Scripture guidance was against the plan of articles being given to the *church* and sold *collectively*. Acts 4:34-37 is clear that persons desiring to devote possessions to the Lord sold them *privately* and laid the *money* at the apostles' feet.

The sisters were loyal. They discontinued the sale and formed themselves into a working party to make garments and *give* these to workers in the gospel.

Interest in work abroad increased steadily and before long God called two from our midst to go to the West Indies. One Sunday morning I spoke on 1 John 2:2: "He is the propitiation for our sins; and not for ours only but also for the whole world." Facts and figures as to the world were given and its vast need of the gospel was stressed. It was my first missionary address and God blessed it. When Mr. and Mrs. Fred Curtis before-mentioned reached home it was to learn that each had heard His call.

Shortly Barbados was laid on their hearts. But some older brethren, of the Bethesda church, urged that the need was greater in Demerara, and they yielded to this advice. I said little, but felt they should adhere to the original direction of the Lord. They sailed for Demerara, but on the voyage Mrs. Curtis was so ill that the ship's doctor refused responsibility for her going beyond the first port of call. So they were put ashore at Barbados, and there the blessing upon their labours proved that the Lord had graciously kept them in His way.

When we had been engaged something over a year it came upon our hearts that there was no good reason for further delaying our marriage, so we announced this and began arrangements. It was a path of faith. My beloved resigned the post held at a large establishment in Clifton, and went to her parents. We had no money put by, for we were agreed in using surplus income in the work of God, which was easy on account of the pressing needs of the poor and the claims of gospel work abroad. But we went on with the arrangements and our heavenly Father treated us generously by moving friends to supply much that my little home lacked.

The marriage was on September 22, 1903, at Copse Road Chapel, Clevedon, where Mr. Brealey had a similar post to mine at Unity. That morning I had only enough money to pay the fares from Bristol of my "best man", my dear friend Thomas Hancock and myself, and to bring my wife and myself back as far as Bristol on our way to London and Brighton. But late the evening before a brother beloved, H. W. Case, at whose second marriage I had been "best man", sent round a cheque for £3. Happily it was an open cheque, so leaving my beloved at the railway station I posted in haste to his bank, and we continued our journey as if we had been millionaires. So long as the peace of God guards the heart it is more satisfactory that our reserves be in His safe keeping than in our own. They will be made available as needed.

The ceremony was performed by Dr. Joseph Morris of Brighton, a retired medical man, whose ministry of the truth had been helpful to many, including the saints at Unity Chapel. He and his wife kindly went from home for three weeks, left their worthy helper there, and generously entertained us as their guests for that period.

He was a quite unusual man. In his unconverted days he had been very worldly. At one time he had two medical students living with him for studies. One was by no means a Christian, the other a zealous but unwise believer. The latter would so often ask to be out at evening meetings that the doctor warned him that he was imperilling the likelihood of passing his examinations. Asking yet again to be excused he urged that the Lord might come that night and he would so much wish to be among the saints. This to two irreligious men was a casting of pearls before swine. The other student administered a salutary rebuke. He fetched a topcoat, green with age, and said, "You may need this. It will be cold going up there tonight!"

After his conversion my dear friend, like so many others, experienced the tyranny of the sin he now abhorred. His quick temper persistently blazed forth. Beaten in the battle he asked that rare saint, Rev. C. A. Fox, the secret of his holy life. The answer was a question: "Doctor, did you ever give your *body* to the Lord?" He thought this through, and saw that his tongue was part of his body and that, if the Lord got control of the whole, victory was secure.

He had a knack of getting into unusual circumstances and dealing with them in an unusual manner. One night he found himself removed by only a thin partition from an old couple who nagged at each other a long while. He heard every word and could not sleep. At last the old man said: "Now kiss me, Mary, and let's go to sleep." The doctor seized his chance, tapped on the wall, and said: "Do kiss him, Mary, and let me go to sleep too!" As Scott wrote:

And silence settled, wide and still.

Dr. Morris had made money, but, like many more, was not wise in investing it. He laid it up on earth, instead of obeying Christ and placing it in heaven. All his eggs were in one nest. One morning he found on his breakfast table a letter to say that the nest had collapsed and all his eggs were smashed. This sharp news he told to his wife by saying that their all had gone. She replied, "It's not so bad as that, my dear." But he had to assure her that it was just as bad as that and nothing less: "We have nothing left!" She did not chide his lack of wisdom or repine at the forbidding prospects, but put her arms around his neck, kissed him, and said, "It's not so bad as that, my dear: *we have Jesus left!*" "The Lord is the portion of mine inheritance and of my cup: Thou maintainest my lot. The lines are fallen unto me in pleasant places; yea, I have a goodly heritage" (Ps. 16:5,6). True are Cowper's lines:

Give what Thou wilt, without Thee we are poor,
And with Thee rich, take what Thou wilt away
(The Task)

Mrs. Morris was a gifted speaker. In the first World War she had been used to the conversion of a number of young women at Burton-on-Trent. After the last meeting several of these were standing around her in the hall when a German bomb blotted out the whole place. There were no funerals. I went to see my beloved friend and found him broken in health but sound in soul. To the end of his life he prayed daily that, if it might be, the man who dropped that bomb might be brought to salvation by faith in Christ.

To have been intimate with such choice souls was an enrichment and inspiration, both rebuke and spur, a living means of grace, provided by the God of all grace. It is good that our friendships be arranged by Him, the Father for the child.

Our only child was born on August 13, 1904. We named her Mary Brealey, the first name being after the Lord's mother and her own mother. Before her birth we offered her unto God for service in a foreign land, if He should so please. He had His own ways of fulfilling the desire of them that fear Him. He never sent her to live in another land, as we contemplated, but in adult life she has more than once visited Germany and Holland, and has toiled in sending there much help after the late war. But beyond this, by remaining with and caring for her mother, she has set me free for years of travel in many lands. And there has been also the service of entertaining servants of Christ of various races who have visited our home. Without her efficient support the past thirty years of my life must have been quite different.

In her earliest months we should have lost her but for a gracious overruling of God. Her mother and the maid were downstairs while she lay in her cot in the dining-room. They heard the cat crying loudly, hurried upstairs, and found the room in flames, clothes before the fire having caught alight. They were able to extinguish the flames. Had the cat not been in the room, or had the door not been shut, the child and the house must have perished. The right-hand pillar of the clock on the mantlepiece was scorched and to this day is a visible reminder that "God is the Preserver of all men, specially of them that believe" (1 Tim. 4:10).

In 1904 Dr. Torrey and C. M. Alexander visited Bristol. The great Colston Hall was well-filled. I co-operated earnestly the whole month and spent all my spare time at the meetings. At the close of their campaign in the United Kingdom it was stated that 90,000 persons had passed through the inquiry rooms. Bristol contributed its quota. It is to be hoped that the final results everywhere were spiritually more favourable than in my experience. Over thirty inquiry room cards were sent to me of persons who had given our large Chapel as their spiritual centre. Of these only one was known to us. I visited all of these repeatedly during six months, and, as far as I could presume to judge, only four had been born of God, one of them being the man already known and whom I had led to decision in his own home the day after he had been to the mission and been truly wrought upon by the Holy Spirit.

This outcome was disappointing and provoked inward inquiry as to possible reasons for only an eighth of the professions being permanent. Dr. Torrey was a fine preacher of the true gospel. Might not the results have been as great had he toured without the "attraction" of choir, singing, and music? The throngs would have been smaller, but perhaps the genuine conversions as many.

Yet indeed we thanked God for four souls saved from eternal destruction, to the praise of the Saviour. One of these was a factory girl, a member of a drinking club. This means that a clique of girls would each put by a sum weekly for some weeks and then pass a weekend drinking it away. But Christ broke the power of cancelled sin and set the prisoner free.

Another convert of that mission was F. E. May. He was on the staff of the Bank of England and was taken to the Colston Hall by my cousin Edward. He was never associated with Unity Chapel, but we formed a close friendship which has lasted for forty-five years and to which I am much indebted.

A few years later another special evangelistic effort was made in our own vast slum area. At that time the clergy, ministers, and other workers in the district were all godly and evangelical and hearty co-operation was possible. The missioner was George Clarke. Some years before he had been distinctly used of God in Clifton. The meetings were held in a tent and we were gratified with large audiences. The preaching was good as to style and matter, plain, direct, logical, without any emotional appeals. Mr. Clarke had a remarkable power over men. The inquiry rooms were filled every night, and at the end of three weeks over seventy persons had professed faith in Christ. Follow-up work was persistent, yet six months later I knew of no convert standing fast, nor could I learn of any in other churches that had cooperated. It would seem that the missioner's influence had been merely psychological, not of the Spirit of God.

Moody and Sankey set the fashion of this modern type of mission. There is no doubt that their first effort was of God. Thirty and more years later I myself met believers who were converted then. It may be that much subsequent effort in imitation of that first has been of human and not Divine arrangement. Dr. Pierson was a personal friend of Sankey, but of his hymnbook he said to me, "It is strong where it ought to be weak, and weak where it ought to be strong."

We need to get back to the original apostolic plan of waiting for *the Lord* to take the initiative in all His work, special as well as ordinary. If *He* sends

Paul to Corinth it will be found that He has much people there. If *He* forbids Paul to go to Ephesus it is because the time for work there has not yet come. His control, when we accept it, is real and perfect.

Unity Chapel stands in the parish of St. Philip and St. Jacob Without. In my time the rector was J. O. West, a true man of God. We had much fellowship. In addition to the open-air meetings of our respective churches, he and I often preached together at the corner of Midland Road and Old Market Street. He would speak at our Hall on occasion. The then Bishop of Bristol, Dr. Browne, greatly disliked what he called this "consorting with Nonconformists of the baser sort." He made things difficult for Mr. West, as by refusing to license a curate and by being even positively rude to him. Standing on the steps of our hall, I expressed my sympathy. He replied: "Our Lord said, 'Woe unto you when all men shall speak well of you.' Thank God I've escaped that Woe, anyhow."

The Secularist Society, militant atheists, had its Bristol headquarters in his parish. Its founder was Charles Bradlaugh. Mr. Shinwell, formerly Minister in the Labour government, was at one time one of its lecturers. Mr. West notified them that he purposed to preach against their view, and that, if they were ready to attend, they could afterward adjourn to the parish hall and discuss his sermon. He asked me to support him in the debate and there I proved the value of my early acquaintance with atheism in disputing with Mr. Hunt.

A smooth-faced and smooth-voiced questioner asked whether foreknowledge does not involve foreordination? Had he expanded the point he would, probably, have urged that a person could not foreknow that an event would certainly occur unless he had the power to bring it to pass and intended to do this.

Mr. West asked me to reply. The idea was new to me. Like Nehemiah, when the king suddenly put an awkward question, "I prayed to the God of heaven," and it flashed into my mind that should the answer be Yes, the atheist would say that therefore God was the author of sin and must be the chief sinner.

To make the point precise I asked, "Does the gentleman put the question in general or in reference to some particular case?" He replied, "Only in general." I then said, "In that case the answer is No; for I may get to foreknow that a burglar intends to raid my house but I do not foreordain it."

Apparently nonplussed, the questioner did not pursue the matter, but the chairman, the leader of the Society, said, "Your own Book is against you" and referred to Romans 8: 29: "whom He foreknew He also foreordained." Exact and minute pondering of Scripture is vital. I replied that the text does not say, "whom He foreknew He *thereby* preordained," but "He *also* foreordained," and that the "also" showed that the foreordination was additional to and not involved in the foreknowledge. To this no reply was offered. The subject of foreordination is discussed at length in my book, *World Chaos.*

The whole debate, of which this was one item, exhibited an aggressive unbelief then much in evidence among working men in such districts as ours. It would come out at the Old Market Street Methodist Bible Class for men led by my dear friend Charles R. Parsons. Though small and unassuming he had a unique influence upon men, many hundreds of whom attended his class. When converted as a youth he prayed the Spirit-impelled prayer that he might be used to the conversion of one thousand souls! According to his faith it was unto him. I heard him say that he believed the Lord had far exceeded that number.

During a discussion an infidel urged that the teachings of Jesus Christ are quite impracticable, and demanded to be shown a man who having been struck on one cheek had offered the other. After a pause a stranger rose and said: "The gentleman wants to see a man who when he was struck on one cheek turned the other. Then let him look at me. I'm the man he wants to see." He then told that he had been a rough, wicked fellow until Christ had saved him. The next day the men in his shop did their best to provoke him to anger. Not succeeding, one suddenly struck him on the face. He said: "I was about to knock him down, which I was well able to do, when I remembered those words of my new Master, and instead I asked if he would like to hit the other side." He concluded his very convincing narrative with the words: "When the Lord Jesus saved me He made a good job of me, that He did."

This is by far the most effective argument against infidelity, and in those days such works of power were frequent, nor were we without them at Unity. But though we saw God working my heart longed for yet more conversions. When I sought Him about this He answered: "The apostles said, 'We will give ourselves to prayer and to the ministry of the word' (Acts 6:4). You have given yourself to the ministry of the word and to prayer: put these things in My order and I will work." Forthwith I rearranged life to give one day a week to prayer, with a measure of fasting, and forthwith the Lord worked more power-fully. They that wait upon the mighty Jehovah change their human strength for His divine strength (Isa. 40:29-31). In the measure that this advances they cease merely to tap at human hearts, but deliver sledge-hammer blows such as break the rock to pieces (Jer. 23:29); they become strong enough to bind the strong and wicked spirits that bedarken and enslave souls, and so they can set their captives free (Luke 11:21, 22).

One Sunday morning, January 15, 1905, I had an inward impulse to pay a pastoral visit before morning service. It was far out of the route to Unity, and was to visit the home of one whose second wife was dying. I found her heart engaged in a fearful struggle to keep moving. Mercifully she was unconscious, but it was a painful sight. By her sat the husband and her mother. I read some Scriptures, offered a few words of comfort, prayed, and went to the service. The battle ended that day; and afterwards the mother told me that she and the husband had watched it all night, simply benumbed, and unable to say a word to help each other. But, she said, "What you read and the words you spoke broke the spell from our spirits, and for the rest of the hours our hearts were quiet and we were able to cheer each other to the end." It is a blessed privilege to be taught and used by the Divine Comforter, the Spirit of Him into whose mouth the prophet put in advance the words: "The Lord Jehovah hath given me the tongue of them that are taught, that I may know how to *sustain with words* him that is weary" (Isa. 50:4). To those withered spirits a bag of gold would have been useless, a bitter mockery. But *words* are either the sword that wounds or the balm that heals, and *His* words are spirit and are life (John 6: 63).

On the way to the visit just mentioned I met on Tramways Centre my dear friend Mr. Sarsfield. He told me that the condition of Mr. James Wright of the Orphan Homes was very serious and his life hung in the balance, and that special gatherings for prayer on his behalf were to be held. At once I had assurance that he would not recover. So as not to seem unconcerned, I attended the prayer meetings but could not Amen the earnest prayers for his recovery. He died on the 29th of the month.

The spiritual state of most of the young men and women then at Unity was marked by stamina. Willie Miles and another young fellow ventured the risky attempt to climb down the 300 feet precipice in the Avon gorge known as Sea Walls. Having descended a good way they reached a ledge from which no further descent was possible and they must try to climb back. The rock above the ledge protruded slightly and in straining to pull himself up Willie pushed himself away, fell, and rolled some 200 feet till some bushes stopped him. His companion was hauled up by ropes some hours later. Willie was taken to the General Hospital. At 11.30 p.m. I was called to visit him. The ward was dim, a mere inch of his face was all that was visible, and it was feared that injured kidneys would prove fatal. But his mind was clear, and the testimony to Christ that all the ward then heard was thrilling. He recovered, and it was to him that the Lord gave May Thompson as wife. That same spiritual stamina had developed in him and carried him through the sorrow of losing her.

Its principal source was the experimental knowledge of Christ as our life, and the secrets of this were: first, plenty of good food—the Living Word supplied through His written Word; second, a pure atmosphere—the presence of God cultivated by prayer; then, healthy exercise, gained in the activities of Christian service already outlined. Where these factors obtain a church can gain, hold, and train young people without adventitious aids and attractions.

Nor is there any point more important than that the children should find their sufficient interests in the family circle itself, not in sectional enterprises.

Spiritually considered the least helpful element at Unity was the Christian Endeavour Classes. The leaders were efficient and devoted, nor were their labours in vain; but in every inter-church organization there is a powerful tendency to cause the heart to feel it belongs to that large outer organization rather than to the local church. This I have observed for fifty years in all the variety of Classes, and similar Youth Movements so multiplied today. Thank God for young folk brought to Christ by such agencies; but from my youth until now that I am old I have seen quite as many saved within the usual church life and fellowship, and their after growth and stability are in general far finer than in any sphere other than the church of God, the local assembly. The latter is the *only* sphere corporate recognized in the New Testament, and naturally God's richest blessing attends it. If it be asked what is to be done for the young believers when the church is dull and lifeless, the answer is: Get it revived! do not start some human organization in hope of supplying (perhaps supplanting) the sphere which is of God's creation. And dying churches *can* be revived, as will be shown later in this book.

The other course, now so general, of humanly devised organizations, is working a subtle yet perceptible degeneration in young Christians of both sexes. It is little likely to produce that stamina before stressed. I was called to address a Youth Rally at an assembly. Some sixty were present, from seventeen to thirty-five years, promising material. The first three-quarters of an hour were spent in singing choruses. That choruses may work some truth into the minds of children is one thing, and even so the benefit is not equal to that of teaching them to learn hymns with a solid doctrinal content, on which some of us were reared to our enrichment; but that believers of the age and type mentioned should want them is pitiful, especially with a precentor striving vigorously to work the singers up to a pitch of merely natural enthusiasm. Nor is it any sound preparation of the heart to profit by the exposition of Scripture to follow.

After that meeting I said to a leader that, in my youth, if the young men and women with whom I mingled had been invited to spend three-quarters of an hour singing choruses we should have felt insulted, as if our time was of no higher value or that we wanted nothing better. We *did* want something better; we wanted the opening up of Scripture unto the knowledge of God and of His Son, and we needed and wanted nothing else. In the wilderness God provided for Israel only manna and water. When they clamoured for other diet "He gave them their request but sent leanness into their souls" (Ps. 106:15). For the Christian God gives only Christ and the Spirit, and other food is needless and harmful. I knew a quite young boy who, when told that there would be a lantern lecture at the children's annual meeting, was sorry and said he would rather have an address.

Another strenuous, united, and God-owned effort was the midnight sweep. At that period those accursed, yet legalized, hotbeds of depravity, the public-houses, were open till 11 p.m. Then they vomited on to the dark and squalid streets a reeking stream of thieves, harlots, and drunkards. I have seen mankind under various conditions in many lands and climates, but nothing so wretched as an English slum, on a wet wintry night, when the public-houses disgorged their victims, despoiled of money, sense, and virtue. Yet is this a fine opportunity for the earnest fisher of men. The publicans and harlots still enter the kingdom of God before the respectable and religious.

The various centres in our slum contributed each its contingent, and singing, or sometimes with music, the whole body marched through the streets as the bars emptied and constrained the degraded to come to the hall. The meetings were held in rotation at our various halls so as to cover the whole area. The night that Unity was the place, I was host to welcome the guests. The first man to arrive was "three sheets in the wind," tipsy and noisy. I showed him to the front seat, and he had not the wits to excuse himself and slink to the rear, as do the stranger, the shy, the sleepy, and the selfish. He talked and sang all through the meeting, but when the call was given for any who wished to be set free from their sins to adjourn to the side room he was the first to rise. Handing to the leader a black bottle he said, "'Ere, guv'nor, you take care of this," and went to the small room. Twenty minutes later he came forth sober and saved. And of him, as of one already mentioned, the Lord made a "good job". Were I young and strong, and the Lord so directed, I would return to slum work with satisfaction and hope.

On March 12 and 13, 1906, I was speaker at an Evangelical Alliance conference at Teignmouth, South Devon. I had no more money than to get there from Bristol. The Alliance did not meet travelling expenses at the time but by cheque from London later. I therefore walked back over Haldon moor to Exeter, some thirteen miles. The day was lovely, the views magnificent, the tramp enjoyable. That day the half-yearly meetings at Fore Street Gospel Hall, Exeter, were held. The next day, March 15, I walked on to Clayhidon, on the Blackdown Hills, perhaps twenty-four miles, for four or five miles of which a farmer gave me a lift in his trap.

I will here introduce to my readers a princess of the kingdom of God, Miss M. C. Rawling. Her mother had died early from arthritis and the doctor had warned the daughter that she would do so unless she fought it by an active life. This battle she maintained so resolutely that she was well into the eighties before having to lie up. Such was her character for strength. For many years she taught in the day school George Müller then supported in Exeter, and later in a similar school at Clayhidon, retiring on a modest pension.

There she tramped the hills visiting families and meetings, knowing everyone and their affairs and loved by everyone. When Mr. Brealey left the district for Clevedon she became the trusted adviser of the elders of the assembly. They ever sought her counsel, and followed it. She did not attend their meetings, but they took to her the minutes to be written up by her. She was the true "bishop" of that region. If the parish registers had been destroyed they might almost have been rewritten from her memory of the births, marriages, and deaths during her time.

She belonged to that spiritual school of which A. N. Groves, George Müller, and Robert Cleaver Chapman were public examples. In her more retired sphere she thought, spake, and acted in the power of the same spirit. In the neighbourhood there was a modest dwelling which had been long a centre of spiritual life. It had been made more commodious and imposing. Miss Rawling showed her sympathy with that older school of saints by writing to me: "It is now the finest house in the parish: *which I regret.*"

Divining why I was walking from Teignmouth to Bristol she supplied, out of her slender means, the money for the train for the remaining fifty miles. This I duly returned.

God entrusted to Deborah, a woman, the chief authority in Israel: He made Miss Rawling the dominant influence at Clayhidon. In her were fulfilled the words, "Ye are the salt of the earth....Ye are the light of the world" (Matt. 5:13-16).

The years at Unity were not only fruitful in direct results on others, but were the period when leisure and regularity of life allowed me to lay the foundation of close study of the Scriptures. Among other measures, and in conjunction with daily consecutive reading, I compared the Revised Version, from Genesis to Revelation, word by word, with three other versions. One was the *Variorum Bible,* a scholarly work giving in notes the changes in the Hebrew and Greek required by various manuscripts, and the changes of renderings supported by various scholars. Another was Newberry's *Englishman's Bible,* giving marginal suggestions as to the strict meaning of many words and changes suggested. There is not much of value in Newberry's margin that is not found in the Revised Version. His helpful contribution is the intimation of grammatical details of the originals by diacritical marks.

The third version compared was J. N. Darby's *New Translation.* Being intentionally literal it is not smooth English, but for giving, with as much fulness and exactness as is possible in a translation, the meaning of God's words it is, in my judgment, the most spiritually valuable of independent versions. Though the first of such translations in recent times it remains, as I think, the best.

The changes from the Authorised Version made by Darby are in much closer agreement than disagreement with the Revised Version.

The general result of these and subsequent studies has been to establish confidence in the Revised Version. No human work in any department is perfect. It had been well if the Revisers could have revised yet more thoroughly, instead of being hampered by the rule that they must assimilate their work as far as possible to the antiquated English of the seventeenth century: but taken all in all, their Version is the most trustworthy of English translations for general and public use.

The years at Unity were profitable not in Bible study only, but also in the preaching and teaching for which it is an indispensable preparation. That may be said of preaching which Moody said of winning souls: "The way to do it is to do it." Preaching is like car driving; one should do much or nothing. In my own earliest efforts I was helped by studying Spurgeon's *Sermon Notes*, and still more by Dr. Pierson's small work *The Divine Art of Preaching*, a collection of talks on the topic given to the students at the Pastors' College when he was filling Spurgeon's pulpit while the latter was ill.

These helped to the formation of the logical treatment of subjects, that is, the laying of a sound basis of Scripture truth and proceeding to sound conclusions and applications.

The epistle to the Romans is a chief model. Facts of history are adduced as the basis of the condemnation of the race of mankind. Facts concerning Christ are laid down as the basis of the Divine justification of the believer. Facts concerning Abraham and David are given as proof that faith, not works of law, is the condition of being so justified. Holiness of life, *sanctification*, is shown to be the indispensable result and proof of the faith that saves. In this connexion facts are given as to the death, burial, and resurrection of Christ (and of baptism as a symbolic union with Him in these), as the basis of the possibility of the believer walking in holiness and working out his salvation into experience. This having been reached, the fact of the *glorification* of Christ is shown as the ground of hope that the one who is thus by the Holy Spirit already associated morally with the Son of God will, in due season, be conformed outwardly to His glory, even as he is even now being conformed to Him inwardly. The whole treatment, though thrilling with animation and movement, is yet severely logical, and it is upon the basis of the facts and truths expounded that the concluding exhortations and appeals from Chapter 12 and forward are pressed. "I beseech you *therefore*, brethren, by the mercies of God."

This logical method tends to the expounding of passages of Scripture in preference to sermons on isolated texts, but when texts are to be dealt with it leads to analytical treatment, so as to expose distinctly the truth as a whole and to arrange its parts in true sequence and connexion. James 2:5 will illustrate.

Hearken, my beloved brethren; did not God choose them that are poor as to the world to be rich in faith, and heirs of the kingdom which He promised to them that love Him?

Here are

(1) the persons addressed, "beloved brethren";

(2) a call for attention, "hearken";

(3) a question, which contains ten principal words, which form five pairs:

(a) *God* and His *heirs.*

(b) God's *choice* of His heirs and His *promise* to them.

(c) He chose the *poor,* rather than the *rich.*

(d) The *world* is one sphere of life, the *kingdom* of God is the other sphere.

(e) The heirs of the kingdom are rich in *faith* and ruled by *love.*

This method of study and of preparation of addresses opens up the purposes of God as revealed in Scripture, conduces to accuracy of study and of statement, and therefore to a lucidity which enables the hearer to grasp easily the truth taught. Such a preacher, being taught and enabled by the Spirit of truth, will have no difficulty in speaking continually to the same audience, without repetition on his part or weariness on theirs. But it is assumed that he has gained the art of speaking pleasingly, as before indicated, otherwise, while uttering the noblest of thoughts he may be as dull and wearisome as a learned counsel who, having argued all day before the House of Lords, asked when it might be the pleasure of the Court to hear the rest of his argument. To whom the Lord Chancellor replied: "We are bound to hear you, and we will try and give you our undivided attention on Friday; but as for pleasure, Sir, that is long since out of the question."

As soon as by such practice the mind has acquired the habit of logical treatment it becomes safe and helpful to forgo the making of elaborate sermon notes. One may then rely more and more upon the Holy Spirit for subject, treatment, and utterance. He takes up the now disciplined natural faculties of thought and speech and uses them as the trained and controlled vehicles of His action upon conscience, intellect, and will. Then preaching is not only logical but spiritual, it has not only light but unction.

Thus led and prepared it came with me, now many years ago, that I ceased to have to seek subjects for ministry. I seek the Lord rather than a subject, and He is pleased to give His message for each occasion. It is my usual experience that a theme, a passage, a text is presented suddenly to the mind with force and clarity. Frequently, without mental effort on my part, I am made to see in a few moments how to treat it; its logical and natural divisions are presented distinctly before the inward vision. This may sometimes be only immediately before the time to speak; but there is assurance that it is the Lord's message for that particular occasion, with confidence that He will unfailingly make it to accomplish His purpose and that it can in no wise return unto Him void.

Of course, it may be long before one hears of definite effects. At Easter 1921 I spoke at Gateshead-on-Tyne. Until July 1947 I heard not a word about that visit. Then at Keswick a lady said: "I was so glad to hear you again this morning. I have not heard you since you were at Gateshead." "Gateshead," I replied, "that is ancient history." "Yes," she said, "but several of us young Christians came over from Sunderland, and we were all helped. One outcome is that for many years I have worked with the gospel in China."

That afternoon a brother in middle life stopped me in the street to say that he had been glad to hear me again. "I was only a youth, lately converted, when you came to Gateshead, and your ministry was just what I needed to set me forward on my Christian life."

The next afternoon a third brother spoke of that visit, and a fortnight later a fourth friend, now a valued teacher and shepherd, told me in another town that the 1921 teaching had been a chief factor in his early Christian advance.

Thus does the gracious Lord encourage confidence to speak His truth though nothing as to results be learned till long after. The above incidents are mentioned to enforce the permanent value of that expository and weighty type of ministry above indicated, in contrast to the only elementary or even flippant style of evangelism thought by some to be necessary today to hold the interest of young people. One of the subjects at Gateshead was the present day application of the Sermon on the Mount. Such serious demands on discipleship and devotion will find response from such young Christians as are most worth our labour.

Financial methods will help or hurt the spiritual growth of a church. All too often the latter is the case. From the time that the minister's salary ceased at Unity, seat-to-seat collections ceased. As a concession, two exceptions were allowed. The Sunday School took up offerings at their Anniversary services, and a collection was taken on Hospital Sunday in the city, the latter being a kind of public testimony that Christians, though not of the world as a system, were ready unto every good work that relieves misery. In place of collections boxes were fixed marked for various objects, the poor, missions, ministry, and other purposes. During the eight years that I analysed the funds every department and section of the church showed a balance, except that on one single occasion the Men's Bible Class had a deficit on the year of a few shillings. And this company of Christians, although composed almost wholly of the poor, maintained for those eight years an average of eight pounds weekly on church funds, not counting the sectional classes and meetings.

This was secured without promises, envelopes, appeals, or pressure. Two chief Scriptural principles were thus conserved: that gifts must be wholly free and must be made in secret, offerings of love given unto God alone. For this the spiritual life of saints must be maintained in vigour, which end is secured by spiritual measures already mentioned, namely, food, prayer, and exercise. Granted this, the financial problem will solve itself, or rather there will be no such problem; for they who first give their own selves to the Lord will abound in the grace of giving to Him of their means (2 Cor. 8).

Of this I saw fine examples. One brother worked a quarry for the Corporation. He was illiterate and gave me the privilege of being his almoner. Each month, after settlement day, he would bring a pocketful of gold to be allocated to various purposes, local or far afield.

Obeying an unusual impulse I went one Sunday before the morning service to visit a sister in the General Hospital. Studying her with care I felt that her trouble was more of the mind than the body. A little tactful inquiry drew out that a year before, being in great need, she had pawned her wedding ring to get food for the family and the morrow was the last day on which it could be redeemed. The Hospital was much out of my way to Unity but on the way I met the quarryman going there. He gladly gave me a pound to redeem the ring. On the steps of the chapel I encountered the husband. Having only bare time to commence the service tact failed me, and I handed him the money rather precipitately with the words, "This is to redeem the wedding ring." Not knowing that I knew of the matter he was overwhelmed and nearly broke down in the lobby. The wife soon recovered health.

A crucial test of the financial system arose when the schoolroom had to be roofed afresh and £300 was required. A simple calculation showed that if each member would set aside sixpence a week for ten or twelve months the sum could be raised. It was therefore suggested to the church that, inasmuch as we could easily provide the money, it would be dishonest to appeal for outside help. This was agreed. Special boxes were put up, and the matter was mentioned regularly for prayer. But the Head of the church saw good to test our honesty and our faith. No one would pray about it at the prayer meetings. There being a lack of public prayer there was a lack of public gifts. Funds came in at the rate of only a few shillings a week.

The work seemed to be required urgently, for some of the principal beams were actually out of the wall, and the roof might easily have collapsed. But private prayer was made against such a catastrophe. I told the Lord that if *He* did not move the people to pray *I* could not do so, and I ceased to urge the point publicly, and thus matters crept on for perhaps two years. At length friends began to pray spontaneously, and I knew that God was about to answer and work. Four brethren who had a few pounds at call then offered to guarantee any balance needed, so that the work could be put in hand. As they were members of the church this would still be raising the money among ourselves. The work was completed, but they were not called upon, for by then all the money had come in.

During that period an anonymous letter reached me. It said that the writer was a seamstress; that both health and work were poor, yet that she had always felt a sense of security because she had £12 in the Post Office Savings Bank. But the Lord told her that He wished that £12 given to the Renovation Fund. Her exercise of heart was described. Suppose health should fail altogether! Whatever would she do without her £12? But she felt she would never again be able to tell her Sunday School girls that it is safe to trust God if she could not trust Him without £12 in the bank. So there lay the golden coins on the table before me.

I made up my mind who was probably the writer and watched her class. In the following two months she saw six or seven of the girls converted. After some years one of the few brethren in the church who had money had the wisdom to make her his wife, and she thus had not only a comfortable home but also the joy of giving money to the needy. Perhaps thirty years later I was in Bristol and she asked me if I remembered the incident, and said, "I don't think I need mind telling you now that I was the writer." She smiled when I said I had decided at the time that that was so, and added: "If I had not found faith to take that step I should never have made progress in the spiritual life; and I look on my present circumstances as my heavenly Father's gracious recompense for having trusted Him then."

Leaving her house one day my eyes moistened as she wrung my hand and said movingly: "Under God I owe more to you in my Christian life than to anyone else." And she was but one of many whose growth and gratitude compensated richly for the strenuous labours of the years at Unity.

In such service with its commingled trials and joys, there passed nine blessed and profitable years. For that period I am ever grateful to the Lord Who was both ordering my way and also preparing me for wider service.

As time went on my mind clarified upon some features of church life and public worship.

The morning service was composite. There was first such a service as might be found in any Nonconformist chapel, conducted by myself as the regular preacher. Then there was the Lord's Supper, which followed the plan usual in assemblies of Brethren, when hymns, prayers, and very occasionally reading of Scripture or ministry, came from any brother whose heart prompted him thereto. Usually, though not invariably or by rule, the distributing of the bread and wine was left to me.

These seasons were not without grace from God, but the plan had patent defects. The hymns chosen, the prayers offered, any Scripture read, almost regularly, almost unavoidably, followed the theme of the immediately preceding address, and there was little freshness of thought or distinct prompting of the Holy Spirit. Moreover, there was little time or inclination for other opening up of Scripture, and new gift in ministry was little developed or likely to be so.

In some Brethren meetings there is today a tendency to this composite service, only that the order is reversed, and a curtailed season at the Table is followed by an address by an arranged speaker. The last result mentioned will most certainly follow: there will be little time at the earlier stage for the ministry of the Word, nor will there be much exercise as to this, seeing that an address is to follow immediately. Thus here also the stirring up of gift by the Spirit will be restrained.

I know of no gatherings so profitable as when the whole season is left to the prompting of the Spirit of God, nor does the New Testament suggest any other type of meeting when Christians come together. Human leadership of worship and human arranging of ministry are equally without warrant from the New Testament. In the Word of God the spreading of the gospel is not regarded as an assembly responsibility, but as the work of each individual Christian, and especially of those gifted as evangelists, nor is such service placed under the control of the assembly or its elders. Still more contrary to the New Testament and to apostolic practice is it that a group of brethren, elected or self-constituted, should have directive influence upon the Lord's servants or upon their financial support. "Power corrupts, and absolute power corrupts absolutely" (Acton).

The other chief matter upon which my mind became gradually settled was that of my own position as the one recognized "pastor" or "minister" of the church. I steadily discouraged the use of either official description, and sought to prepare minds for an abandonment of the office. When the time came for me to leave I told the fellowship that, as I judged, the Head of the church had Himself raised among them a true shepherd, and that they would do well to encourage him to devote his whole time to this service, if he felt so led of the Lord; and that they could safely trust the Head of the church to provide for the public preaching, either from among themselves or from elsewhere. This course, however, was not followed; two ministers were chosen in succession, but neither stayed long. In spite of the steadfast devotion of a few beloved brethren and sisters, the church and work gradually declined. This exhibited once again the inherent weakness of the system which makes too much that is vital to a church to depend upon one servant of God, and so far diminishes in the believers a direct working faith in the Head of the church and His Spirit.

Much as I learned and gained at Unity Chapel, and much as we saw of the gracious working of the Lord, I could not again accept such a formal "pastorate"; though most readily do I admit that God may put into such positions faithful men who have not more of His mind on this matter than I had at first, and who can therefore serve Him well up to the light gained.

How my own service at Unity ended as it began, under the ordering of the Lord, will now be related. The Good Shepherd led me out as distinctly as He led me in, and went before me.

CHAPTER 5

Travel

Egypt and India. 1909

My learned friend David Baron, of the Hebrew Christian Testimony to Israel, told me in Egypt that by preference he would not have travelled, but gladly have pursued his studies and the writing of books; but that the Lord had seen fit that he should take long evangelistic journeys seeking lost sheep of the house of Israel. It is thus with me. By nature retiring and studious, I have yet been constrained to spend the more part of forty years away from my home and books, wandering in many lands. Apart from effects produced in others, this has been the best for my own character and growth, for the discipline of doing what one would not choose is deeper and finer than that of doing what one would prefer. Surely the Son of God would not have chosen incarnation and humiliation, not for its own sake; but He showed His moral perfectness by delighting to do the will of the Father. This was inherent in Him, but it has to be developed in us by discipline, which must often take the form of tasks not congenial to nature.

Across the will of nature
Leads on the path of God:
Not where the flesh delighteth
The feet of Jesus trod.
If now the path be narrow,
And steep and rough and lone,
If crags and tangles cross it,
Praise God! we will GO ON.

Oh bliss to leave behind us
The fetters of the slave;
To leave ourselves behind us,
The graveclothes and the grave!
To speed, unburdened pilgrims,
Glad, empty-handed, free;
To cross the trackless deserts
And walk upon the sea.
                                        (Tersteegen)

Life in one city and service at one centre had been a living on *terra firma;* now I must learn the lesson and the joy of walking on the sea, of getting to know God amid the uncertainties of foreign travel.

Towards the end of 1906, after I had laboured at Unity for seven years I began to notice in my mind an impression that my service there was not to continue for long. There was nothing to occasion this: the church was harmonious, the work encouraging, and I was happy in it. But the impression steadily deepened. I asked of the Lord, that, if this was to prove the case, He would grant still greater prosperity on the church, so that, when I had to leave, there should be no reproach that I was leaving because of failure or disunity. Forthwith there were more conversions and more growth in Christians, and the more this increased the more sure I felt that the impression was of God.

This continued for two years, and not a soul was aware of my exercise except my wife. During 1908 Miss Brealey asked by letter if I had ever thought of serving in India. I answered, No, adding that I believed the climate of the Arctic circle would suit me better than the tropics. So little had I any thought of India. At that time Miss Brealey went to Coonoor on the Nilgiri Hills, in South India. This is a district from 6,000 to 7,000 feet above the burning plains, where the Government of Madras Presidency sat for eight months of the year, where retired English officials and others resided, and where missionaries resorted in numbers for the hot months. The chief centres were Coonoor and Ootacamund.

In addition to Church of England buildings and chaplains, there was at each of these places a Union Church, where all other denominations worshipped, and which were served by recognized pastors. Miss Brealey learned that these churches would shortly be without ministers, and she thought of myself in this connexion. On Friday, October 23, 1908, she came to visit us at Unity Lodge, and that evening, sitting together by the fire, for the first time I felt an impulse to mention the exercise of my heart as to leaving Unity. For a while I hesitated, so as to be sure that this impulse was of God; but presently I told her. She said nothing to me, but going upstairs told my wife of the need of the Nilgiris, which a little later my wife repeated to me. I said at once, "My dear, this is the call for which we have been waiting," and she, with that simplicity towards Christ and His will which characterized her, replied, "Yes, I know it is."

It was wise and gracious of the Lord that Miss Brealey did not, as would have been so natural, tell me of the need while we were conversing, but mentioned it to her sister first; for so my wife heard the call direct from God and I did not have to persuade her that it was of Him. Living, as we did, without reserve or resources it could not but be that she must herself rely wholly upon God for her support, and that of our child and home, while I should be away;

but having herself been assured of God that this separation was of Him she found faith to rely on Him apart from me. And we presently felt clear that I should be away for not less than two years. It proved to be two and a quarter years.

If it be asked why I did not take them with me, the answer is that the Lord gave no such direction. Neither then, nor during the forty years since, have I had any leading to settle in any other land. Times not a few have believers in different parts begged me to settle with them, but it has never been my call from God, however this may have been with other servants of Christ. It is clear from the New Testament that men "separated unto the gospel of God" (Rom. 1:1) did not establish themselves in any place. They were ready to remain two years (Acts 19:10) or eighteen months (Acts 18:11) or three months (Acts 20:3), or shorter periods, always as the Lord might indicate or persecution might compel. Philip, the evangelist, having four daughters, must needs have a home for them (Acts 21:8,9); but there is no hint that he moved his home from one land to another, or that any other apostle or evangelist did so. It is a modern development, feasible in such an exceptional period of world order as was the Victorian era, but unsuitable to unsettled times, and not contemplated in the New Testament.

Being now sure of the call of God I mentioned the matter to intimate friends and after a while asked a few of these to meet at my house for prayer and consultation. Not that their advice was needed but their fellowship was valued. Among them were those two men of God E. S. Bowden, of the Godaveri Delta, and H. Handley Bird, also of long service in India. Their endorsement was of use in commending the project to the wider circle of Christians.

Shortly I told the church at Unity Chapel I should be leaving them for India. There was general and genuine sorrow as regards themselves but equally cordial support and financial fellowship. At a large farewell meeting Handley Bird, in that blunt style of his that made his remarks ever forcible, told them that he did not in the least pity them but hoped that they would later send to India others such as myself. It reminded me of a farewell meeting at Bethesda Chapel, Bristol, a few years before, when that nobleman of the kingdom of God, F. S. Arnot, was leaving for Central Africa. Speaking of the dignity of carrying the good news of God to the unreached peoples, Dr. A. T. Pierson had said: "Our brother Arnot does not need our pity."

By February 1909 preparations had been completed and tickets for the journey taken, when two serious difficulties arose such as the all-wise God frequently permits so that faith may be tested and strengthened.

It became necessary for our home to be removed by March 25. It was not till the day before I left Bristol that another house was secured. Yet our hearts were kept in perfect peace, for we were sure that our God and Father would keep His promise never to fail them that trust in Him before the sons of men. I could not see to the actual removal, but my very capable elder sister, Ella, lovingly shouldered this task in my stead.

Then also news arrived that the need of both of the Union Churches on the Nilgiris had been met. To Coonoor there had come a Mr. Hercus from New Zealand, and Mr. D. R. Logan, of the Ceylon and India General Mission, who had been serving at Ootacamund, had decided to continue there. Thus the occasion for my journey seemed to have ceased. But I knew that I had heard the call of God and I went forward.

The last day or two were passed at the house of my parents at Folkestone, whence I was to sail. What according to nature should have been a time of tension and sorrow to my wife and me was actually, according to grace, a time of heavenly joy in the power of the Holy Spirit. In the richest possible measure we experienced that the joy of the Lord is strength. The only moment of strain was at breakfast the morning I was to leave. By my side was our sweet girlie of four and a half years and it suddenly rushed over me that I was not to see her for a long indefinite period. I was almost overwhelmed and it was only by the sternest effort that I restrained myself for that brief spasm. But it passed with the recollection that the privation was to be for Christ's sake.

Nor did the child fail altogether to enter into this new element in her life. It is blessed how early a young mind can grasp the truth of God. The Spirit of truth works in the very young, especially if their parents do their sacred duty of instilling the truth into their minds. When Mary was but three I sat her on my knee and asked her to tell me why the Lord Jesus had died. She gave a clear and correct answer. When she was five years old her mother wrote to me in India to say that the child had just come and said, "Oh, Muvvidie, the Lord Jesus has taken away all my naughty sins and He is going to keep me from doing them now." That so young a child should take hold at once of both sanctification in Christ as well as justification is noteworthy, and may well encourage parents to expect such workings of the Holy Spirit.

A year after I had left my sister wrote: "If Mary's prayers can do anything they will bring you home quickly. Dear little soul, she is torn between two opinions. She loves you to be telling the gospel to those poor people, but she sometimes feels she 'cannot do without my Daddy any longer'". Thus do heavenly and earthly emotions mingle in this present condition, and the sacrifice of the earthly is sanctified by the purity of the heavenly.

It was March 2, 1909, that I left England. On the 7th, bespeaking prayer for those who have left loved ones and those who are left, I wrote as follows: "The particular need to be borne in mind is, that the presence of the Lord Jesus, by the Spirit, may be a vivid reality to the spirit; for it is *persons* they have left, and it is the personal presence of Christ that needs to be known that the void may be felt less acutely." The special promise which the Lord gave to me for this new course in life was Isa. 41:10: "Fear thou not, for I am with thee; be not dismayed, for I am thy God: I will strengthen thee; yea, I will help thee; yea, I will uphold thee with the right hand of my righteousness." Gracious fulfilments of this vast guarantee will be narrated.

The journey to India was to be broken by a week in Egypt, the occasion being to visit Miss J. S. Jameson of the Egypt General Mission. A few years before we had met at Great Yarmouth in connexion with the Open-Air Mission seaside work. An address I gave on living by direct faith in God had influenced her to leave a Church of England missionary society and join one where such faith had more definite place. But much more than I foresaw was to come from this passing visit. Miss Jameson had thoughtfully sent a card of introduction to the head of the customs at Alexandria, named Rickard, which facilitated the formalities there; and from this also more was to arise than one knew at the time.

Miss Jameson being then at Ibrahimia, a suburb of Alexandria, I stayed a day or two at Miss van Somer's Home of Rest, "Fairhaven" at Ramleh, a little further from the city. There I met William L. McClenahan, a member of the American Presbyterian Mission, and Miss Tula D. Ely, a young American lady with private means, who had dedicated her life to the spread of the gospel among Moslems. Much co-operation with these friends was to grow from these contacts.

As Miss Ely knew the land and the language, and was going to Cairo, she kindly consented that I should accompany her. In the train the subject arose of the Christian so failing to walk with Christ that he may be accounted unworthy to share in the first resurrection and the millennial kingdom. Most of the four hours' journey was spent in examining the Scriptures as to this. When parting at Cairo she remarked that the Scripture said: "Let him that is taught in the Word communicate unto him that teacheth in all good, things" (Gal. 6:6) and that she would write to me in India. Knowing then nothing of her circumstances I set no store by this remark and shortly forgot it. God will have our faith to rest on His promises alone: "My soul, wait thou *only* upon God. For my expectation is from *Him*" (Ps. 62:5). But Miss Ely duly redeemed her promise, as will appear later.

Mention has been made of Mr. W. R. Moore. A few years before this time he had taken a house in Clifton and lived there during school terms, because his family were being educated there. It was at this time that I was privileged to be treated as a personal friend, and thenceforth to have the support of his daily prayer. The evangelist James McKendrick and F. S. Arnot of Africa were two others whom he thus served. For this foreign tour he had given me the signal benefit of bringing with me Dr. Edwin Hatch's most valuable study *The*

Organisation of the Early Christian Churches. It was an unusual mark of confidence to allow such a book to be taken on an indefinitely long tour abroad. I have never ceased to thank God for the insight into church history therein gained. It had a determining influence upon the forming of sound opinions upon church life and order and upon the methods of Satan in corrupting these. It is worthy to be written upon the sky that the book came back to England after long wanderings and was duly restored to its owner. I wish I could say this of all books I myself have loaned. In this matter there is in many Christians a regrettable lack of common honesty.

At this time Mr. and Mrs. Moore were in Egypt and with them I made the first of several visits to the Great Pyramid. It is a truly wonderful structure; yet not so wonderful as some theories about it of a chronological and prophetic character. After 4,000 years the Pyramid stands firm on its base: the theories have no basis.

A few days were now spent visiting some of the Egypt General Mission stations in the Delta, a pleasure afterwards renewed, as will be related. At Ismailia, on the Canal, I was kindly received for one night by Mr. Wilson Cash, of that Mission. He told me that he was studying for orders in the Church of England. Naturally I regretted this purpose to draw back from a "faith" Mission to the servitude of a State Church having as a system no real relationship to the New Testament. We did not meet again for thirty-eight years, when in July 1947, as the Rt. Rev. Wilson Cash, D.D., Bishop of Worcester, he gave the morning Bible Readings at the Keswick Convention. I thanked God that his beliefs and statements had remained evangelical. At Bilbeis, the station of the beloved William Bradley, I experienced my first dust storm. Sand and dust filled the air, darkening the light. Sand and dust penetrated everywhere, mixing with the food itself. On susceptible persons the atmospheric effect was something like that of a thunderstorm.

I embarked at Port Said on March 16, 1909. It was a German vessel, and we were aroused each Sunday morning by the ship's band playing two verses of "Nearer, my God, to Thee." I had left England in a blizzard. In the Red Sea my cabin was at 84°. I lay sweating and panting, thinking I never could survive to reach India. Two years later I found a permanent temperature of 80° comfortable.

Colombo was reached in the early morning of Sunday, March 28, 1909. Mr. A. F. Witty had kindly purposed to meet me, but as we arrived on Sunday, he could not do so, being four miles from the harbour and having four meetings that day. This could have left the inexperienced traveller the unpleasant job of getting along through the customs and finding an inexpensive lodging in that Eastern seaport. But God had graciously taken in advance His own measures to meet this difficulty and show His loving care. Without a word to me my friend Rev. J. O. West, already mentioned, had written to a clerical friend of his asking him to meet me. Being far up country he could not come, but he had sent the letter to Mr. Ferrier, the Accountant of the Church Missionary Society, who kindly came on board, attended to all formalities, and took me to their centre, where the Secretary, Mr. Dibben, gave me a warm welcome. That day and night I was their guest, and in the evening spoke at one of their Mission halls.

This manifest interposition of God for my comfort and help, by putting me at once into the arms, as it were, of the Church of England missionary society, emphasized the line He wished me to take in relation to His children I should meet in such systems and Societies. The systems and Societies as such I could not sanction or support: with the true people of God in them I was to show fellowship, and to receive it from them on the basis of our common heavenly life in Christ, and for the mutual furtherance of that life. Those of their views or practices which I believed unscriptural I could not recognize and might on occasion be compelled to oppose; but I was not entitled to separate from anything evidently of God, such as prayer, Bible study, preaching of the Word, winning men to Christ. When later I read the life of Anthony Norris Groves I was impressed to find that this was the practice of those great men of God whom He had used eighty years before to recall His servants to the true principles of Christian fellowship. And now after forty years' experience in many lands, I am more than ever satisfied that it is the path wellpleasing in His sight.

That first day Mr. Dibben gave me insight into one of the needless burdens involved in the plan of Societies for gospel labours. He remarked that I would do all missionaries a great service if my visiting various fields should reveal some way of saving them from the immense labour of filling up statistical forms and compiling reports. But one does not need to travel far for the desired solution. Drop the plan of Societies, and let each worker depend directly upon the Head of the church for all guidance and support. Then the only obligatory report will be that shown in Luke 9:10: "And the apostles, when they were returned, declared unto Him what things they had done."

In Colombo I learned to what moral depravity young Englishmen, including Christians, can sink when they go out on business to Eastern cities. Greatly do they need to be fortified in advance by having experienced that Jesus is able to "save his people from their sins" (Matt. 1:21). No other power can do so.

At the foot of the Nilgiri Hills lies the important town of Coimbatore. On Friday, April 2, 1909, I was kindly entertained there by Mr. (afterward Sir) Robert Stanes, and met there Mr. D. R. Logan above mentioned. He had that week been ordered to Scotland, his health having broken down, and thus

I arrived as he left, and the sphere of service which seemed closed was opened exactly as my six weeks' journey ended. Thus admirably does the Lord control and arrange the ways of one submitted to His ordering. In fact two spheres were available, the Union Church at Ootacamund, and "Brooklands", the large home of rest at Coonoor.

Miss Bishop who conducted this home was a gracious and devoted lady. Her life was given unreservedly to caring for the servants of Christ who resorted to one or other of the homes she provided and superintended at Colombo and Coonoor. She smilingly remarked to me that had she chosen to live in England she could have had a flat and a maid and a visitor now and then; but here she had these lovely houses in these lovely districts, with many servants and many visitors. In reality, she was everybody's servant and therefore shared the joy of Him who said, "The Son of man came not to be served, but to serve" (Mark 10:45).

When I reached "Brooklands" on April 5 I had ten pence in hand. This would not have been the case but that Miss Jameson had lovingly met the cost of my days at "Fairhaven". But for this I would not have had money for incidental expenses on the further journey. But on reaching Coonoor I found Ernest E. Winter in business in South India, with whom I had been a playmate when as boys we lived next door to each other at Sidcup. Knowing nothing of my circumstances, he kindly gave me a sovereign, and I had not need to be ashamed of my empty purse.

The spiritual service now available was varied and fruitful. At "Ooty" (short for Ootacamund) there were three services weekly at the Union Church, and sundry gatherings at "Montauban", a home of rest similar to "Brooklands". The influence was not measurable by numbers but rather by the indirect help to the work of God all over South India, and indeed much further away, by workers coming to the Hills to recuperate being instructed and strengthened in spirit. This applied also to the many Christian officials and men of business who returned to their spheres refreshed for the wars of the Lord.

In a heathen land it is perforce better understood than in England that life is verily a wrestling against wicked spirits in heavenly places. The servant must be also a soldier. These evil beings have gripped and ruled these lands for thousands of years. All minds are blinded by their ideas, all feelings dulled or fired by their cruelty, all morality debased by their vices, the whole atmosphere is poisoned by their satanic spirit. It is this that makes it so foolish and dangerous that young men and women, from a comparatively elevated Protestant land, should go to a heathen or Moslem region before having understanding of, and real experience of, this spiritual warfare, and of the secrets of victory over demons. It is especially necessary to know by personal experience the part that prayer conflict has in this warfare. For want of such training in advance the young recruit too often goes under in the conflict, of which the following is an instance.

There came to me at Coonoor an earnest young woman, a teacher in a school. She bemoaned that for a long while she had found herself plagued with jealousy of her fellow-workers. If the Principal but spoke kindly to or looked kindly at another of the staff she felt wickedly jealous of her. So obsessed was she, and so ruined was her inward life, that she felt she must return to her home in America, unless deliverance could be gained. Now it is important to make sure that such a disease in the moral realm is not a symptom of disease in some physical organ. This can be the case. But in this friend there was no reason to think this was a factor. She had never been so troubled in earlier years and her general health was good.

I told her that the Bible gave an explanation of her case, but that it was sorrowful and humiliating. James 3: 14,15 says that where bitter jealousy is found it is earthly (not from heaven), soulical (not of the new spiritual nature), yea, *demoniacal:* and that in some way, no doubt unrecognized by her, she must have given access to a demon to infect her with this evil feeling. I then pressed upon her that, if she would humbly accept this as God's explanation of the matter, then she could claim such a promise as 1 John 3:8: "To this end was the Son of God manifested that he might destroy the works of the devil." With bitter tears she bowed before God, claimed the promised deliverance, and was set free immediately and permanently.

In the text cited above the word "destroy" (*luo*) means to loosen, untie, disentangle, and so set free, as a bird from a snare or a captive from the cords of his captor.

On another occasion at "Brooklands" there came for conversation about the "Tongues" movement and its claims a lady of perhaps fifty-five years. She had been used of God in a notable and difficult service among fallen women in a distant part of central India, and was had in reputation by all who knew her. We were to resume the subject the next morning, but very early it was impressed upon me that we were not to renew that theme but that I was to explain to her the opening part of Ephesians 2. I pointed out that it is involved in our being seated in heaven with Christ that His authority over the powers of darkness is ours and it is for us to use this right. Thus when Paul would drive the demon out of the girl at Philippi he did not ask the Lord to do this but did it himself, using the name of Jesus Christ: "I charge thee in the name of Jesus Christ to come out of her. And it came out that very hour" (Acts 16:18).

It was suggested that all too many Christians are like the wrestler who is under his opponent struggling to rise, instead of being the man on top holding his adversary down. To illustrate the position I remarked that the Lord Chief Justice has a wide authority over the whole judicial system of England, but the village policeman has authority only in his small area and limited measure. Yet within his sphere the policeman has the same authority as the Lord Chief Justice, for they both act in the name of the king. Similarly Christ can command the whole system of Satan everywhere, and they must obey, whereas I can act only in my small realm; but within that realm they are bound to obey me, acting in His name.

After some time this friend wrote from the north to say that from her youth she had been perpetually urged by Satan to commit suicide. She is not the only Christian I have met thus harassed. What a brave and stern battle must she have waged those long years, and with success so far as that she had not yielded. But, she said, that from the day she had seen her place and right in Christ she had dared Satan ever again to tempt her like that and he had never done so! Thus at last was she more than conqueror through Him that loved her. But how much better it might have been had she been instructed in her youth in the methods of the Adversary and had gained deliverance then. How much fuller all those years could her testimony have been to Christ as the Conqueror and Deliverer.

For myself, in England, on race courses, in slums, in gospel work in a priest-ridden village, and, indeed, and alas, in the church of God also, I had been given preliminary experience of Satan's kingdom, its atmosphere, dangers, and strength. I had been in active and varied labours for eighteen years before the Lord sent me to India in my thirty-sixth year. But for this I could easily have collapsed under the moral and spiritual assaults not to be avoided on such Devil-ridden territory.

In India this experience was greatly enlarged by being privileged to join in one of the strenuous battles of that doughty soldier of Christ Amy Carmichael of Dohnavur. Were the longdrawn fight to rescue a girl from Satan described in full it would indeed instruct and inspire many in the warfare for souls. Among other lessons it showed how real and strong can be the work of the Spirit be in a Hindu Christian, for the barrister who fought for her in several hearings in the Courts, not only bravely endured opprobrious treatment from a British judge, but would take neither fees nor travelling expenses, though he journeyed several times from Madras to Polamcottah, many hundreds of miles each way.

It was this battle that prompted me to write the booklet *Prayer Focused and Fighting*.

Another experience of prayer conflict, taken from this period, is given on p. 14 (ed. 1949) of *Praying is Working*. It reads:

> Again, in a certain heathen land a serious difference arose in a very large circle of missionaries. It threatened to issue in a public cleavage and

this before the native Christians and the heathen. The centre of the trouble was a wholly sincere but very determined man, one always difficult to persuade or turn. For months negotiation and prayer had proceeded, in view of the annual missionary conference before which the matter would come; but to within two weeks thereof no sign of reunion was seen. The tension was great, and forbearance was much taxed.

At that point three friends joined for a half-night of prayer, seeking general reviving. About midnight their hearts were powerfully drawn to deal with this special matter, and they found great liberty in spreading out the whole case before the Lord. They specially committed to Him for His definite dealing those mainly responsible, and in particular the beloved worker who had precipitated the crisis. Nor did the spirit of intercession cease to impel them until they were fully assured that the situation was mastered, and that the Lord would effectually intervene.

The conference duly met, and for six long sessions, occupying two whole days, discussion proceeded, but without result; and at the close the feeling expressed was that matters must take their course. But one of those who had prayed that night was convinced to the contrary. He had observed that throughout those wearying hours of debate a remarkable restraint had been upon all, so that, in spite of the acute feeling existing, not a speaker had said any word which hurt another. He therefore pointed out that the Lord's ideal for His church is a oneness that the world would see and be impressed (John 17:21); and that the Lord could be trusted to bring this to pass, if faith did not fail but patiently waited upon Him.

The next morning the subject was unexpectedly resumed, but without any progress to agreement being apparent. But shortly, to the amazement of nearly all, the very brother who had brought about the crisis said that, *contrary to the wishes of those who thought with him,* he had resolved, for the sake of peace, to desist from the course upon which he had thought it right to enter! The happy result was the restoration of harmony; and the Spirit of the Lord, being no longer grieved by dissension, was shortly able to show the solution of the original matter of disagreement.

In *Earth's Earliest Ages* (p. 316) Pember narrates the beginning of the modern spirit outburst in the Fox house in America in 1848. The advance was from the side of the spirits, by means of raps on the wall of the chamber of two young girls. Alongside of this put the following fact. At Ootacamund, the chief Government station of South India, on the Nilgiri Hills, I saw often, in 1909 and 1910, an earnest Christian woman, whose witness to Christ was clear and owned of God. She knew nothing of the Fox incident, but narrated to me a precisely similar experience of her own when a girl, peculiar and systematic rappings on the wall of her room having occurred, though, happily, failing to lead her into the toils, as the Fox family were led.

She was of a susceptible temperament. In her worldly days she had been much in demand for amateur theatricals. I suggested to her that, on this account, the spirits had probably judged her to be a likely subject for enticement, and had approached her. This led her to tell me the further incident that, when once, in those unconverted days, she had been at a party at a European bungalow, she observed a tall gentleman leaning on the piano, listening to the lady playing. She was struck by him, because his clothes were of a somewhat out-of-date cut. After the party she asked the hostess who he was, and described him. The lady replied that she must have been dreaming, for no such person was known to her, or had been present. She, however, was sure she had seen him; and on the matter being mentioned to the oldest resident of the part, and the description being repeated, he said at once that he knew quite well who it was, a Mr. So-and-So, and that he had been murdered in that bungalow.

These two incidents seem capable of one or two explanations. Either, as the heathen believed, the dead, or some of them, can on occasion re-visit their old haunts, and re-enact their former experiences; or spirits, designing to alarm or attract the living, can reproduce former events, and afterwards cause the facts to become known to the persons they would entice. In either case, how important it is for us to be fortified with the knowledge that God had most sternly forbidden such intercourse from either side.

On July 22, 1909, a baptism deserving of record took place at Coonoor in a mountain stream. Thirty years before a heathen had been converted in connexion with the Church Missionary Society. He had great natural gifts of memory and speech. The power of God was upon him. He was appointed by the Society an evangelist and was used in innumerable conversions. Thomas Maynard of Tinnevelly told me they numbered thousands. He was brought to England, more or less lionized, and thereby injured in soul. He returned to India weakened spiritually, and presently lapsed into a life of vice lower than before his conversion. It was a sorrowful reproach throughout South India. After several years he was restored and was again used in the gospel, and now was baptized by immersion as a believer.

After having spoken in his native Tamil, he did so in English, giving a brief outline of his life as above, and adding that not very long after his conversion he had seen in the New Testament the true meaning and method of baptism; but that he knew that, were he immersed, he would lose his post and salary as an evangelist under the C.M.S.; that on this account he fought against what he saw to be the will of God, which was the beginning of the decline of soul that issued in public collapse.

Such was the story of V. D. David ("Tamil" David). It rebukes the fallacy that one who backslides deeply and long can never have been born of God. It reproves the want of faith that doubts if such a one can be restored. It exhibits the peril attaching to human arrangements in the things of God, such as an official position and a stated salary. It exhibits the love and fidelity of the Good Shepherd Who goes after His lost sheep until He finds it. Let us join Him in His search.

My time was divided roughly between "Brooklands" and Ootacamund. At the Union Church, Ooty, I preached three times a week and visited. I lodged mostly at Shoreham Hotel, which had a large compound nearly surrounded by tall mimosa trees. In the flowering season the scent was almost overpowering. It was one of the only two places in India which I knew where it was safe to drink the water unboiled. The house stood higher than the surrounding parts, so that no water could percolate from higher levels and huts or houses and contaminate the well. Yet this was kept covered and locked. "A garden shut up is my sister, my bride; a spring shut up, a fountain sealed," and so undefiled (Song of Songs, 4:12).

There stayed at the hotel a man named Coleman. Miss Brealey had dealt with him about his salvation and had asked me to continue this. But he had sealed himself against me. Only once in some months did I entice him into such conversation, and then after a few minutes he closured the talk by saying with a laugh, "You missionaries are clever beggars: you deserve to succeed: I made up my mind that you should never speak to me about these things, and yet here you are at it."

He was Irish and had the customary humour. It was his regular daily routine to walk at the same hour in a park. One often there asked him why he came so habitually. He replied that he did not like to have his private affairs talked about, but if the other would promise never to repeat what he said he would tell him. The promise being given he said: "I am minding my own business." He had been in the police in Burma and gave an instance of what a fine command of English Orientals can gain. He asked a native official if he would do him a certain favour and the instant reply was: "To be sure; of course; why not? yes; certainly." It would defy an Englishman suddenly to string together these expressions more appropriately or emphatically.

But Coleman had lived a vicious life and was hardened. On the eve of my leaving the country, and burdened in spirit with his state, I resolved on journeying specially to his town to make one further attempt to reach him. On arriving, the monsoon rain was pouring steadily. When I reached the bungalow where I was to stay it was just the breakfast hour, and an inward discussion arose as to whether I should, as inclination prompted, go in and refresh myself after the journey, or trudge on through mud and rain and first see my man. I finally decided to do so. He met me with unusual cordiality, and, to my great wonder and delight, in a very few minutes we were engaged in close, personal converse as to his life and eternal prospects. The change in his attitude was altogether extraordinary; but on my return to the place whence I had started the explanation was found. Shortly after I had left, Miss Brealey had gathered twelve other praying workers, and for over two hours they had continued in steadfast supplication for this one case and concerning my interview with him. They had commenced praying just before I had to decide whether to breakfast first or not, and had continued in powerful intercession until a little after I had left him, although they had no knowledge as to what part of the day I might be with him.

Such concentration of supplication may be compared to "barrage" artillery fire, by which a desired objective is isolated from opposing forces, and thus is the more easily relieved or captured. We would not unduly press a preposition beyond its normal force, but let it be remarked that when our great Advocate spoke of a spiritual conflict in which He had intervened by intercession, He said to the subject of that conflict, "I made supplication *around thee*" (Luke 22:32), and so, though Simon was suffered for his own good and for his after usefulness to weak brethren, to be severely mauled in the battle, his faith, being protected by His Lord's intercession, was not finally overwhelmed. A high privilege does the Captain of salvation share with His faithful followers in enabling us to take hold of shield and buckler and stand up for the help of the oppressed: a blessed thing it is to be able to draw out the spear and stop the way against those who pursue after souls for their ruin (Ps. 35:2, 3).

I had one more opportunity of meeting Coleman by making a special journey to a Jesuit boarding house in another part whither he had removed. He was then softer and spoke feelingly on religious topics. It was interesting to learn that the Catholic priests had convinced him that his fornications were wicked in the sight of God and rendered him liable to judgment. But they had not shown him the way of forgiveness through the blood of Christ. This I did, and could only leave him, with the prayer that ere life closed he might seek and find that abundant pardon.

Another man at Ooty was named Booth. He was born in Yorkshire. His father was a churchwarden, but led a double life, of which his wife did not know, though the boy did. It turned him wholly against the evangelical faith which his father professed but disgraced. He went to India as a locomotive driver on the Southern Marathi Railway. For thirty years no one spoke to him about his soul. He married a Eurasian and had four children. Leaving the service he took the toll gate on the Ghaut road from Ooty to Coonoor. It was a mile or two from Ooty. He was a violent man and threatened to kill his wife if she read the Bible to the children.

This summer he was taken to hospital with pleurisy, where, in August, I visited him by desire of a lady who was being kind to his family. Only because I came at her request was he civil to me, and whenever I spoke of Jesus as the Son of God, or of His atoning blood, or of the eternal doom of the sinner, he became angry and would say things hard for a Christian to hear. At such outbursts I would quietly rise to leave, but he would promptly ask me to stay, from which I inferred that his Unitarianism was superficial and unsatisfying.

Returning to his little house he commenced secretly to read the Bible, and coming to John 6 he read the words: "I am the living bread which came down out of heaven; if any man eat of this bread he shall live for ever" (ver. 51). Under the influence of the Spirit of truth his mind for the first time worked rationally on these themes. He said to himself: "I always allowed that Jesus was a good man; but if He was a good man I ought to believe what He says, because good men do not tell lies. So as He says He came down from heaven I ought to believe it." Believe it he did. As he said to me: "I ate of the bread"; and the result was the reception of the new life promised. He knew it and was joyful. And his wife knew it and said: "It was a tiger changed into a lamb," an apt figure borrowed from the jungle around their home.

He was now seemingly well, but in only a week or two an internal abcess developed; he was hurried to hospital and died. "Is not this a brand plucked out of the fire?" (Zech. 3:2). It would have been well worth while to have gone from England to India for the salvation of Booth alone. But more was to follow. His wife was left without means and the matter of the children was acute. I knew not whether there were Protestant orphanages at all accessible; but God's arrangements work like smoothest machines. Exactly then there came to me Miss Mergler, a Eurasian and Secretary of the Eurasian Missionary Society. She said that the folk at Ooty contributed annually the support of an orphan in their Orphanage. But the child came from a distant place, and she thought they would contribute more did they know they were supporting a local child. Did I know of one? I replied, that I knew of three, urgently needing a home, and we drove out.

But Mrs. Booth said No; decidedly, No! Her father had lately married a Romanist, and there would be no end of trouble if she gave the children to Protestants. They must go to the Catholics. I said to Miss Mergler that we should not get the children unless the mother was brought to Christ. The whole of the next morning I spent in prayer concerning her, went out in the afternoon, and she was led by the Spirit to receive the Saviour, and we had the children. There lies before me a grateful letter from her written as I was leaving the district in December.

On these remote and high mountains, the Nilgiri Hills, there have wandered from of old wild tribes, Irulas, Badages, and Todas. The last seem to be acknowledged by the others as in some sense lords of the soil. Their social life is low. At the time I was there, indeed, for years before, Miss Ling, of the Church of England Zenana Mission, had laboured among them and a few had professed faith in Christ. On one occasion I went out with her to a group of huts.

Their religion centred in their buffaloes, and the head dairyman of the tribe was the chief priest. Wandering one day over the open country I came suddenly upon a burial hut, and took the liberty, and perhaps some risk, of crawling through the very low entrance into the hut. It was divided into three parts: the outer into which the corpse was brought before cremation and into which women as well as men might enter; the second, beyond a low barrier, into which only men might pass; and the furthest in, to which the high priest alone had access.

Until the British opened up these Hills last century these tribes had been apart from all the world, completely so from the world beyond India. How shall we explain the correspondence between that hut and the Tabernacle in Israel? The latter had an area to which all had access, then a holy place to which only men (priests) had access, with an inner sanctuary to which only the high priest had right of entry. Trace back very ancient religions far enough and they converge towards a common original knowledge of God and of how to approach Him.

During the days I was at Coimbatore, on the way to the Hills, there came into the office of Mr. H. C. Golden, a Brahmin lawyer, the Public Prosecutor of the district. He was learned and wealthy, and was later a member of the Governor's Council of Madras Presidency. Hearing that I wished to go to the other side of the town, he courteously drove me in his brougham. The next day, on entering the second class railway carriage to go to Coonoor, this gentleman was seated there. He did not see me. Shortly there came in a rough, blustering Britisher and ordered him to leave the seat for he had already taken it. The lawyer expostulated quietly, pointing out that there was no article on the seat to show it had been taken. But he had not noticed a small parcel on the rack above. As he did not at once rise the other seized him by the shoulder and dragged him up. The Brahmin's eyes flashed furiously, but, with the admirable self-control that marks them, he said nothing and quickly left the compartment.

I said at once to the uncouth man that, as a newcomer from England, I regretted greatly to see a native gentleman treated so rudely: that only the day before he had been very kind to me, a stranger; that he was a public official, learned, and rich. The other replied savagely: "Then let him go first class." This he had done, and at the first halt I went to him and expressed my sincere regret that he had been treated thus and repeated what I had said. He was touched that an Englishman should champion an Indian against an Englishman. As a rule the British, especially officials, behaved fairly and justly to the Hindus; but one dead fly causes the ointment to stink and one sinner destroys much good. Such arbitrary and offensive behaviour, even if only occasional, did much to forment a spirit antagonistic to British rule. And it was not the only instance I saw.

I met the lawyer again at Ooty and he asked me to his bungalow. There I drew him out to tell me his Hindu philosophy of the universe. He explained that Brahmah, the Creator, made the universe and ruled it for an inconceivably vast period. Then Vishnu, the Preserver, took it over and maintained it for a further inconceivable period. Then Siva the Destroyer would take the rule and would, through another immeasurable period, destroy it. Whereupon Brahmah would again create and the whole immense cycle would be repeated; and so on endlessly.

Whilst he was dilating fervently upon the majesty of this stupendous programme a postcard was handed to him and his enthusiasm was struck dumb. It said that his brother's little son had been drowned in the fishpond in their garden. Then was seen the vanity and emptiness of human philosophy. It left his heart blank. He was an illustration of Deck's lines:

> *The people sit in darkness; yea, in death's dark midnight gloom:*
> *No ray to cheer the passage to the dark, devouring tomb:*
> *The mourners weep despairingly around the open grave;*
> *No hope is known to enter there, for they know none to save.*

It was a bitter exposure of the false notion that Hinduism is good enough for the Hindu and he should not be troubled by Christian propaganda. This is a working of the Strong One to keep his goods in peace, a wile of the Devil to hold his blinded captives. When leaving the Hills I saw this man once more in his office, and pressed upon him the difference between salvation by faith in a Substitute and the heathen plan of our works, and later I sent him a Revised Version of the Scriptures.

During the eight months I was at Ooty the Union Church, at my request, had suspended the plan of paying a salary, but they had been faithful and generous, my needs had been met, and I had even been able to send sums to my wife in wealthy England.

Fruitful and happy as was service on the Hills it was not to be prolonged. On December 11, 1909, Mrs. Keary, of Shoreham hotel, gave me a card with these lines copied from an old manuscript:

> *Though scoffers ask "Where is Your gain?"*
> *And mocking, say you work in vain;*
> *Whate' er the works that be forgot,*
> *Work done for God it dieth not.*
>
> *Work on, work on, nor doubt nor fear:*
> *From age to age this Voice shall cheer,*
> *Whate' er shall die and be forgot*
> *Work done for God it dieth not.*

I left on December 13, and, after a few days saying farewells at Coonoor, was in Coimbatore on the 18th. This note is from my diary:

> This afternoon my host had to tea six young men from the Agricultural College near. It was deeply interesting to learn that these, and two other Indian Christian students, had this week unitedly objected to attend a field demonstration tomorrow on the ground of its being the Lord's day. After some objection the Principal, an Englishman, exempted them from attendance. This is a Government College and senior officials from Madras are coming to give this instruction on the Sunday. Here therefore is the spectacle of English officials disregarding the fourth commandment in their dealings with Hindus and native young men under them setting them an example in fearing God.

On December 20 I reached the town of Cochin on the Malabar coast to visit Ernest Winter before mentioned and his wife. As the day cooled they took me to a district where lived an ancient community of some hundred families of "white" Jews, who claim to be descended from those of the Babylonian captivity. They were really quite fair. They kept to themselves, were mostly poor, and devoutly attended the synagogue. This was an unusually interesting building. It had a pavement of large, patterned, blue Chinese tiles, brought thence by a former Rajah of Cochin, and given to the synagogue as a token of respect for his Jewish subjects. The brass work was handsome, and there was a very old clock with enormous weights. They courteously showed us the five or six rolls of the Pentateuch (one having part of the prophets) well written in Hebrew, and two having silver crowns at the head of the rollers.

There is something striking and solemn about this age-long witness of scattered Israel to the true God; but the veil is upon their darkened mind; they have the letter of the law but miss its spirit, and, for want of knowing Him of Whom Moses and the prophets spoke, they still grope for the wall like the blind. Yet "Israel shall be saved by Jehovah with an everlasting salvation. . . . I, Jehovah, will hasten it in its time" (Isa. 45:17; 60:22). "Amen, come, Lord Jesus" (Rev. 22:20).

Leaving Cochin on December 21, the next journey was by boat down the very lovely backwater which runs about a hundred miles southward, a little inland from the sea. Having to change boat at Aleppi I met on the little wooden pier a young Englishman and his wife. There were thirteen Europeans, with five children, in the business colony, and no spiritual provision for them. The C.M.S. missionary who visited them at times was in England, as his wife was ill, and there was no certainty of his return. When these friends saw me coming down the pier they wondered if I was a new padre come to them. "Sheep having no shepherd."

The next day I reached Quilon, the railhead of that part, and was soon at Kottarakara, welcomed by P. F. Marmen, a native evangelist. Handley Bird and I had come for a conference. Many hundreds attended. A brother of the land named Thomas interpreted for us and did it well. During the three days, with all day meetings, he hesitated but once. Mr. Bird was speaking of Satan as a roaring lion persecuting the early Christians. He intended to explain that this method of opposing the gospel failed, and that the Enemy turned to that of corrupting the church, by joining it to the world, Constantine making it the State religion. Mr. Bird exclaimed, "But the Devil found the roaring lion did not pay." The idea of a roaring lion paying something was baffling, and the interpreter hesitated and said, "I beg your pardon." It was a useful lesson to me as a novice in speaking for interpretation. Each sentence should be a complete grammatical entity, and curious English idioms ought to be omitted.

Life here was purely Indian, as to food and quarters. I slept in a tiny lean-to, with a leaf roof and sides. The litter of straw was a comfortable bed. An old-time Welsh itinerant said that, as he traversed the mountains, sometimes he was lodged like a bishop, sometimes like an apostle. When the squire gave him a sumptuous meal and a feather bed, it was the former; when a goatherd gave him black bread and a pallet of straw, he was lodged like an apostle. That hardened and iron-nerved traveller, F. S. Arnot, told that one night, lying in the dark in such a lean-to, he heard a gentle rustle and purr and knew that a snake, attracted by the warmth, was making its way to his side. Had he moved the creature would probably have struck him. It could see and he could not. His comment was: *"When I awoke in the morning* I remembered my bed-fellow and cleared from my blankets at a bound." The snake was then killed. At Kottarakara I was spared any such test of nerves and fortitude.

On Christmas Day the train took me over the mountains and plains to Palamcottah in Tinnevelly. My late hosts had kindly provisioned me for the journey. To a friend in England I wrote that for breakfast I had had bread and water and bananas, and for lunch, by way of a change, I had had bananas and water and bread, and that probably my Christmas fare had done me more good than much that had been eaten that day in England.

An ox cart took me by the afternoon the fifteen miles to Dohnavur, where Thomas Walker, Miss Carmichael, and Muttumal gave a warm welcome. It was partly to see the child for whom I had prayed much that I came. Dohnavur was a fairyland, with its hundred or more dark brown sprites, in greens and pinks, chasing each other in and out of the shrubs and flowers. These girls were the choicest for beauty, for the heathen give to their gods their best, and these would have been dedicated to a life of shame as temple girls.

Children in the days of innocence are alike in all lands. As Mr. Walker took me over the compound to my room Chellalu (whose portrait at that age is in *Lotus Buds*) hauled along one of my smaller bags and prattled in Tamil. Mr. Walker checked her quietly and said to me: "She is saying, 'I wonder what you have got in this bag?'"

Dohnavur was, firstly, a place surcharged with the prayer spirit; therefore, it was filled with the presence of the Hearer of prayer; and therefore, thirdly, it was a home of miracle. I wrote thus forty years ago, and I hope earnestly that it is still all true.

Thomas Walker was a rare man of God, a saint and a scholar. We met at Ooty, then at Dohnavur, and lastly at Keswick. His sudden death from cholera when far from home was a loss to the work of God far over India. I wrote a line of sympathy to Miss Carmichael. She replied that she did indeed miss him sorely, but added characteristically that she "would not so write to one who would say, 'How strange!' I cannot bear to hear our heavenly Father's will called strange. It is good and acceptable and perfect. Our little children should teach us better. They give us pleasure by looking up into our faces and trusting us. I want to give Him pleasure". Then she added: "Mrs. Walker is wonderful. 'And now shall my head be lifted up.' That is so much better than 'keeping up.'"

The night I left Dohnavur a long procession of helpers and children, with lanterns and songs, followed my bandy down the drive to the entrance gate. The last sound that gradually died away was sweet voices crying "Good-bye, good-bye". The angels can see in the dark, and knew that eyes that seldom wept were wet that night, as the bulls stumbled on in the darkness and Dohnavur became but a happy memory.

There followed six days and five nights in trains. I slept well on the bare boards of 3rd class carriages, with a leather Bible bag for a pillow. Visits were paid to Gunjur and Bangalore, with a few days at Hyderabad City in the Deccan. This was to visit the head of the municipality of that city of half a million Moslems. It was an insight into life to go round the city with him on a tour of inspection. The poverty, dirt, and misery in which most lived was pitiful, though a capable Englishman, with a native staff of 500, had done something to improve conditions. It was in shocking contrast to the luxury of the wealthy. The Nizam was said to be one of the richest rulers of India. It was interesting to watch proceedings as my friend investigated disputes regarding buildings. This man wanted to put a window in a wall. The neighbour protested that then his women could be seen. And so on. When he gave his decision the parties salaamed and seemed satisfied. But when he told his clerk that the matter would be referred to the native Committee then all faces fell, for now must begin what is called expressively the "oiling of palms", and he who could give the larger bribe would be favoured.

His wife was the daughter of an invalid who used the enforced leisure to compile the first birthday autograph book. She was a Christian and it was strongly against her father's wish that she married one then an unbeliever. She paid the price of thirty or more years of spiritual loneliness in her home, her husband being wholly worldly. Then God answered the prayers of herself and a converted son. The husband was brought to the gates of death with very severe typhoid. He bethought himself that, big and strong as he had been, he would not live for ever, and what then? But he did not know the way of salvation, had no Bible, and was too proud to inquire of his wife. In misery of heart he thought he would look round her room in case he might find help. He even turned over some dresses and there fell out a book she had brought from England. It was Andrew Murray's *The New Life*. He said to himself, "That is what I want. I am heartily tired of my old life." Now the book did not so much quote Scripture as put the references in the margin; so he could make little of it, being without a Bible. He was then commissioned to build the camp when George V, as Prince of Wales, went to India for the Durbar. This took him to Bombay, where he bought a Bible, and between the BOOK and the book he found Christ.

His conversion was thorough. Horses, liquors, tobacco, novels, theatres were all discarded. The gramophone was converted and played "Rock of Ages". His stand in the city was fine. But a high church cleric misled him, and, upon his retirement, turned him from the simplicity of the Spirit to the deceits of formal religion. He was ordained and I visited him more than once in his parish in England, but he made no progress in grace and his end was sorrowful. A fine start, good running, but a poor ending; this is not how the racer wins the prize, but how painfully frequent it is. "Let us press on."

On Friday, January 7, 1910, I reached Chettapetta, Mr. E. S. Bowden's home in the Godaveri Delta. This was the region opened by the earlier Messrs. Bowden and Beer, the first from England to follow A. N. Groves to India to spread the good news on apostolic lines. It was deeply interesting to visit most of the centres of work. During the more than seventy years God had wrought blessedly in saving souls. Yet there was manifest weakness as regards the churches. There were few men ready or fit to shoulder responsibility in the house of God. Practically everything depended upon the "missionary" and his money. This was sad after so many years. Yet it is scarcely to be avoided where the foreigner who starts the work remains permanently at hand, a feature unknown in the apostolic age. And the practice of paying a salary to native workers in the gospel is baneful. It makes them dependent upon him and not on God, prevents a working faith that can surmount difficulties, and keeps the foreigner in the dangerous position of being the employer and master. It is difficult for him not to be a lord over God's heritage. This is discussed at length in my life of Anthony Norris Groves. It is good that of later years some English workers have laboured on better lines, studying to bring on Indian leaders.

Oh, how dark and evil is a land without the truth of Christ! Sailing with E. B. Bromley up the Godaveri I saw the whole situation epitomized in one horrid scene. A dark and naked corpse was floating down the stream, and when it touched the bank savage dogs rushed at it and tore fiercely at the limbs. Thus is man, dead in spirit, carried ever downward on the stream of sin, with evil spirits gratifying their cruel delight in his destruction. But this is a dependable saying, and worthy of the fullest acceptance, that Christ Jesus came into the world to save sinners (1 Tim. 1:15). And He does this, as the Godaveri Delta showed.

At Tatipaka, one beauteous moonlit night, E. C. Adams had gathered under the palms perhaps thirty educated English-speaking Hindus to hear an address. The subject was the plan of God to elevate some from the sons of men to share the throne and glory of His Son, in a coming kingdom which should fill heaven and earth with peace. The audience listened long and carefully as this scheme was unfolded step by step. As shown above, the cultured Hindu has his mind filled with vast, though purely imaginary, philosophical conceptions of time and the universe. It is not enough to tell him only of the forgiveness of sins, essential as this is. To displace from his heart his false scheme it is necessary to unfold to him the far nobler plans of God and to show that these centre in Christ Jesus, His Son. This the apostles did. They preached the *kingdom* of God, and the place in it of the Lord Jesus Christ (Acts 20:25; 28: 31). Even to young converts they explained the *"mystery of God"*, that is, His secret counsels, in general (Col. 1:24-29), and in details, such as the part in that programme of the visible return to the earth of Christ (1 Thess. 4:13-5: 11; and 2 Thess. 2:1-12, especially ver. 5).

I explained to that company the steps by which men of the earth would be fitted for the honour of reigning with Christ. The resurrection of the dead, the rapture of the living, the removal bodily from earth to the upper realms, at the descent of the Lord, were mentioned. Suddenly I stopped and said: "I wonder what you gentlemen are thinking about this programme?" An elderly hearer blurted out the single word "Impossible!" "No, sir," I replied, "it is not impossible; it has already taken place in one instance, and therefore can take place in other instances, if the same Power chooses to exert itself, and this is promised." I then pressed the fact and meaning of the bodily resurrection and ascension of the Lord Jesus Christ.

The resurrection of the body of Christ is central and vital to the Christian scheme of things, as Paul showed to the lately converted Corinthians, whose minds were still darkened in measure by the same philosophies which still darken minds. Hence the Athenian philosophers mocked when they heard of resurrection (1 Cor. 15; Acts 17:32). Here is the explanation of why Satan labours still to deny that bodily resurrection, as when a London minister asserts as his opinion that the body of Christ evaporated into gases as does another dead body, only more quickly. It is destructive of the gospel, thoroughly and completely anti-Christian.

It had been pleasant to see my sister-in-law in her sphere of service and the dear Bowdens in their home, but the road lay northward and on January 22, 1910, I reached Calcutta. It was a privilege to stand in Carey's Baptist chapel, erected in 1809, where Adoniram Judson was baptized in 1812, proceeding the next year to his heroic labours in Burma.

Before going myself to Burma I stayed for three days in a second class boarding-house in Daramtolla. An Exclusive brother was there, so we sat together at meals and talked quietly of the things of God. Next to me sat an English lady, who presently expressed her surprise and pleasure to hear Englishmen speaking of things divine and carrying Bibles in their pockets. She proved to be a real believer and she asked me to try to help her daughter and son in Rangoon. This I did.

The daughter remarked that her mother need not have lived in Daramtolla. They had had a lovely home, but her mother had fallen under the spell of Seventh Day Adventism and had made life unbearable by insisting that Saturday must be kept rigidly as a sabbath. After long patience the father, an unconverted man, could endure it no more, had broken up the home, and was making his wife an allowance. How much more pleasing to God it would have been had this devoted Christian remembered the plain and emphatic command of God that the wife is to be subject to the husband, not to domineer over him. Various circumstances call for the humility and trust expressed in Faber's lines:

When obstacles and trials seem
Like prison walls to be,
I do the little I can do
And leave the rest to Thee.

Chapter 6

Travel

Burma and India. 1909-1910

While on the Nilgiri Hills a plan had formed in my mind to visit China, and a number of circumstances seemed to confirm it. I was to meet John McCarthy, of the China Inland Mission, at Bhamo in Upper Burma, cross the mountains with him to Yunnan Fu in Western China, and thence to work my way to the northern province of Shansi, where lived my esteemed friends Mr. and Mrs. Albert Lutley.

I was not yet sufficiently versed in the matter of divine guidance, either from Scripture or experience, and had yet to learn caution in accepting coincidences as being by themselves the leading of God. The south wind blowing softly may mislead. Looking back I see that the project to traverse China was not of God. What was in His mind was that I should get as far as Rangoon, and the anticipated road to China lay through that city.

I arrived there on Friday, January 28, 1910. The voyage up the Irrawaddy in the early morning was charming, with the rays of the rising sun glinting on the golden bell-shaped dome of the Shwe Dagon pagoda. The preceeding year Handley Bird and his wife had visited there a young Englishman in business. His name was Benjamin Sayer from Ipswich. He was worshipping with a group of Burmese Christians with a history. The senior was a man of God named Maung Maung. He was a spiritual grandchild of Adoniram Judson, his father in the faith having been led to Christ by him. The assembly met in his house, the apostolic practice.

There had been a division in the Baptist church in Rangoon, when several had seceded. This new circle also had divided. The group in Maung Maung's house was visited by an English Exclusive brother, who had instructed them more fully in Scripture. He had passed on further. The meeting welcomed Benjamin Sayer, were glad of his help, for he was spiritually minded, and they were happy when the Birds added their aid. But two British soldiers who were stationed in Rangoon joined them who, alas, were rigid Exclusives. They were shocked that one from Bethesda Chapel, Bristol, was allowed to break bread, and through their graceless insistence B. Sayer and the Birds were excluded. The latter returned to India.

But the soldiers were shortly transferred, and the little group was bereft, whereupon the sisters of the assembly saved the situation. They urged that it could not be the mind of the Head of the church that they should be starved for want of the food which the English shepherds could supply to the sheep. After deep and wholesome exercise of heart the brothers concurred, Benjamin Sayer was invited back, and thus when I came among them I was heartily welcomed by a chastened, warm-hearted, and hungry circle.

But it was no intention of mine to remain with them. The following Wednesday I was to leave for Bhamo. Mr. Johnson of the American Baptist Mission kindly found me a room at the Y.M.C.A. hostel. This good brother told me that he had lately conversed with a Burmese recently returned from the Middle East where he had met Abbas Baha, the founder and leader of the Bahai sect. He was thoroughly convinced that the claim of the Baha to be Jesus Christ returned in the flesh was true. Mr. Johnson had said that in that case Abbas had of course shown to him the wound prints in his hands and feet as proof that he was Jesus. But equally of course Abbas had not done so.

In these days I found kind friends in Mr. and Mrs. Testro. He too was in business. His wife had been formerly a worker with the China Inland Mission. The evening before I was to start on the long journey to Bhamo, which would take some days, first by train and then by steamer on the upper stretches of the Irrawady, I went to say farewell to them. Money in hand was sufficient for the actual fare to Bhamo, but not for food on the journey. This did not distress me, for the Lord has called His servants not to be anxious as to daily bread, assuring them that those things shall be supplied to such as seek first the kingdom of God. But I was secretly wondering that He was sending me to so out-of-the-way a part as Upper Burma and Western China with no funds. Yet the apostles had taken such ventures and had proved God to be faithful.

Mrs. Testro knew nothing of my circumstances; no one but the Lord knew; but she told me of some former experiences of hers when, having to take journeys, God had more than once supplied the need at the railway station itself. I pondered why she was telling me these things, and wondered if the Lord proposed to work for me at the station the next morning. He did so work, but not in the same way. I reached the station an hour and a half before the departure time, a precaution commonly advisable in the East, but found that the time had been suddenly changed, and the daily train had left an hour before.

That was answer enough for that day and I returned to the hostel. I could have gone the next day (Thursday) but it would have involved travelling on the Lord's day, which I had long ceased to do; and there being no necessity to depart from principle, I decided to stay till the following Monday. This was well, for on the next night I developed a sharp attack of Rangoon fever and was deeply thankful not to be on a train or an upcountry river boat.

That night, February 4, 1910, will be for ever memorable. I lay in my tiny cubicle, in the damp heat of that unhealthy district, feeling terribly ill, with but one or two newly made acquaintances in the vast city, practically moneyless. The sense of isolation rushed upon me as an enemy bent on destruction. But in that hour the One who stood by Paul that dark night, after the beating in the temple, and the excited meeting of the Council (Acts 23:11), drew near to me in personal presence, a presence which for one ecstatic moment I felt physically, as if He touched me with His hand. The sense of loneliness was gone, for I was not alone, nor has my spirit ever felt so through the forty years since that blessed night, though many times in equally trying circumstances.

On March 17 my sister Ella wrote as follows:

> I am so glad you have got over the fever so well. I wonder what date you were bad, because on Friday, Feb. 4th, I had come off duty and was very tired, so quickly went to sleep, but waked again about 11 p.m. with terrible neuralgia which prevented more sleep; and yet I hardly thought about it, as my whole self seemed concentrated in thought on you, and I had to pray desperately for nothing in particular, as I did not know what you were needing at the minute, but felt most vividly you were in need of Divine help and succour. Of course, I imagined you in some mountain pass with Mr. McCarthy.
>
> Flo sent me a copy of your paper *Prayer Focused and Fighting*. It is very good. I think I "prayed through" that night for you. There seemed quite a black wall round me at first. It was an awful feeling, and all the time I was thinking of you. After a long time, a real battle, Psalm 91 came to me, especially verses 4-7, and I went to sleep.

This Spirit-wrought prayer it is that has prevailing strength (Jas. 5:16); this Paul earnestly asked from brethren who could not know his exact circumstances, saying: "Now I beseech you, brethren, by our Lord Jesus Christ, and by the love of the Spirit, that ye strive [agonize] together with me in your prayers to God for me, that I may be delivered" (Rom. 15:30, 31). Thus did I strive that night, and thus did my sister, by the Spirit, strive together with me, and I was delivered, being brought through the fire and water into a wealthier place than I had before reached.

This effectual prayer differs radically from the routine mention of names found on a prayer list: for the latter has the distinct element of routine, and therefore the definite peril of formality, both wholly foreign to the former; and this routine is determined by the human mind, that is, of the compiler, whereas the former intercession is by the immediate impulse of the Spirit of God (Rom. 8:26, 27).

That advanced experience of Christ had its effect upon those I was to serve in Rangoon. The Lord took His own measures for keeping me among them, without my planning it. The money that I had thought to spend on the journey to Bhamo was soon spent at the hostel and on postages. My native "common sense" and human prudence had caused me to give an address in Yunnan Fu for letters and thither they were sent from England and none reached me for two months. Thus possible supplies from that direction did not come. I resold an English saddle purchased for the journey, and when this sum was gone there occurred a touching token of the love of God and of a native brother, a poor man, an evangelist. While in bed with a second turn of fever, a month after the first, he kindly visited me though we had not met, and when departing he said he felt it of God to leave two rupees, then 2*s*. 8*d*. It was very rarely that such ever thought of helping an Englishman. It seemed the common notion that every Englishman was in perpetual contact with the Bank of England and had only to turn a tap and gold would flow. It may be that the style and ways of many missionaries encouraged this idea.

A week or so further and the wet season on the mountains was due, Mr. McCarthy had to leave Bhamo, and it was clear that I could not join him. But meanwhile the work of the Lord in the group of Burmese Christians went forward. The exact ecclesiastical problems and heart-searchings which they had lately known I had experienced in earlier years and so was the more fitted to serve them at that juncture. Nor have I ever seen the word of the Lord have freer course or be more glorified. Their united sorrows having softened their hearts it needed only that the mind of the Lord be shown from the Word and at once they acted upon it.

Thus an address upon the value and power of prayer was followed immediately by the commencing, at their own suggestion, of a weekly meeting for prayer. The duty of every disciple to witness for Christ having been pointed out led one to take a weekly service at a native Y.M.C.A., which before he had refused to do. Younger men were provoked to spend the Easter holiday preaching in the villages, and later to get time off from daily duties to go as a band to preach for three days in the jungle. They left in fine weather in cotton clothing and returned drenched from heavy rains, but simply radiant with heavenly joy.

The right of all godly persons to come to the Lord's table being shown, a believer from the Baptist Mission was welcomed, which formerly would not have been the case. Without any ministry upon the subject (which I did not give lest a personal reason might be suspected), the Lord Himself showed them the privilege of giving of their means to this work. They had exercised their Oriental memories upon the New Testament and had a great command of its letter. This was particularly the case with young men, and specially with two who had been converted from Romanism only two years. One of these went on with the Lord and after forty years is still a leader in the church, the other lost his way in what Lord Rosebery, Gladstone's successor as Premier, called the "evil bog" of politics. He became the pro-Japanese Quisling in the late war, and only escaped with his life by the clemency of the British.

Behind Rangoon there had been formerly low swampy ground. A British engineer raised a long and winding mound across the lower side and caused the stream that made the morass to form a lake. Planted with glorious, flowering shrubs—giant croton lilies, far-stretching banks of brilliant bougainvilleas and the like—and noble palms and tropical trees, it was a paradise of beauty. One morning at dawn, while the fairy mist still lingered over the blue water, shimmering under the first glints of sunlight, old Maung Maung led a young woman, lately come to faith in Christ, down the marble boating steps into the water, lifted his hand above her head in patriarchal style, blessed her, and immersed her in the name of the Father, the Son, and the Spirit. The brilliant garments of the Christians gathered, with the lovely setting, made it a charming outward scene; but more beautiful to heaven must have been the sight of a soul escaped from the kingdom of darkness and sin passing in symbol through death, burial, and resurrection into the kingdom of God, the realm of righteousness, peace, and joy in the Holy Spirit.

I was asked to visit the leading barrister of Rangoon, a Parsee, also a member of the English bar. His wife was a Christian, himself a Theosophist. He was courteous, but wary, excused himself from religious discussion, and referred me to the Brahmin Secretary of the Rangoon Theosophical Society, a learned Sanscrit scholar. This gentleman lent me books and we had conversation. I pressed for a definition of sin, he was driven to assert that there is no essential difference between right and wrong. It is right to do a thing if you think it right, wrong if you think it wrong. This applied to, say, adultery or murder. "So then," I said, "if an anarchist thinks it right to throw a bomb under an emperor's carriage, it is right." "Yes," he said, "if he thinks it to be right." "Well then," I added, "suppose I draw a pistol and shoot you on the spot, will that be right or wrong from your point of view?" He started, as if wondering what the sahib might intend to do, but answered, "Oh, it would be wrong from my point of view, but it might be right from your point of view."

This is Theosophy stripped of its theory and verbiage and exposed naked in its native immorality.

The barrister threw a lurid light upon the moral impotence of Buddhism on public life, which we may compare with the influence of Christian teaching. He said: "The difference between our practice and that in England is, that you believe a witness unless you are prepared to prove that he is lying: here we disbelieve him unless he can prove that he is telling the truth." This low condition was confirmed by a leader I read just then in the Rangoon *Law Times,* edited by two Burmese barristers. It described the bribery which corrupted the whole legal administration from the senior judges downward, and said that the system could never be purged until the High Court judges were appointed direct from England and so not be subservient to local pressure. It was parallel to what an English magistrate had said to me in South India a few months earlier, that they never believed a witness unless he was incriminating himself, and not always then, because some one might have made it worth his while to go to prison for a time.

Yet we are assured by certain deceivers that heathendom is good enough for the heathen—why disturb them? For the same reason that night needs to be disturbed by the sunrise.

There was a young Englishman sick. I found him naturally intelligent, but wholly beclouded and muddled by Buddhism, Hinduism, Theosophy, and other cults in which he had dabbled. When I quoted the Bible he said that it was no use quoting that book because he did not look at it in the same way as myself. But I remembered what Dr. Torrey had said—that were he attacked by a robber, and threatened him with his sword; and should the robber say he did not believe it was a sword; I should not, said Dr. Torrey, discuss that but should push it into him and let him find out that it was a sword. So I kept quoting the Bible.

I said that such as he did not approach the Bible with fairness. If it were a book on any other subject they would read it as being true until they found it false, but they assumed the Bible to be false and demanded proof that it is a message from God. A timetable they would assume to tell the trains correctly unless they found errors. I had lately taken a cycling tour of 500 miles in a part of England I did not know, and bought a cycling map. But I did not ask the bookseller to prove that the roads were shown accurately or I could not be expected to buy it: I bought it for what it professed to be and went away to test it. If they would accept the Bible as being God's Word, as it claimed to be, and would test it honestly, its truthfulness would be felt.

I further pressed that God had provided a way of salvation for all men and was not going to make a special way for his private benefit. To his demand that God should prove the Word to be true and then he would believe it, God gave only a refusal and required that he should believe the Bible and then He would prove it to be true by fulfilling it. "Well then," said he, "tell me something I must believe."

The critical moment had come. Lifting my heart to God for the exact answer needed, I said: "Here is something you can believe: 'If we confess our sins, He is faithful and righteous to forgive us our sins'," and he finished the quotation, "and to cleanse us from all unrighteousness" (1 John 1:9). "This verse," I continued, "says that, if a man confesses his sins, God forgives them; but you must understand on what ground God does this. It is for the sake of Christ, His Son, Who paid the legal penalty of our sins by dying for them; even as it says in verse 12 of the next chapter, "Your sins are forgiven you *for His Name's sake.*" "Yes," he answered, "I know that is what the Bible teaches."

"Well, then, the question is, are you a sinner?"

"Yes, there is no doubt about that."

"Now do not say that just because I have led the conversation to this point. God reads your heart as you lie there, and knows whether you really are honest in owning that you are a sinner."

"Oh, yes, there is no doubt at all that I am a sinner."

"Then God sees that you confess to Him your sinfulness. Now, what does the verse say He does when a man confesses his sins?"

"It says that God forgives him."

"Then are your sins forgiven?"

"Well, but—"

"Excuse me, there can be no 'but' about it. The verse either tells the truth or does not tell the truth. Either God has forgiven your sins, or He had not forgiven them: which is it?"

"But—"

"Pardon me, I will allow no 'but' in the matter. God says that, for Christ's sake, He forgives him who honestly confesses his sins, and he expects you to believe Him. If I owed a grocer half-a-crown, went into the shop in a hurry, put down the coin, and said, 'I won't wait for the receipt; just mark off your book': and if later I went in again and said, 'You marked off that half-crown I paid' and he replied, 'Yes, you won't hear any more of that half crown'; I should not ask him to show me his ledger but should believe his word. Exactly so does God expect you to believe His word that He has forgiven your sins."

"But is this all there really is to it?"

"Well, the Bible speaks about a great many other matters, but upon this subject of the forgiveness of sins this is all that counts."

He turned his white face away on the pillow and I saw a tear trickle down his cheek. Then he looked at me and said, "I suppose it isn't the way to speak about these things, but I feel I could dance a hornpipe."

"Now," I asked, "what has happened to change your feelings so suddenly? Just now you were doubting and distressed; now you are relieved and happy. But I have not been working on your feelings but speaking only quietly and unemotionally. What has happened?"

"I don't know."

"What has taken place is this—that you have at last accepted what God says as true and He by His Spirit has proved it to be true by giving you peace and joy as He has promised to do."

Another day I learned that he was indeed a sinner, even as men reckon. Having a wife in England he was entangled with a woman in Rangoon. When he asked what could be done, I confessed that I did not see any way out of the situation, but I assured him that his newly-found Saviour could solve the problem, and together we asked His intervention. Immediately thereafter the woman herself set him free, without action on his side, by writing to say she declined to have any more to do with him.

But he did not go on to confess Christ to others. I asked why? He replied that he was manager of a large bookshop; that they sold certain French novels that as a Christian he could not sell, and he felt it better not to talk much about the Saviour until he had cleared the shop of such books. And he added that the proprietor would not like this step, for that line of books was very profitable. It was proof that the new life had at once produced a quickened conscience and a determination to be holy in walk. The proprietor was the Parsee lawyer mentioned, which partly explains why he had preferred Theosophy to Christ.

When my time came to leave he much wanted to give me a token of gratitude, and was amused to have met a man who found it hard to think of anything he wanted. At last, we thought of binoculars, which I still treasure.

While I was in Rangoon an event occurred which will not be repeated. There was an ancient tradition that at the death of Gautama Buddha (483 B.C.), the king of Peshawar, now in Pakistan, caused some pieces of his bones to be inclosed in a golden casket and placed in a vault beneath his palace. A Government archaeologist discovered this casket and now it was brought to Rangoon on its way to the great temple at Mandalay. Rangoon went on holiday; there were vast processions, headed by vicious, arrogant priests, most repulsive objects, borne on men's shoulders with every sign of rapturous excitement because these relics had come among them.

The following Sunday evening, at the Y.M.C.A., an English speaker, whose name I have not preserved, emphasized the radical difference between Buddhism and Christianity, pointing out that were any authentic relics of the body of our Lord discovered, Christianity, so far from exulting, would go into mourning, and close down as an age-long fraud based on the deception of the bodily resurrection of its Founder.

After a third attack of fever it seemed clear that I ought not to face the dangerous climate longer, especially as the intense heat of summer was at hand. But how shall one take a journey, and a long journey, who has no money and no human likelihood of receiving any? About this I looked much unto God, and there formed in my mind a clear conviction that it was His good pleasure that I should return to "Brooklands", Coonoor, for the coming hot season. One morning therefore I wrote to my sister-in-law, who would be already there, to say that I expected to leave Rangoon for Madras by a weekly boat, leaving in ten days' time, and that I hoped to reach Coonoor on a given date. After having written the letter I spent some four hours still seeking the face of God, and, feeling sure of His mind, about noon I went downstairs to post the letter. In the hall of the hostel there lay a letter which had only just arrived. It was from Miss Bishop inviting me, if I had no other guidance, to return to "Brooklands" as her guest and minister the word to the household during the hot season. That letter had come 500 miles by land and 1,200 miles by sea and had been delivered exactly as I was writing to say I thought to go to that very house. Later I learned that, after writing, Miss Bishop had deferred the posting for ten days until fully assured of the mind of the Lord. Thus perfectly does God dispose minds and co-ordinate actions.

As to monies needed, the beloved Burmese friends at once gave a loving gift, Mr. E. S. Bowden sent from India £7. 10s. 0d., and a cheque arrived from England for £10, for which the bank gave £10. 3s. 6d., such being then the value set on English money. This last letter had been sent from England via Siberia to Shanghai, had travelled some 3,000 miles up the Yangtze valley to Yunnan Fu, had then crossed the Burmese mountains to Rangoon, some 700 or more miles, and reached me precisely when needed and in conjunction of time with the other gifts. All charges at the hostel were cleared off, the ticket taken, and I sailed on the date announced, April 19, 1910.

The voyage to Madras was very delightful, one of my most pleasant trips at sea. The ship was crowded below with 1,700 Tamil coolies. They sat at nights in small groups back to back while they slept, there being insufficient space for all to stretch out. There was plague among them and they crossed from one deck to another past the second class cabin I used.

On board there was an English railway driver fleeing from Burma. Poor fellow, he was a heavy drinker. But he seemed to sense that I might help him morally, and inquired how I found it possible to keep from wine and women. It gave opportunity to tell him of the One Who saves His people from their sins. But the last I saw of him as we left the ship was lying under a bench dead drunk. Such is too often the servitude of the Devil.

On May 4, 1910, I reached Coonoor, enriched in personal knowledge of God and praising Him for the mercy that endureth for ever.

The next two and a half months were occupied with service similar to that of the year before, only mainly among the Lord's servants gathered at "Brooklands".

On arrival I had an experience not known before or since. In spite of the abundant grace lately enjoyed, my soul seemed dry and barren, destitute of heavenly emotions and largely so of earthly. The subtle temptation was pressed upon me that it would be needful to defer helping others until my own heart was refreshed. But this was of the Devil. I recalled that in his *Narrative* George Müller had mentioned that he gave an address with no comfort to his own soul, but that before long he had heard of eighteen persons who had been helped. Against the suggestion of Satan I opposed the promise of God. Dr. Pierson said that his special text as a preacher was Isa. 55:10, 11: "My word shall not return unto Me void, etc.," and that he did not remember an occasion when he had claimed that promise but that he presently heard of some fruit. The promise upon which I have relied is John 7:38, 39: "He that believeth on Me. . . out of him shall flow rivers of living water. But this spake He of the Spirit." On the occasion in question I reflected that the waters will flow through an open pipe even though the pipe does not feel anything, and I kept on speaking daily.

We have to work in faith as much as to walk by faith. In this case faith was soon justified. Before the workers returned to their places there was a testimony meeting. Miss Hastie, chief English helper to Pundita Ramabai, was kind enough to say that a talk I had given had showed her the secret of overcoming wandering thoughts in prayer. Privately she added that not once during the late weeks had she heard me speak, but it had each time exactly suited her soul's need. This must have happened at least fifteen times during the period that my own feelings were cold. The vitality of the heavenly seed is not dependent upon the feelings of the sower, but upon the perpetual energy of the Spirit of truth.

My dear friends, Mr. and Mrs. H. C. Golden, of Coimbatore, were at Coonoor. They had booked passages for England by the Italian S.S. *Balduino*, sailing from Bombay on July 15, and they were very urgent that I should join them. But I had neither guidance nor money and could only defer the matter. Mr. Golden, however, without mentioning it to me, asked Thomas Cook and Sons of Bombay to offer me a berth, which they did. By the same post, or perhaps the next, a letter came from Miss Ely, before mentioned, saying that she would be in charge for that summer of the rest home "Fairhaven" at Ramleh and intended to place on the seashore a tent in which to hold meetings for missionaries and for Moslems. She asked if I should be returning about that time, and, if so, would I break the journey in Egypt, and join in this service? And she redeemed her promise, which I had forgotten, by enclosing a draft for £20. It was drawn on Cooks at Bombay and I had only to send it and book the passage. So exactly does God work as to time and measures.

On the way to Bombay I paid a short visit to workers in Belgaum district, and had an hour at Poona with Soonderbai Power, an Indian lady conducting a Christian training home for Indian women purposing to serve in the gospel. There followed two days at Mukti with the cultured and spiritual Pundita Ramabai. This learned lady was engaged in printing the Bible on her own press—the Old Testament in Hebrew, Marathi, and English (both A.V., R.V., and Newberry's emendations), and the New Testament in Greek, Marathi, and English.

It was a new experience to hear a thousand women and girls praying aloud at one time. The sound rose and fell like the roar of the sea or the wind in a forest But what to a Westerner might seem mere confusion did not so strike me, for I had before heard in Egypt a whole school of boys similarly learning and reciting their lessons out loud. Yet the mind of each was on his own recitation, undisturbed by the noise around. Similarly each woman and girl was oblivious of the rest and when each finished praying she rose quietly from the ground and left the hall. What is the force of Acts 4:24: "And they. . . lifted up their voice to God with one accord and said..." Was it that the whole company were suddenly moved by the one Spirit to say unitedly the same words? The New Testament was not written as a description of modern and Western meetings!

On the ship there were two British officers, captains. One had won his commission in the South African war. He was quiet and religious, but a Freemason. He loaned me one of their books, but when he found that I was beginning to fill in correctly the blanks in the book he would no more converse on the matter. It reminded me that in South India a young Englishman had tried to kindle in me an interest in Freemasonry. Asked what was the advantage of being a Freemason, he replied that it was knowledge. Each grade that one advanced, more knowledge was imparted. Asked what was the nature of the knowledge that could be imparted only behind locked doors and under revolting vows of absolute secrecy, he would say no more. I pressed upon him the extreme contrast of this secrecy with the statement of Christ before His judges: "I have spoken openly to the world: I ever taught in synagogues and in the temple, where all the Jews come together; and in secret spake I nothing" (John 18: 20). The Book of God contains indeed high mysteries, but they are written there for all men to read. There is no esoteric teaching declared only to initiates, as in the ancient pagan Mystery societies or in modern Theosophy or Freemasonry.

The other captain was of the older type of officer, a man of some position in Society. After a long close talk upon salvation and the divine life he revealed the darkness of mind of many such men by saying: "All I can say is that never in my life did any man talk to me as you have done tonight."

As we neared Suez, where I was to disembark, my loving friend H. C. Golden wished to know how I was placed as to money. I answered evasively, not wishing to tell anyone but my Master. My dear brother gave me five pounds. Without this I could not have reached Alexandria, where the next service waited.

CHAPTER 7

Travel

Egypt and Tunisia. 1910-1911

I landed at Suez on July 26, 1910, and reached Ramleh on the 28th. The meetings for Christians in the tent helped many. For six Sunday evenings gatherings were held for Moslems, concluded by two on week-nights. Many attended, mainly from Alexandria, six miles distant. Not a few remained late for conversation. Fierce opposition was shown in the Moslem newspapers. The city authorities were against us. The Prime Minister, a Moslem, was in the city and lent support to the agitation, as did a chief British official. He would have closed the tent, but Miss Ely was American. The United States consul came several times and reported the threat to the Legation in Cairo, who declared they would refer the matter to Washington if there was attempt to interfere with the rights of an American citizen. So we were let alone, though Miss Ely on her part made no appeal to the consul, who came and acted on his own initiative.

Here is seen the wisdom, we may almost say the strategy, of the Lord. British policy in all lands has been to hinder gospel efforts among Moslems. One known to me went from Canada to Khartoum to do such work. When he applied for a permit to reside and evangelize, the British Chief Secretary to Government asked why he had not applied in writing from Canada, for he could have saved him the journey, and he added that he had already refused thirteen such applications. No permit could be had save to work among the *pagan* tribes.

But God is not to be thwarted. Almost a century earlier the Church Missionary Society had tried to work in Egypt, but having found the field sterile had withdrawn. Later the American Presbyterians entered and established themselves. Thus when the British took control of the country in 1882 the work of God was in hands they could not tie, nor was it feasible to hinder officially English people from doing in Egypt what Americans were allowed to do. One who knows the ways and judgments of God can see His recompense of this false policy of Britain in the cessation of their rule over the chief Moslem areas, as Pakistan and the Middle East.

The fear of disturbance in our little tent on the shore was not unfounded. A plot was laid to make a riot and afford the authorities pretext for suppressing us. But this came to nought. Four of us had spent the whole of the day in prayer in the tent, though not knowing of the plot for that night. The powers of darkness were bound and defeated. It was this circumstance that led to my booklet *Controlling the Situation,* incorporated now in *Prayer Focused and Fighting.*

When this effort ceased in September guidance came to other work in Egypt. It is happy to be without local ties or fixed plans and so to be available for special service. Mr. Dickens of Ramleh proposed a series of midday meetings to attract the English-speaking young men of Alexandria. These were held in the Scotch church with encouragement.

An English lady living in Paris had given me the name of an English Christian lady in Ibrahimia who had married an Irishman. He was prominent in British business circles, but not a member of the kingdom of God. They kindly asked me to be their guest while holding the meetings at the Scotch church, and the Lord responded by leading my host to the knowledge of Christ as we talked on his verandah on January 22, 1911. He has gone forward throughout the forty years since. It may be instructive to some to mention that he began to suffer from facial neuralgia, severe and prolonged. No remedies helped, but upon his giving up smoking the attack ceased.

On January 29, 1911, I crossed Lake Menzaleh from Mansourah to Port Said. The steamer stuck in the mud and the night had to be passed on deck without food. There was a tiny cabin, but sixteen Arab merchants packed it, all smoking. So I went outside. Though I was ponderous with clothing, rugs, and a counterpane of coconut matting, it was nevertheless bitterly cold.

For several months I visited up and down Egypt, sharing the toils and joys of godly people of various missions and churches. One of the first was William Fairman of Shibin el-Kom in the Delta, a godly man, a master of colloquial Arabic. He gave an illustration of how phrases current in Christian speech may seem ridiculous to the unconverted and are better avoided. In his worldly days, he, with two godless companions, stood at an open-air gospel meeting. An elderly lady with white hair commenced with the announcement: "Dear friends, I am two years old today." They booed at her and passed on.

While staying with J. Gordon Logan at Zeitoun another instance came of the value of being free for sudden calls. Dr. Samuel Zwemer was expected as a speaker at the American Mission annual meetings. When he reached Egypt by sea the ship was quarantined and it fell to me to fill the gap until his arrival.

Near the Logans' house were patches of open desert. On one of these a Greek lived and kept four large dogs. As I was passing in the gloaming these beasts rushed down on me. With true military instinct they encircled the foeman, and dodged easily the blows I aimed with a heavy ash stick. Not until I began to stone them did they retire. Artillery succeeds where small arms fail. As I described this incident a humorous friend told me the best way to scare dogs. He said, "You turn your back on them, stoop far forward, and stare at them between your legs." He had a large head, prominent eyes, and huge mops of hair. I told him that I thought the plan might succeed in his case.

My host at Ibrahimia had asked me to see his brother, who was in the R.A.S.C. at Cairo. I saw him in barracks, and the following Sunday evening he came to the American Mission church where I was to preach. After the service he remained in his seat. All others left. I spoke to him and prayed, prayed and spoke, yet he, though Irish, said not a word. I appealed to him, prayed, appealed. We sat thus for two hours; it was now ten o'clock; the stone building was very cold; and I knew it must soon be locked for the night. At last, with sweat pouring from his face under the pressure of his spirit, he uttered a few words of confession of faith in Christ, and we departed.

We did not meet again until my next visit to Cairo three years later. Upon asking him if he could say Christ was his Saviour he at once answered in the affirmative. I asked how long this had been the case and the prompt reply was, "Ever since that night in the church." Thank God that I had not given up until that battle had been won. The good shepherd "goeth after that which is lost *until he find it*" (Luke 15:4).

It was at this time that I made the acquaintance of that excellent woman Mrs. Todd Osborne, famous for gospel work among troops of the Mediterranean garrisons. She took me to Abbassia to the vast camp then being formed. On a spot at the highest and central point she said that for the Home she proposed to build "they" wanted to give a site at the bottom corner of the camp, right out of the road the soldiers would use. She asked that we should pray together that the Home might be on the exact spot where we stood. And there the King George V Soldiers' Home was erected.

I was often at the Russell Soldiers' Home near Shepheard's Hotel, Cairo, her centre at that time. She sought advice under the following circumstances. The Home had been bought many years before from the executors of a Greek. Some while afterwards a woman put in a claim for £600, alleging that she was a beneficiary under the will and had not been paid her share. The Mixed Tribunal gave judgment in her favour. Mrs. Osborne's lawyer was the leading French advocate in Egypt and said the judgment was bad in law. An appeal was entered and had been lying unheard for years: what should she do? Of course, if either party had given a sufficient bribe to the clerk of the Appeal Court the case could have been called early; but Mrs. Osborne would not do this and the other party did not. I told her that it was no concern of hers how long the appeal lay: she had nothing to lose; let the other woman stir it up, if she wished.

Fourteen years later, at Keswick, I asked Mrs. Osborne about the matter and learned it had just been settled. A clerk in the Greek consulate, clearing a drawer of papers, found a document connected with the case, and took it to her lawyer. The hearing came on immediately and as soon as the President of the Court saw this document he dismissed the action.

Such was the state of things when English and French judges dealt with matters affecting non-Egyptians. Delay and bribery will be far more prevalent now that, with the abolition of the Mixed Tribunals, Moslem judges act. One who knew the facts told me of two farmers who went to Court under Egyptian law. One took £10 to the clerk and it was arranged that he should get the verdict; the other took £20 and it was arranged that *he* should get the verdict. The case had not yet been heard. Presumably the clerk would leave the judge to decide the matter, and so excuse himself to the party that lost.

Only where the Word of God has had public influence has it been reasonable to expect justice in the Courts. Why is this? The explanation is in Psalm 82. Evil *angel* judges secretly pervert human judges so as to defeat justice and corrupt mankind. Consider also 1 Kings 22, especially verses 19-23.

At table one evening there was occasion to mention that in Rangoon I had visited the Synagogue on Passover Day and had held a long conversation with an intelligent Jew, speaking English fluently. I asked him if I had not read in the Torah that God forgives sin only when there has been the shedding of blood of a victim in place of the sinner? He assented. I remarked that there was no shedding of blood in their present services. He replied that there could not be, because they had no temple or priesthood. I urged that this did not alter the requirement of the law of Moses. His answer was pathetic: "Yes, we do all these things, but we do not know if it is acceptable." I replied, that they might be sure that it is not acceptable, seeing that it did not fulfil the just requirement of God. Such is the uncertainty of even the pious Israelite.

I added that this Jew, surprised to meet an Englishman who seemed to know the law and the prophets like a rabbi, said: "May I ask, sir, if you are a Hebrew?" Mrs. Todd Osborne quietly interjected "That is just what you are, Mr. Lang"; from which I learned that this fine Christian was misled by the theory of Anglo-Israelism. Not appearing, however, to notice this, I went on to narrate that, in a train in Upper Egypt, a German had said: "But you are not English! I thought from your appearance that you were a German professor"; and I added that, as the fact that a Jew mistook me for a Jew showed that I was a Jew, that a German mistook me for a German showed that I was a German. My dear friend did not pursue the subject.

At Port Said I stayed several times, and I think on every occasion some person was blessed. The first was a Greek. In the Greek-Turkish war he was called to the army, where he distributed tracts written by himself. After the war he ran a Sunday school of his own, and so continued till his death. Another was a leading Englishman, who received Christ as we walked the beach on New Year's Day 1911. I have reason to think that the truth found entrance to the heart of an English governess met on the shore with the children she taught.

Light and shade chase each other across life's sky. My friend, C. T. Hooper, agent of the B. & F. Bible Society, kindly let me use his bathing hut on the shore. Some genuine humorist, able to rise above the sad events of life, had drawn on the wall a tombstone, with skull and crossbones at the top, and beneath the following inscription: "In fond memory of 5*s*. which departed from this hut on such and such a date. 'Tis better to have loved and lost than never to have loved at all."

On January 10, 1911, I witnessed in the Muski, Cairo, at night a procession of Persian Moslems. It was an annual event in memory of the death in A.D. 680 of a grandson of Mohammed, and is thus an ancient ceremony. It was a spectacle characteristic of the cruelty and barbarism in which Islam was born and nurtured, and which properly belong to it as a system.

Down the narrow and poorly-lit streets of the native quarter came many men and lads in loose, open files, some bearing banners, richly worked in colours, and others carrying torches of wood flaming in an iron framework at the top of a pole. By this lurid light was seen, first, a young boy riding a horse, both boy and beast being covered in white and much splashed with what may have been blood, but was more likely pink colouring. But the boy's face being freely smeared, looked hideous. Presently followed in the procession a disgustingly filthy dervish, a beggar, with matted, tangled hair and unwashed person, who was earning a reputation for sanctity by living in rags and dirt. Shortly, amidst the motley crowd, where all sorts of Eastern garbs mingled, appeared men stripped to the waist flogging themselves with scourges made of many small iron chains fastened to a short handle. My impression was that, whilst one or two were hurting their persons, the more part of these men caused the chains to clank more in the air than upon their body. And last of all, came some fifty men, in two long lines, walking sideways, each with the left hand holding the man coming after him, and each in the right hand brandishing a fierce, cruel scimitar. As they moved they chanted a weird, monotone dirge; and at short intervals the procession stopped—but not the dreadful dirge—whilst these poor fanatics cut their heads about with the swords. It was too horrible to hear the keen, hard edge of the weapon click against the skull bone, and to see, by the red glare of the torches, the scalps of all cut and gory. The white outer robes also were stained and blotched with blood, where others had used them to wipe the faces of the wearers, and had staunched for the moment the flow from the gaping wounds. Crowds of men, women, and children watched the ghastly sight with enthusiasm.

Such scenes were far more common in former days when Moslems only ruled, and Islam revealed its native ways unhindered. As in India, so in Egypt, British rule, though with less vigour than formerly, counted for much against these public horrors. This procession was prohibited a few years later.

Let none be deceived by the specious writings of some who in modern days, and for English readers, would present Islam as a virtuous, pleasant system of thought. In its home spheres Islam is cruel, vice-encouraging, and inhuman—and therefore demonic, Satanic.

I was now so accustomed to the heat that the summer did not tax me though the temperature rose at times to 115⁰ in the shade. But by May 1911, I felt the Lord's time had come for me to move towards England. I therefore bought in Cairo a ticket from Alexandria to Tunis, proposing to see the work of the Lord in that Moslem country.

There being a little time before sailing I paid farewell visits in the Delta.

Tanta is the third largest town in Egypt. The mayor was a pasha who had been virtually insolvent, but, securing this position, after only a few years was very wealthy. This was attained by crooked means; but, omitting this ungodliness, the change of his circumstances illustrates the honour and advantage to which the Lord pointed in the reward the King gave to the servants who had been faithful to his interests in his absence: "have thou authority over ten cities" (Luke 19:17).

Tanta was fortunate in having the tomb of some ancient Moslem saint. Quite possibly his sanctity lay in having endured for years more filth and vermin than other men. The advantage to the town was an annual pilgrimage to this tomb which brought perhaps 200,000 visitors to spend money in the shops. Pilgrimages are lucrative affairs for keepers of shops and hotels, and guardians of sacred shrines. In connexion with this pilgrimage there was a vast fair. At night (April 11, 1911) I wandered around the booths, and spent hours sitting with the folk in dimly lit tents watching the religious dance known as the *zikr.*

A number of men joined hands and moved round and round in a circle with a slightly swaying and slightly springing motion, chanting continuously a sentence from the Koran. The motion increased steadily in rapidity and energy, the chanting becoming proportionately louder and faster. After some while the faces grew frenzied, the voices screaming, the forms jumping and twisting violently. This would continue until the desired climax was reached by demonic possession imparting supernatural energy, so that the fierce dancing might go on for long hours, until the possession ceased and the devotee collapsed with exhaustion. It was obviously the same as the devil dances of savages.

The night was very cold, so I sat with others near a brazier where burnt the cobs of Indian corn from which the grains had been eaten. It gave a most pungent smoke severely irritant to the eyes. Unfortunately I had not brought my overcoat and could not stay the whole night and watch the dancing at its fullest development. Oh, with what fetters of deceit, excitement, and destruction have the powers of darkness bound their slaves. Only Christ can set them free.

He breaks the power of cancelled sin,
He sets the prisoner free.

The Lord strengthen and own every Christian to strive to make known His victory by the cross and resurrection.

After buying the ticket to Tunis I had only enough money for the visits between Cairo and Alexandria where I was to embark. But a comfortable assurance was given that I should find needed funds at the port. A large English mail awaited me at the house of my kind and godly host Dr. Finney, of the American Mission. In my mind I had taken for granted that this would be the means by which the money needed would reach me. But the Lord wished to teach me again the important lesson not to look to England but to Himself. The heavy mail brought much news but no money, not a penny. "Now," said the Enemy, "you are stranded. You cannot even put your bags on board tomorrow." But the promises of God preserved my heart in peace. Considering how to spend the evening I thought of two houses which I would visit to say farewell. But they were miles apart on opposite sides of the great city and I had only enough pence for the tram fare to one. Which should it be? Waiting upon God I decided to go to the Rickards, the customs officer mentioned. There I learned that the other friends were from home, so a visit to them would have wasted my pence. After a long talk with two unconverted daughters, Mrs. Rickards kindly proposed that I should stay the night, rather than return to Dr. Finney's in the dark. No sooner had I closed the bedroom door than it opened gently, my hostess put out her hand and put into mine a packet containing five golden sovereigns. I had found the needed help at the port, but not by the means that "common sense" had forecast.

The American Mission was housed in fine premises on the chief street in Alexandria. Dr. Finney told me the story of this. For years their schools, teachers, and missionaries had been scattered in different directions and often in unhealthy premises. One of their number went to Pittsburg, the wealthy area of U.S.A., the centre of the Presbyterian churches with which the Mission was associated. A loan of £20,000 was secured at five per cent interest. The central site was bought, shops (including a Bible depot) were built on the street, also a fine auditorium for 500 persons, with commodious school rooms, flats above for workers, and above these other flats to be let. It was expected that in twenty years the rents of shops and flats would repay the loan. In addition, there was the saving of the rents of the many scattered premises and the convenience of the work being centralized.

I remarked to my kind friend that it was a first-class business scheme, with only one drawback—the spiritual! He had a little before told me sadly how disappointing they found their converts from Islam, for these became mere dependants of the Mission, expecting to be supported by its funds, developing little faith, stamina, or spiritual vitality. I asked how it could be otherwise? Upon turning from Islam these converts found themselves cut off and beggared. Was it not natural that each should think that as it was these Christians who had led him to this, of course they will support me; they are wealthy; look at the style in which they live!

During these months in Egypt I visited some of the ancient monuments, as well as on later visits, but space does not allow of writing of these.

TUNISIA

Leaving Egypt on April 19, 1911, we touched at Syracuse on the 22nd, and reached Bizerta the next day. The day following, on the train to Tunis, I gave a gospel in French to a young man. He read it from beginning to end without even lifting his eyes save once, when the door of the compartment closed with a bang. Thus fascinating is the story of the Lord Jesus to one who evidently had never before read it.

On April 29 Mr. Liley took me over the ruins of Carthage. The theatre is largely intact. Its acoustics were perfect. The heart was moved when standing in the arena where in A.D. 202 or 203 Perpetua and Felicitas were martyred for Christ's sake. In this city Tertullian, the lawyer, wrote his "apology" for the Christian faith. Here Cyprian, the bishop, was beheaded in A.D. 257. He was another instance of one so devoted to Christ that he would die for Him, yet who led the churches far astray as regards unscriptural and ruinous church organization. It is good that the heart be sound, bad that the mind be misguided.

The city of Tunis is well worth a visit. Its bazaars are famous. It was instructive on Saturday to pass at a step from the thronged and bustling Moslem bazaar into the closed Jewish bazaar, as silent as a graveyard. The Moslem is required by Islamic law to go on Friday to the morning prayer in the mosque, but the rest of the day he may do as he pleases.

My host had lived in Tunisia many long years. He told me that fifty per cent of Moslems there drank intoxicants regularly, that twenty-five per cent were heavy drinkers, and ten per cent habitual drunkards. This is a shocking effect of Western influence, for wine is prohibited to Moslems by the Koran (Muir, *Mahomet and Islam,* ed. 3, 244).

In Mr. Liley's house, in other houses, and in the assembly of Italians gathered by Miss Alice Case of Bristol, there were many opportunities of filling the five weeks in Tunis. The first week in May I visited Kairouan. The great mosque is noted for the number of carved marble pillars. It is the one mosque known to me where "infidels" (non-Moslems) may enter without removing their shoes, or putting on over-shoes, as an acknowledgment of the sanctity of the building. As I was not free in conscience to admit this supposed sanctity in a building where the Son of God is blasphemed I never entered a mosque save this one. The exception is made on the ground that when the French captured Kairouan after an obstinate defence, the Commandant spitefully marched his troops into the mosque and so defiled it. Since then, in contempt, the Moslems permit the defiled infidel to enter it.

In a small yard behind a house I was gravely shown a wondrous sight— the two large anchors with which Noah fastened the ark!

Sfax was visited, and on the way to it the vast colosseum at El-Djem, said to be the next best ruin of a colosseum to that at Rome. At Susa there are catacombs bearing their silent witness, as do those at Rome. In these three towns there were brave and isolated witnesses for Christ whom it was a privilege to visit, as well as at Nabeul.

But the time was come for this long tour to end. On May 29, 1911, I sailed from Tunis. It was a most miserable cold night, with a strong cross wind tossing the tiny ship. Going to the cabin late at night it was to find a lady already in bed, and looking very ill. Finding the second officer I succeeded in making clear that I objected to the situation. He was astonished, it being a French way of things. But he fetched the unhappy husband, who poured out streams of arguments in voluble French, fearing lest I should disturb his poor wife. But all I wanted was another berth. This the officer found in a tiny cabin where three other men were in possession. It opened on to the small dining-saloon, reeking with fumes of French cooking. I was dreadfully ill, and understood the remark about sea-sickness that at first one is afraid one is going to die, and then afraid one is *not* going to die!

But the worst night ends in morning. As soon as the ship reached the long entrance to Marseilles and the rolling ceased, I was well, and the warm welcome to their home of Mr. and Mrs. Thorpe banished the cold of the night.

Here I believe I missed the exact way of God for me. I was over-anxious to get on to Switzerland and home. I had word that a letter with £10 was on its way. On the strength of this I borrowed a few pounds from Mr. Thorpe and went forward the next day. Had I waited only one day more, as my kind hosts proposed, the letter would have reached me there and the loan would not have been needed, nor the disclosure of the need. "Rest in the Lord, and *wait patiently* for Him" (Ps. 37:7).

In the village of Blonay, above Vevey, on the lake of Geneva, Miss Ely had taken a chalet, so as to provide, at nominal cost, a holiday resort for workers from Egypt. She had furnished it with taste. A devoted, self-denying friend had objected to the pictures, lounge-chairs, and general refinement. Why did missionaries need such indulgences? But she worsted him with the argument that when God made the garden ugly she would make the house ugly! Yet in Egypt her own quarters were plain and unadorned.

After a few days in Paris I reached England on June 8, 1911, to praise the Father of mercies for the joys and trials that my loved ones and myself had been granted during the two years and four months of our first separation.

CHAPTER 8

England

On July 3, 1911, we moved from Bristol to Clayhidon on the Blackdown Hills in the north-east of Devonshire. Some fifty years before, my wife's grandfather, George Brealey, had invaded that remote and neglected district with the gospel. After his death her father, W. J. H. Brealey, had continued to superintend the six mission halls that had been acquired or erected, with Clayhidon as the centre. Later he went to Clevedon, Somerset, as pastor of Copse Road Chapel, while still responsible for the work on the Hills. His home being vacant, and the work needing help, we went there; but I accepted no binding tie and was free to visit other places as guided by God.

By October Mr. Brealey's vigour was reduced and a long rest was needful; he and his family therefore came to Clayhidon and we went to his house in Clevedon, where I undertook the ministry until May 1912, when he returned.

The work at Copse Road had been commenced by a lay Churchman who outgrew that State-bound system. In due time Mr. Victor, whose labours had resulted in Unity Chapel, Bristol, took up the work. It developed, and a fine chapel was built, too handsome for serving the best purposes. The work was on the same lines as at Unity. One preacher was responsible for the ministry, though he could invite others to speak, which was often done. The morning gathering was first a usual preaching service conducted by the pastor, followed by a short open meeting for the breaking of bread. The same features as at Unity were evident, and the same defects; particularly that gifts of ministry did not develop, nor spontaneity of worship. To this day the church is too weak to dispense with its fixed ministry and function healthily in the energy of the Spirit. Yet good men and good ministry have been its portion for eighty years, and many have been saved and helped. But feed people never so well, if they always have a crutch they will never walk freely or safely.

The rest of 1912 passed in ministry of the word on the Hills and in many places in the south and west of England. At Yeovil conference in September there was present Lieutenant Willie Lange from Germany. He was a strong witness for Christ, and forwent his chance of a post on the Imperial General Staff because he would not abandon the principles of the New Testament as to church life and join the Lutheran church, at that time a condition of being on the Staff. This I learned from his brother Major Ernst Lange, whom later I knew well. Yet when this sincere and brave Christian was asked at Yeovil by an English brother what he would do were their two countries at war and they met in battle, without hesitation he replied, "I should kill you; it would be my duty." Thus does the spirit of the world cancel the Spirit of love, and it is made manifest that no man can in this matter serve two masters, the State *and* the Christ of Calvary, for no one can act at the same time by law *and* grace.

The year 1913 was full with the same labours in various parts. In March Walter H. Clark held evangelistic meetings in the tiny hall in the hamlet of Stapley, three miles from Clayhidon. On Wednesday, March 5, there took place here a notable miracle. There lived near by a notorious ruffian named Buttle. He had put in twenty-one years in the Army and finished his education in wickedness. He was a poacher, a drunkard, a curser. His boy dreaded his return from the inn, for he and his mother had known what it was to be driven out of the cottage to pass the night on the hillside.

This evening Walter Clark finished his address abruptly and said that Mr. Lang had something to say. I whispered that I had no notices to give out or anything to say. He replied: "I am spent. Test the meeting or close it." Now I am not enamoured of the plan of "testing" a gospel meeting, and on the few occasions I had done so it had been to no purpose. But seeing Buttle present (for I knew him, though he did not know me), I said a few words as to the power of Christ to save us from the power of sin. Then, while all heads were bowed, I asked any who might wish to experience this salvation to put up the hand and Buttle's hand was raised.

He remained behind alone, and in that small hut, by the dim light of a single small lamp, we talked. He began by saying, "I want to tell you, sir, that I have been a very wicked man; I've committed every crime a man can commit except murder, and I've been near that more than once."

I let him talk awhile, checking his story against what I already knew, and it was plain that he was honest and sincere. So I said: "Well, Buttle, the question we want to get at tonight is, Do you want to get quit of your sins?" "That's what I came for," he replied. "Then we can soon get at that. You know that Jesus Christ is the Son of God and that He came down here to pay the penalty for our sins, by His death, so that we may be forgiven." "Yes." "Do you know that He is now alive and ready to deliver us from our sins?" "Yes." "Then get down on your knees and tell the Lord like an honest man, just as simply as you have told me, that you have been a wicked man and that you are going to trust Him to save you."

This he did. It was probably the first time he had ever prayed, and the wording was what may be easily supposed; but he spoke out of his heart into the heart of God. I prayed briefly and we rose and sat again. He looked at me and said: "I don't know what's happened, but I feel very different to what I did just now." I replied: "Of course you do: you have asked the Lord Jesus to save you from your sins, and He has kept His promise and done so; so of course you feel different."

And different he was, a new man in Christ. Some while later he told me that his Foresters' Club met monthly in the inn where he used to get drunk so often, but that now he did not even want to go into the bar. He had no difficulties with his pipe; the craving to smoke simply ceased at once. But the most miraculous change was in his language. He was so habitual and confirmed a swearer that he poured out volleys of curses in his dreams; but many weeks after his conversion his wife told me that since that night she had not heard an oath, waking or sleeping.

Let this be considered carefully. Let a man accustomed to use habitually any one word—say, "awfully" or "tremendous"—decide not to use it for a week or even a day; and let him ask his wife or a friend how often he has used it; and he will feel how extremely hard it is to banish from his speech even one word. What then shall be said of the sudden and complete removal from the mind of a whole class of words, so that no watch had to be kept against their use? Such a mental miracle can be effected only by the Creator of the mind.

I said to Buttle that night: "You must be fifty-five years of age." "Just about," he answered. "What has begun to trouble you about these things?" "It was a hymn sung last night." (It was Dr. Watts' lines:)

> *Alas, and did my Saviour bleed?*
> *And did my Sovereign die?*
> *Would He devote that sacred head*
> *For such a worm as I?*
> *Was it for crimes that I had done*
> *He groaned upon the tree?*
> *Amazing pity, grace unknown,*
> *And love beyond degree!*

Said he: "I went through the battle of Abu Klea." That was on January 17, 1885, in the Sudan war, twenty-eight years before we were conversing. He continued: "After the battle, as we lay on the sands at night, a lad of my company was bleeding to death at my side, and as he lay there he sang that hymn. It made no impression on me: I was already the ruffian of the regiment: and I never heard it again until last night. As it was sung I suddenly saw that lad singing it as he lay dying. It was more than I could stand and I had to leave the meeting to get control of my feelings. I went home and said to my wife, 'Wife, we must change our lives.' She said, 'Then you change yours first'; and that's what I came for tonight."

That dying boy cast his seed upon the waters, and the fruit was found after many days. Let us sow the truth beside all waters, even the foulest; in the morning and at evening; in season, out of season; for we know not which shall prosper, whether this or that, or whether both alike shall be good. That dying singer shall come again with rejoicing, bringing his sheaf with him. One soweth and another reapeth, and we shall rejoice together.

But it is startling and solemn that his wife, as far as I knew, was never converted, though she had seen and benefited by the work of grace in him. She had kept straight and respectable in spite of him, and seemed not to feel a need of his Saviour. Still do the taxgatherers and harlots go into the kingdom before the self-righteous (Matt. 21:31).

During our time at Clayhidon another unusual case was as follows. There came to Clayhidon a quiet, respectable man, with his wife and child. The wife was a keen Christian and was commendably concerned for her husband, who made no profession. Sitting in their big chimney corner, by the log fire, I asked him why he had not believed on Christ as his Saviour. He replied that he had done so. I asked when? He said it was three years ago. His wife had been given up by the doctors. He was dreadfully cut up; went into his smithy, shut the door, turned unto God, and accepted Christ. In astonishment I said: "Man alive, you had that experience and yet have managed to keep it so utterly secret that not even your wife has had any suspicions of it!"

How little we can judge of the state of the heart of another. With the heart he had believed unto righteousness, and three years later he made confession with his mouth unto salvation. Now his inner and dormant life began to grow.

About this time the Lord opened the door to one of those usually inaccessible places, a large county mansion. The Colonel sometimes read prayers in church, which seemed to be the sum of his religion. The lunch hour was dismal. I was a fish out of water while they chatted about dogs, racing, and theatres. But the lady of the house was a smothered Christian, starved and hungry, whom it was good to cheer. She wrote later to ask whether I thought it allowable to paint her face. Her husband wished it, as he did not like to see her looking old. She was well on in years. What troubled her conscience was the thought that she was deceiving people. Making allowance for her childish spiritual state, I put upon her no burden that she was not likely to bear well, and said that, if she felt free to please her husband in so foolish a desire, I thought she might do so; and added that she need not feel any trouble in conscience as to deceiving people, for no one was likely to be deceived.

How important is the desire of the apostles that the regenerate shall *grow up* into Christ in all things, shall cease to be children and become men, having their senses exercised to discern between good and evil, becoming full of the knowledge of God's will in all spiritual wisdom and understanding, to walk worthily of the Lord. For this growth from babyhood to manhood the Word of God, the sacred writings, are indispensable and sufficient (2 Tim. 3:14-16). It is ignorance of this holy Word that accounts for such infants as this poor lady.

During our residence in Devonshire I was one evening stricken down without warning with influenza, the fourth such seizure known. Utterly prostrate, and with severe nausea, my first thought was to send for some brethren to pray. But this being found impracticable, my wife and I prayed together; and faith was given to plead that there should be a prompt raising up to fulfil a preaching engagement in a distant city the next day but one. In particular it was asked that the distressing nausea might subside. My wife rose, and at once left the room; but ere she had closed the door I recalled her to say that the nausea had instantly gone, and that I was already well.

Many who adopt no such opinions as that sickness is always from the devil, or that it is sinful to use remedies or to consult a physician, nevertheless know experimentally the power of the prayer of faith in severe sickness.

That God does not always immediately heal all infirmities is evident from the cases of Trophimus (2 Tim. 4:20) and Timothy (1 Tim. 5:23). Some bodily weakness is permanent, being for spiritual benefit and is cause for glorying (2 Cor. 12:7-10); some is disciplinary, and can be relieved only by repentance, confession, and prayer (Jas. 5:15, 16; 1 Cor. 11:29, 30); some is but the unavoidable wear and tear upon the physical machinery which is incidental to all strenuous effort. God will instruct prayerful hearts as to the nature of the ailment, and what measures, spiritual or medicinal, or both, are proper to each case.

During the autumn of 1913 Miss Ely wrote from Egypt that she purposed to erect a large native tent in the heart of Cairo for another gospel attack upon Moslems. Mr. McClenahan would lead the Arabic work; would I join them to take meetings in English? She also invited my wife and daughter. I knew this was a call from God. But to take them also nearly trebled the expense. Yet what is that to God? Sometime before, my cousin Musgrove had arranged that I should address a gathering at the house of Mr. F. W. Byrde at Weston-super-Mare. This kind friend, hearing of the purposed visit to Egypt, sent £30. Miss Ely sent £25; other smaller gifts furthered the project, and we reached Alexandria on December 22, 1913, with 11s. 4d. in hand. Here a quite unexpected difficulty met us. Miss Ely had intended to receive us at once at Heliopolis, near Cairo. But her arrangements for a house were delayed. Perforce we had to stay at Ramleh, and for some weeks we were greatly tested as to funds. Yet money came in small sums from as far apart as England, Egypt, and South Africa, and we were brought through, with faith tried and strengthened.

CHAPTER 9

Egypt

The most famous street in ancient Cairo is the Muski, crooked, narrow, fascinating. The principal thoroughfare in modern Cairo is Sharia Kasr el-Nil, broad, straight, imposing, yet commonplace. Here is the Savoy Hotel, where, in the ampler days before the First World War, royalty stayed. Beside it, under its walls, there was in 1914 an open plot of building land. Here, behind a high hoarding, was erected the large native tent, constructed of long curtains hanging over high poles and crosspieces. It was entered by one gateway, on which was fixed, over the pavement, a small board announcing the meetings, with the words, if I remember them aright, "What must I do to be saved? The question answered here." Also, handbills in Arabic were scattered widely, especially at the open-air cafes.

Members of the established Missions were much perturbed by this bold attack on Islam at the heart of the city. "Oh, yes, you will get Moslems to come; but there will be riots, which will give the authorities pretext for suppressing your effort, and our whole work among the Mohammedans will be prejudiced."

But we replied that riots in connexion with aggressive gospel work were quite apostolic; so we went ahead, protecting and enforcing the effort by intense and persistent prayer. In this last all-important service we were strongly supported by a few sympathetic friends.

Moslems came, generally forty or fifty each of the five nights a week, and smaller numbers to my afternoon talks in English. We did have riots, every Thursday night. Students from the great El-Azhar university, having no lessons to prepare for the Friday sabbath, came in groups to interrupt. They switched off the electric lights, chanted the Koran, booed, upset the seats, and caused general confusion. But the authorities gave no sign that they knew of the tent, though we were only a few hundred yards from the British consulate.

One night the tent was set on fire during a meeting. But the heavy curtains did not burn fast, and sand (of which Egypt has abundance) is a quick extinguisher. Another time it was set on fire during the day when empty. The flames took hold. The occupier of the next adjoining building summoned the fire brigade, who saved perhaps half the tent, and reported to the police. A big handsome Moslem officer in plain clothes came to interrogate us. It was explained that we recognized it was the duty of the police to punish crime, only we had to beg them to recognize that it was not our business to help them in this. Our business was to tell all men that God was very willing, for Christ's sake, to forgive them their crimes; and therefore, if they could catch the miscreants, all we could do would be to assure them that we also forgave them. The officer listened with polite wonder to this strange talk and went his way. We heard no more of it, and not even then did the British officials utter a sound. It was to a ruler of Egypt of old that it was said, "against any of the children of Israel shall not a dog move his tongue" (Ex. 11:7).

The Moslem youths of Cairo were well primed against Christian doctrine. I have seen a boy of ten engage eagerly in controverting the truth that God has a Son, even Jesus. The El-Azhar university boarded free and educated some ten thousand students, sending them into the professions and commerce, all trained to propagate Islamic doctrine. Those who came to the tent were keen controversialists. But my earlier observation of missionary work among Moslems had satisfied me that the controversial method was wrong. I had urged upon those so engaged that it was a false move to attack Mohammed and the Koran, for it provoked resentment, just as it would be the wrong approach to a lover of Christ were a Moslem to attack Him and the Bible.

C. T. Hooper of the Bible Society had told me that he and a friend had gone from Suez to Jidda on a pilgrim ship on purpose to be among pilgrims going to Mecca on the annual pilgrimage. His companion was one of the most widely read and able missionary students of Islamic law and literature, and in discussion he defeated easily the learned sheikhs. But his attacks were so severe that shortly they shunned him, and so he defeated also his own good desires to enlighten them. It is noticeable that Paul laboured two years in a chief heathen stronghold, Ephesus, and quietly undermined respect for the abominable goddess there revered, yet the town clerk was able to assert that he had not spoken disrespectfully of Diana (Acts 19:10, 37).

I had further stressed that the controversial method was false psychologically, because to discuss Mohammed and the Koran was simply to keep the mind of the Moslem more deeply occupied with the very subjects which one wished to uproot from his mind. Occasionally one will be met already sufficiently suspicious as to his beliefs to make it helpful to show him their fallacies and errors, but in general controversy is unwise.

My fellow-workers agreed, and we made for ourselves a fixed rule that we would on no account discuss Islamic questions. At first our contentious visitors were annoyed that we would not fight. "No," we replied, "you must excuse us; we are not here to do that. We are only messengers. If you send your servant with a message, when he has delivered it his duty is done; you do not expect him to stop and discuss your message. We are messengers of God sent to speak about His Son. If you do not want to hear the message you need not come; but you must not expect us to discuss our message." But they came again and again, and shortly they were saying: "What we like about these meetings is, that you do not say unkind things about our prophet and book."

Three young men were particularly troublesome. One afternoon, as I walked down the tent feeling weary, they were waiting as usual, and I said to myself that I really could not further battle with their unreasonable opposition. But the leader rose and said quietly and seriously: "The Lord Jesus has changed my heart this afternoon." When a keen Mohammedan thus spontaneously calls Jesus LORD, one knows that the Spirit of truth has wrought. His spirit and attitude were different from that hour.

During the three months the tent was up, I conversed closely with some hundreds of young men, of various social orders, and was secretly satisfied that some thirty were definitely convinced that Christ was the Son of God and did in some degree regard Him as their Saviour. But of these only four came out on His side by being baptized in His name. One of these was a special joy. He was a pure-blooded Bedawi, his family having migrated from Arabia. He was proud to be descended from a tribe as ancient as the Prophet and that he spoke the pure Arabic of the Prophet. His contempt for Egyptian Arabic was profound. His father was dead but his grandfather was living, the head of the clan. They lived in the country, he was boarding in Cairo while at school, and they supplied him freely with country produce and needed money.

The lad in the house where he lived told him of our notice board and they came in. He had never before heard the gospel and knew scarcely more of Jesus than that his elders cursed by that name. Miss Ely conversed with him and he espoused Christ that first night, was shortly baptized and continued stedfast. He was thirteen years of age. He was at once cut off by his people and reduced to poverty and was homeless. His grandfather tried to get the army to call him up, but his diminutive size saved him. He then threatened to get him killed.

After some months, when we were having meetings in a house, his elder brother came to endeavour to reclaim him. A terrible dread seized the lad, thinking that his brother would kill him, and he would not go in. Knowing that this battle must be won or he would relapse in defeat, some Egyptian brethren and I reasoned with him and prayed. I urged that the Lord would protect him, and that, in any case, his brother would not attack him in the presence of an Englishman, for that would secure his own death as a murderer. It was long before he consented to face his brother, but then there came a demonstration of that word, "God gave us not a spirit of fearfulness, but of power and love and sobering" (2 Tim. 1:7). Without waiting for his brother to speak he commenced to set the gospel before him with energy and boldness and sobriety.

After the conversation had ended and the brother had departed, he told me that the family had offered to receive him back and to start him in life comfortably. I asked why he did not accept the proposal. With a dark look in his eyes he gave an answer which was a flashlight as to the moral state of Moslems: "They are all liars."

Miss Ely and Mr. McClenahan went to Europe for the hot season, while I remained in Cairo to shepherd the group of converted Moslems and Copts we had gathered. I saw Abdel Messiah (his name by baptism, meaning "servant of the Messiah") almost daily. How he should support himself, and not be dependent on others, was an early problem.

I got Mrs. Todd Osborne to consent that he should be official shoeblack to the Russell Soldiers' Home. It was a humiliating occupation, but I felt it would be helpful against his native pride. At last he consented, and one morning I took him into the dining room, told the soldiers that here was a young Arab who had become a Christian, had lost everything by his stand, and now wanted to earn an honest living by blacking their boots, and I hoped they would encourage him. I then blacked the first pair and he continued the task. This he did for quite a time.

One day he said that he had had only bread and dates for breakfast. I replied that I had had only bread and bananas. From the hour that he thus learned that the English *hawaga* (gentleman) was actually down on his level, and for his sake, his heart was mine, the truculent Arab spirit subsided, and he accepted instruction and counsel as never before. It was a proof of the definite advantage of the servant of Christ being poor, as Christ Himself was.

In 1915 the British army took him to Mesopotamia as an interpreter. His last word to me as we parted testified that God had indeed cleansed his heart by faith: he said: "One thing I ask of my heavenly Father—that He will keep me holy." A few years later a Christian officer in Bagdad made inquiries about him on my behalf and learned that he was giving every satisfaction, and was standing as a Christian.

But the work of the gospel brings sorrow as well as joy. For forty nights in succession a young man attended at the tent. He was the son of a landed proprietor in Upper Egypt; had ample means, no occupation, and just indulged his pleasures in the capital. His English was excellent. For those six weeks I had no contact with him. He began coming to the prayer time for workers before the evening meeting, and at last the Voice said in my heart, "Take Mohammed away and talk with him." We went to the other end of the tent and within ten minutes he made a hearty confession of Christ.

At once he witnessed openly and proved a most efficient helper to me in translating with those who did not speak English. One evening at our rooms he gave an illuminating instance of the Oriental habit of thinking and speaking in figures. We had explained the way of salvation to a visitor, and at length I asked him to say that there was nothing more to be stated, that the visitor must either accept Christ and be saved or reject Him and be lost. He spoke a few sentences, and then said, "I have told him that there are two ways of leaving this house; he must either go down the staircase or jump out of the window."

He brought others to the meetings. One of these was the son of the Arabi Pasha who led the rebellion which took the British into Egypt in 1882. Presently he wished to be baptized. This was arranged, but courage failed and he did not come. Who can throw stones? How many Englishmen of standing and wealth will incur the loss of social position, home, inheritance, and for Christ's sake accept poverty, reproach, danger? It was long before I found him. He earnestly averred that in his heart he still believed in Christ. I did not doubt it, but could only press upon him that until he was baptized his friends regarded him as still a Moslem and so must we. This he recognized. On later visits to Egypt I did not meet him.

A law student of much ability came to the tent. He was very disputatious. I gave him a gospel of John. This gospel is the more suitable because it forces the Moslem to face the most crucial of issues, the Sonship of Jesus. He brought it back with the demand that I should explain its opening statement. "This book speaks of one called the Word of God and says he was both with God and was God. How can a person be with himself? Explain this!" I replied that I could not explain it, nor could any one else do so. "Then why do you ask me to read a book you cannot explain?" he asked angrily. I answered as Christ answered Nicodemus, by asserting the truth positively and assuring him that unless he believed the book he could not be saved. After a further outburst, I added that there was one suggestion which he could ponder. "If there were a problem in mathematics which you could not solve, and you took it to your tutor and he could not solve it, it would at least be clear that neither he nor you had invented that problem. Now here is a problem not in mathematics but in theology, that is, the Being and nature of God as a trinity. Thousands of the ablest minds of the centuries have pondered this problem, and no man has been able to explain it; who then invented it? What man can invent man can explain: what man cannot explain man cannot have invented. It must be a revelation."

He found no answer to this, nor have I ever known a Unitarian to do so.

Near Heliopolis there lived an Englishman, a man of commerce. His wife was a believer; he was not, but was blinded by Christian Science. In the hope of helping him I toiled through Mrs. Eddy's literary desert *Science and Health*. On February 18, 1914, we spoke together on the divan in his hall. He was of a cool, unemotional nature. I explained that it was not of the essence of repentance towards God that the feelings should be deeply stirred. Sometimes, indeed, the sense of shame, the fear of wrath, the thought of being loved by a holy God did overwhelm the heart and cause intense emotion; but this is not necessary or invariable. I showed that the word repentance means a change of mind: that an accused might enter the court thinking he had a good case and should be discharged, but if the judge declared him guilty in law he must simply change his opinion about himself and accept the verdict of the judge. Thus does God declare of each man that he is guilty before Him, and repentance consisted in humbly bowing to that verdict. Also, a man may think that he can produce works suitable for acceptance by God; but God says it is impossible and that the only work He can accept for the good of the sinner is the atoning work which Christ wrought on the cross on behalf of man. The sinner must therefore change his mind as to how to be saved, and obey God by transferring his trust from himself and his works to Christ and His work.

This he did there and then in the most matter of fact way, sitting on the divan. It was an instance of the truth that, in the last analysis, it is an intelligent act of the *will* that secures salvation, and the decisive step may be taken with or without emotion. He shortly proved that his heart had been reached by his pocket being reached. Upon the sale of some property he brought £5 as a thankoffering to the God of his salvation.

During this tent effort we who were co-operating lived as Miss Ely's guests in a suite of rooms at Heliopolis. My room was very large, furnished sparsely with a narrow bed, a box for washstand, a small table, and a chair. The humorous brother who told me how to scare dogs came in, looked round the spacious apartment, and said, "Well, brother Lang, before you put out the light make sure where the bed is, or you won't be able to find it." The life was typically American, one steady rush all day, with visitors, letters, prayer seasons, and at nights the meetings in Cairo five days a week, from which we did not return till 11 p.m. City life in England, with its late hours, had caused me to forgo my boyhood's habit of early rising. I now saw that unless it could be resumed there would be no leisure for indispensable privacy with God and soul nurture. But how resume early rising with days so taxed and retiring so late at night? I besought the special help of the Lord, Who in the days of His flesh had Himself been an early riser (Isa. 50:4; Mark 1:35), and immediately I found myself able to rise at 5 a.m. This profitable practice has continued ever since.

One day there came a Moslem convert of twenty years' standing. He was a ticket collector on the State railway. Like all others he augmented his small salary by taking bribes from passengers; for instance, to allow a traveller to ride in a higher class than his ticket warranted, without charging the extra fare. At last his conscience had commenced to prick and he sought counsel, secretly hoping that we should excuse him. But we told him it was robbing the Government. He was offended; but others he asked said the same, and finally, with his wife's consent, he drew from the Bank all his life savings and the sum was handed by an American missionary to the Treasurer of the Railways as conscience money.

His name was not mentioned, but as he was the only Christian collector it was easily decided who had done it. God rewarded him with a radiant happiness. But I feared lest he was a little proud of having done something no one had done before him, so I said, "If you had a giant before you, you would not see a little man standing behind him; but if the giant moved out of the way you would see the little man. God has shown you this giant sin and has enabled you to put it away; now you must be prepared for Him to show you lesser sins, that you may cease from these also, by His help." Shortly he sent me a message that he had seen the "little man" and had put him also away. It was his cigarettes! Many other Christians need to put away this same "little man". To do so would increase their joy in the Lord. Slavery is misery; liberty is bliss. "For freedom did Christ set us free; stand fast therefore, and be not entangled again in a yoke of bondage" (Gal. 5:1).

The tent meetings continued until May 24, 1914. It was now full midsummer heat. The climate suited my wife well, but our girlie of nine years drooped like a flower without water. Miss Ely lovingly took tickets for them to London, and they sailed from Alexandria on the 28th, I saw them off. The steamer took some three quarters of an hour leaving the berth; they on deck, I on the quay, looking at each other, but too far to speak. It was a trying farewell.

On June 4th Miss Ely left for Switzerland and on the 23rd Mr. McClenahan followed. As mentioned I remained to shepherd the group of young men, Copts, Moslems, a Greek or two, and others, whose hearts the Lord had touched, and most of whom had been immersed in His name. For twelve centuries the Moslems, the ruling race, and their Coptic subjects had nourished bitter hatred, racial, political, religious, for Copts are nominally "Christian", though for the more part as wicked as Moslems. It was a deep joy to see children of God from all these races walking together in love and breaking bread at the one Supper of their one Lord. One of the Coptic young men, who had been converted a few years before, and whom I had known in Port Said, was my devoted helper in scouring the city for Moslems I might wish to track, and for translating for me into Arabic. He has continued a zealous disciple and worker until now. Nothing of native animosity survived the working in him of the love of the Spirit.

We held regular meetings in a hired room in a large house in Shubra, not far from the Central Railway Station. To these there came a Coptic student. He was a gentle, attractive youth. For quite a while I did not converse with him, but on Thursday, June 25, 1914, while an Egyptian was speaking, he left the room, and the Voice said in my heart, "Go after him and talk with him." In the court of the house, under the graceful palms, by brilliant moonlight, we spoke together, and in a few minutes he was rejoicing in assurance of acceptance by God in Christ.

Presently he said: "But, Mr. Lang, what am I to do in my home and school?" I knew what he meant. The atmosphere of his home was very probably poisoned with wrangling and cursing. The conversation of his fellow-students would be disgusting and lust-provoking. How shall a youth with a new longing to be pure be pure? I spoke as follows:

"You know now that Jesus Christ is your Saviour and that God has forgiven your sins, do you not?"

"I do tonight."

"How do you know anything about these matters?" He thought a moment and answered, "From the Bible."

" Yes; God has taken care that we should have no other channel of information concerning His Son. Now the Bible says that Christ died for our sins, and it promises that he who will rely upon Christ shall be forgiven his sins. You have believed on Him and your sins have been forgiven, and in your heart you have peace with God; is this not so?" He assented heartily, and I continued:

"So that the promise of the Bible has been fulfilled in your experience. Well now, the same Book tells us of another Divine Person Who came into this world after the Son of God had returned to heaven. He is called the Holy Spirit of God. He did not come to atone for our sins because the Son of God had done that completely. He came for this reason, among others, that He might give to us the moral strength of the Lord Jesus, so that we may become like Him, pure in heart and clean in life. Now you have never seen the Son of God, yet the promises of the Bible as to those who trust Him have been made good to you. And you will not see the Spirit of God, but exactly as you have accepted the promises concerning the Son of God and they have been fulfilled, so you are to believe the promises concerning the Spirit of God, and His work in you, and they also will be fulfilled to you."

He pondered a little, and then said, with simplicity and decision:

"I see; *that meets my case.*"

Such presenting to the newly-born soul at one and the same time the work of both the Son of God and the Spirit of God is apostolic (Acts 2:38). The Christian gets nothing but what he takes by faith. If he does not know of the promised gift of the Spirit of Christ he cannot accept the Spirit by faith, for faith can exist and act only upon a promise of God.

To tell the converted that he does automatically receive the indwelling of the Spirit by being born again is contrary to both Scripture and experience. That indwelling can occur at the moment of a first faith in Christ (Acts 10:44); but often it does not do so, as witness the first disciples, who believed on the Son of God unto eternal life while He was with them, yet did not receive the Spirit till after Christ's ascension. So also the many who believed when Philip preached at Samaria, but did not receive the Spirit till Peter and John came among them (Acts 8:14-17). So also Saul of Tarsus who did not receive the Spirit until Ananias visited him three days after his conversion (Acts 9:9, 17); and those twelve disciples whom Paul found at Ephesus (Acts 19:1-7).

The reception of the Spirit by faith in the promises is as much part of the good news as is the reception of Christ by faith. As certainly as the joy of pardon is experienced by faith, even so, and as distinctly and as consciously, are the presence and energy of the indwelling Spirit to be experienced by faith.

When the First World War broke out in August 1914 I saw the mercy of God in my loved ones having gone betimes to England, so saving her and her people from anxiety about each other. Yet in fact Egypt was probably the quietest country involved. The British officials managed affairs to general advantage. I know the sensation of sitting in a land expecting invasion; but the Turks had attacked and been repulsed before we knew of it in Cairo. It was known earlier in London.

Just before the war I was granted a singularly gracious ordering of God. Archibald Forder, of Jerusalem, the fearless traveller among the Bedawi camps east of the Jordan, came to Cairo, on his way to visit the tribes in the Sinai peninsula. He wished me to accompany him. Why he invited me I scarcely know. Maybe he had heard that I had just before (July 21, 1914) gone alone to visit the lonely ruins of Pithom. I was in fine form physically and would have loved such a tour with so experienced and interesting a companion. But funds were scarce just then, nor could I feel that it was of God to leave so soon the care of the group at Shubra.

Forder started off alone, but he had gone only a day or so into the desert when he had a strong presentiment that he should abandon the journey and return to his wife in Jerusalem. Scarcely had he got into Palestine when the Turks joined the war against the Allies and the British at once closed the Sinai frontier. It was well that neither of us was in that area.

Through this period, I lived upon the almost daily bounty of God my Father. Possessing all things in Christ I had little or nothing in kind. Yet food and lodging were enjoyed. Miss Ely paid the rent of the rooms which I occupied, so that we should have them for the next winter service. My own living expenses averaged 16*s*. a week. For food I had bread, fruit, eggs, water, and twice a week an ordinary evening meal at the Russell Soldiers' Home in Cairo. This diet suited me well. My brain was never clearer. The severe heat caused me to pass the days in the cool of my rooms. No one called, so I had whole days of prayer, meditation, reading, and writing. During that six months I read more books than in any other six months of my life. It was then that *Firstborn Sons* was written, though it was not published till many years later, after further reflection had deepened my conviction that its teaching was scriptural.

Temptation approaches from many directions. Week after week alone is not good for any man. On Sunday morning, November 22, 1914, I spoke at the meeting of the American Mission, then held in a shop. Several thanked me warmly, but not one of them asked if I would return home and lunch with them. I felt neglected as I returned to my large and silent flat. It was foolish; perhaps not one of them knew of my circumstances—Americans are usually most hospitable. But I thought of the words, "They went every man to his own house; but Jesus went to the Mount of Olives" (John 7:53; 8:1). That afternoon the ever-present Lord the more endeared Himself to my heart, and I wrote the lines:

LONELY BUT LOVELY

The men He had made to their homes repaired,
*   To their homes with their joys and pleasures;*
But the Man Who had made them, a Stranger here,
*   Possessed neither home nor treasures;*
The Pharisee turned to his lordly house,
*   To his loaded board and his cushioned bed,*
While the Teacher went to the lonely mount,
*   On the bare, cold earth to lay down His head.*

The languid lawyer was lulled to sleep
*   By the plaintive pipe and the rhythmic song,*
Nor a moment was kept from his slumber deep
*   By the orphan's wail or the widow's wrong;*
But the only music the Saviour heard
*   Was the wind as it rustled the olive trees;*
And few were the hours that He spent in sleep,
*   And many He passed on bended knees.*

The cold night air chilled His weary frame,
*   But His spirit rose undaunted;*
For to share the sorrows of men He came,
*   By His Father's will appointed:*

And the whole of the burden He needs must bear
   Of the poor and despised and neglected;
And so that the Helper of all He may be,
   He, though Lord of all, is rejected.

And on that lonely mountain side
   What joy and sorrow are blended:
O'er the sin of the world He weeps, and yet
   His heart has to heaven ascended,
And thrills with the bliss of His Father's love
   An ecstasy deep, refreshing:
And again in the morning He meets the crowds,
   And pours out the rivers of blessing.

O lowly Saviour, I choose with Thee
   Thy portion so satisfying;
To be scorned of the world that knows not God,
   To share both Thy life and Thy dying:
Far better to walk with Thee and weep,
   Than to laugh with the godless worldling;
For Thou art Thyself my boundless joy,
   When my soul is Thy company sharing.

And who that has watched on the mount with Thee
   Will crave for a night of pleasure?
Or who that has tasted Thy love most sweet
   Will leave it for other treasure?
My choice is to share Thy toil and pain,
   Thou lonely but lovely Saviour;
Accounting Thy cross my richest gain,
   To win Thine eternal favour.

To know e'en now Thine entrancing bliss
   Of helping the weary-hearted;
Till the guilty soul shall praise Thy name
   For the dread of doom departed:
To know at last Thine eternal joy,
   And to share Thy heavenly glory—
This, this is my choice, Thou Despised of men,
   And Thyself my unchanging story.

I had companions in the flat, a nest of small ants. It was instructive to watch them. The large wing of a hornet found its way in. Scores of tiny ants seized it on all sides to haul it to their storehouse. They did not drag it along the floor, I suppose because the friction would have sensibly increased the toil. But they pulled it up above the skirting and bore it along the wall but not touching the wall. In this way they carried it round the room, out of the door, round the wall of the passage, into and around the kitchen. At last a serious obstacle was met in an inch-and-a-half water pipe. At first they tried to edge it behind the pipe, but this not being possible they maneeuvred it round the pipe, and so to their hole. Not once did the wing fall to the ground, though the journey was long and took perhaps an hour-and-a-half. It was a remarkable feat of skill and perseverance and co-operation. "Go to the ant, thou sluggard; Consider her ways, and be wise" (Prov. 6:6).

The flat was at the top of a four-storied house, and had entrancing views over miles of desert. It was a joy to watch the changing tints as the sunlight fell from different angles when the orb rose and sank. But though high above the ground, as soon as food was on the table near the French doors hornets would appear. To test whether they came by sight or smell, as well as to enjoy my meals in peace, I would close the doors. The upper panels were latticed, so that air could ventilate, though hornets or locusts could not see or get through. But no sooner was food on the table than the hornets would be buzzing at the doors. For size they were like several queen wasps in one. The sting is very painful. I escaped, but one can understand the force of Ex. 23:28: "I will send the hornet before you." No army of men could resist an army of hornets.

It was from these doors that I watched more than one flight of locusts. The sun and the air were literally darkened as if by a cloud of smoke, out of which the individual locusts seemed to dart forth (Rev. 9:2, 3). That the locusts of this Scripture are not to hurt any green thing is strikingly contrary to nature, which suggests that the beings in view are not literal locusts. It is painful to see a field of grain after locusts have dealt with it. Only bare stalks are left. They find the field a garden, they leave it a waste (Joel 2:3).

Can God prepare a table in the wilderness (Ps. 78:19)? It is deeply important for gospel workers from England to bear in mind that their God is not dependent on English money. During the first seven months of 1914 sums reached me from Egypt, South Africa, Canada, and India, as well as England; of the total less than a third came from England. Directly war was declared at the beginning of August 1914 all foreign exchange ceased. Therefore gifts of money from England ceased. Here was a new and serious emergency. During the months of January to August money in hand had been reduced to sixpence, a penny, and once to nil. But always the need had been met. By the beginning of September I had fourpence. But on the 6th of that month abundant help arrived. Miss Ely's kind heart had pondered the need, but she was blocked in Switzerland, nor would banks grant remittances. But she remembered that W. L. McClenahan had money lying at call with a large *commercial* house in Cairo. She wrote to him in England and asked him to send an order on that money for £50. But it took three days for the firm to find so much English money. To meet this God had moved a friend in England to send a postal order for 5s. This was payable at any post office in the Empire, and thus food could be bought and tram fares were met for the three days.

But more. I wished to send some of this money to my wife in England. How could this be done at such a time? I felt guided to ask the Treasurer of the American Mission if perchance they had money lying in England which they could not get out. They had, and were most happy to give me a draft on this in exchange for twenty golden sovereigns. "Is *anything* too hard for the Lord?"

Late in the autumn Mr. McClenahan returned and we put up a tent well out in the Shubra district of Cairo and evangelized there. But British troops having camped in thousands between Zeitoun and Heliopolis, the tent was brought there, and we and the Logans, of the Egypt General Mission, worked at nights among these lads. Many were grateful for the quiet hours and quiet talks in that small and dimly lit tent at the far end of the camp. Presently the Y.M.C.A. was appointed the official controller of religious work among troops. Worldly methods were introduced which curtailed, and virtually nullified, our purely spiritual work, and we returned to our labours for Egyptians.

At this time there came often a young man, a Copt. He was sincerely desirous of salvation, but mourned that he *could* not believe, greatly as he longed to do so. It occurred to me quite suddenly to ask if he had had any contacts with spiritism. He replied that his brother was a medium and that he often attended the seances. I pointed out that were a strong man to grasp firmly the upper arm of a child, just below the shoulder, the child would be unable to use the arm. Similarly he, by going on to the Devil's territory, had given opportunity to an evil spirit to grip and suspend his faculty of faith. Was he sincerely willing to be relieved of this bondage? He affirmed emphatically that this was fully his desire; he longed to trust in Christ. By the authority of the name of the Lord Jesus I commanded the spirit to depart from its victim, and forthwith he became a definite believer, and went on his way rejoicing.

Has such a case a bearing upon the ancient controversy as to the bondage or freedom of the human will? It would seem that bondage to sin may in measure be broken by the will of man in even the unregenerate, as when a heavy drinker facing ruin and shame, and his loved ones with him, by a supreme effort of the will breaks that fetter and walks soberly. But if the will is paralysed by a demon it cannot act freely until released by a superior force, yet thereafter the liberated *can* exercise his will and believe on Christ unto salvation, present and to come.

Life was much varied. Many Sundays of this summer (1914) I went with the Wesleyan Chaplain and spoke at two or three of his morning parade services in the different barracks. This increased acquaintance with the life of British soldiers in camps and barracks abroad.

Visits were paid to Port Said. One was from December 12 to 17, 1914. To one meeting in the Seamen's Rest there came a well-built English gentleman about sixty years of age, and his small wife. Hooper of the Bible Society had told them to see me and get addresses in Cairo and Heliopolis where they could stay while the war might last. In Port Said, where all kinds of folk come and go, one does not "lay hands suddenly" on strangers, so I drew them on to talk of themselves. His name was Edgar Shelley. He looked for all the world like an old-fashioned English squire, with coloured waistcoat, knickerbockers, and stockings. And, in fact, years later he showed me the family tree, a Sussex family going back to the time of Henry V. One of the family was Percy Bysshe Shelley, but he was not proud of his connexion with the brilliant atheist. He was a tea merchant from Australia, had retired, and had in mind to settle in Jerusalem or Mesopotamia, where they would give themselves to Christian service for the rest of their days. He had not been in England since he left as a young man, and had no wish to return, nor in the issue did he do so. He died in Cyprus in 1949.

The fact that he was a tea merchant somehow sent me back to my boyhood, for I had known one such. I said to myself that I ought to know this lady. Drawing a bow at a venture I said, "May I ask if your maiden name was Rouse?" She looked surprised, and assented. "And you were one of seventeen children?" More surprised, she replied, "No, fifteen." "And you had a rather clever brother, who knew a good deal of botany?" "Yes, my brother Martin." "And you lived in a big house on Chislehurst Common?" More and more bewildered, she assented to this. "And on Sundays you all attended the small hall of Exclusive Brethren at the other end of the village, on the London Road?" The lady eyed me almost as if she thought she had encountered Sherlock Holmes, but admitted that it was so. "Yes," I said, "and so did I when we were girl and boy".

In the good ordering of God something came out of this interview, of which more anon.

During one of these visits to Port Said I had finished what work the Lord seemed to require and felt guided to return to Cairo on a certain train. I had no money at all, but went round and said farewell to friends, the last being Mr. Locke of the Seamen's Rest. I had left his house and was already round the corner of the road to the station when he came hurrying after me, put into my hand just enough for the ticket, saying, "I think the Lord means this." I thought so too, and thanked the giver and the Giver.

It was a change from our work in the city to take a horse now and then and visit untouched Moslem villages in the Delta. Entering one it was asked if they had any Christians there. Yes, they had one, and led us to him. He was the Greek shopkeeper, who helped to make them more than ever vicious by selling liquor! Thus did the only "Christian" they knew encourage them to break one of the few salutary rules of the Koran, that which commands Moslems not to use intoxicants. What a subtle triumph of Satan to get the name of the Holy One degraded by putting it upon *nations* and so upon unholy individuals.

On one of these trips we were riding single file along a narrow, greasy path by the edge of a wide ditch of black water. W. L. McClenahan was in front, I followed, and Miss Ely was in the rear. Glancing over my shoulder to see if she was all right I saw her horse slip on the wet mud, and plunge into the ditch. The rider was a fine horsewoman and kept her seat, but as the animal struggled to climb the opposite and vertical bank, her weight and the tight rein that kept her in the saddle toppled him backward and he pinned her beneath in the muddy water. Throwing my rein to Mr. McClenahan I cleared the ditch at a bound and reached her in time to grip the horse by the bridle and hold him down so that he could not struggle to rise and crush the lady. Quickly McClenahan came, and being very tall was able to reach Miss Ely and draw her from under the horse. She was bruised, but not injured seriously, and the animal was unhurt.

The head man of the village was profuse in his apologies. No doubt he feared lest he should be reported and be reprimanded for the bad state of the path. Men took the horse and cleaned it well. When these came on the scene I was wiping the mud from her face with a handkerchief. They gazed in silent wonder. They had never seen a man tenderly concerned for a woman. "Is he your brother?" they inquired. Such is Islam towards women. The unpleasant occurrence gave quite exceptional opportunity for explaining the message to deliver which had brought us among them.

These visits gave excellent occasion for watching and admiring my friend McClenahan in purely Egyptian surroundings. In English and American company he was the most silent man I ever knew. I have seen him sit for half an hour "conversing" with a visitor, that is, the other doing *all* the talking and he contributing nods of his head or movements of his hands. He reminded me of Dean Ramsay's tale of the Scotch farmer who lived alone with a tame goose. The candidate for Parliament called to solicit his vote and talked and talked and talked, the farmer saying not one word. After the visitor had gone the farmer looked at the goose the opposite side of the chimney-corner and said, "I'm thinking, yon windy chiel'll no tell many tales of what you and I said to him." At length I came to think of my silent friend that he would have much less to regret than I when giving account to Him Who has said, "By thy words thou shalt be justified, and by thy words thou shalt be condemned" (Matt. 12:37).

But seat W. L. McClenahan among a group of men in the village hall where the omdeh and his elders met, or in the goat's hair tent of the rough Bedawi, and he was all animation, and they were all attention, while Arabic poured forth as copiously as his English came in but a trickle. He had lived and moved among the villagers in many parts and for so long that they understood each other well, and he had straightened out their tangles and reconciled their squabbles until they had given him the heavenly title Abu Salaam, the father of peace! A handful of such men are more real benefit in a land than are all its statesmen and all its soldiers. I watched the 3rd Coldstream Guards entrain at Cairo for the 1914 front in France. There was much waving and cheering, but in a few weeks came the melancholy tidings that these and tens of thousands more had fallen in battle. Such is war, glorious, horrible, futile; but "blessed are the peacemakers: for they shall be called sons of God," "and the fruit of righteousness is sown in peace by them that make peace" (Matt. 5:9; Jas. 3:18); though in this world of strife such sowing is often hard work and dangerous.

Returning from another of these visits to villages we had to cross a piece of water in a barge. I was holding the heads of two horses and as we reached the bank a British voice said, "Let me have one horse," and a soldier led him off the barge. My companions rode on while I chatted a few minutes with the lads. By the time I started it was nearing sunset, and in the gloaming sandy tracks look much alike and I missed the road. My Arab horse, wanting his friends, sped fast, but before long he, as well as I, sensed that we had lost our way, and he slackened his pace. The dusk showed only far stretching sand and scrub, with nothing to indicate direction.

The prospect of spending the night thus, with a restive horse, was not pleasant. But He Who saw Hagar in the wilderness and sent guidance, had His eyes on me, and sent guidance. Riding slowly I happened on an old Egyptian on a donkey, a rare circumstance, for the Eastern is seldom out in lonely places in the dark, unless he be a robber. He got down and salaamed. "Fan el Materiyeh?" I inquired, "Where is Materiyeh?" He got on his donkey and went forward. It was interesting to note how my intelligent and proud Arab steed was content to follow slowly his humble relative, the ass. Presently the aged man dismounted, pointed to lights twinkling in the far distance, and said, "Materiyeh."

Whether the high-spirited horse knew the name of the town, or whether he saw the distant lights, I do not know, but immediately he became so eager and restive that it was with difficulty I kept the saddle; I could not get my hand into my pocket, but was carried away so quickly that, to my great regret, I could not leave my deliverer a coin or a gospel to show my gratitude. Of this point I ought to have thought in advance when jogging along quietly, and have been prepared.

Before long I came up with my good friends and the horse with his. We were both content. My companions seemed so blissfully satisfied with each other that there was no need to explain my delay. Not long after this they were married, of which pleasant prospect I did not then know.

The months passed quickly in such strenuous and congenial labours, and the burning heat of midsummer returned. On Thursday, June 17, 1915, I was sitting at dawn on the verandah looking over the deserts and looking up to God, when suddenly the Voice said distinctly in my heart: "This, and that, and the third purpose of your coming here are finished, now you can go to England." I announced this at breakfast, left Cairo on July 3, and Port Said, on the Japanese S.S. *Hirano Maru,* on the 15th. Shipping was scarce and it was remarkable to get a berth so soon. German submarines were about, and the ship sailed at night without lights.

There were twenty-six Englishmen on the second-class deck, all coming home to enlist. As far as I could discover I was the only one that could put his head on the pillow at night feeling that, should anything happen, I was safe as to eternity. Poor fellows, they tried to forget the present and ignore the future by carousing. The night before reaching Marseilles they spent nearly all the night drinking in the saloon and roaring and bawling songs. I slept on the deck above. Waking about 1 a.m. the smell of beer was heavy, and I saw that some joker had placed a bottle of it near my pillow, with a glass. The bottle went overboard, but the glass belonged to the ship. When I awoke later it was to find the prank had been repeated.

As companions from Marseilles to London I had two Englishmen, who had come first class on the boat, and an Australian proposing to enlist. The two former were wicked, the one reserved and dangerous, the other frank and engaging though depraved. The Australian was pleasant, but every other sentence was marred by the misuse of "O Christ!" Before long, as we chatted, I said, "If we are to travel happily to London you must stop using the name of my Master as you do. Were I an officer, and the King's name was thus misused, it would be my duty to protest, would it not?" He expressed regret and promised not to repeat the expression, and he did not do so. But he added: "I have just put in six months on His Majesty's Ship *Queen Elizabeth,* and it's a place to finish your education in bad language."

As the train to Paris sped on I suddenly put a paper before the frank and vicious man. He glanced at the title and exclaimed "*No,* I'm *not.*" The title read:

"God is satisfied, are you?" Drinking of the world's waters, he was ever thirsting. I gave him *Safety, Certainty, and Enjoyment.* On the train from Dover to London he politely handed it to a young woman next to him, with the easy manner of a practised tract distributor.

But before we reached Paris the point came up of one of us arranging for crossing the city and the others sharing the expense. The Australian promptly proposed that Mr. Lang should be responsible. Why did a man of the world prefer to trust a Christian rather than one of his own sort?

On July 21, 1915, I reached my father's house in north London at 11.30 p.m., whither my dear wife had come to meet me. We all rejoiced together and gave thanks to the Preserver of all men, our Father of mercies.

CHAPTER 10

England and Scotland

THE next seven and a half years were spent ministering the Word of God in all parts of England and in the south-west of Scotland. My readers being able to picture this service, only special incidents need be narrated, such as will evidence that God is the same to faith in this land as abroad and that the principles of the life of faith are the same everywhere.

While we were in Egypt, in the early part of 1914, my father-in-law found it needful to leave Clevedon and return to his house in Clayhidon. It was necessary that our furniture should be removed in our absence. This difficulty was met by our dear friend William Rouse, evangelist, and his wife, who had been using the house. He kindly prepared all for removal. As I prayed for light as to where the goods should be stored my mind was directed to Weston-super-Mare, rather than to Taunton or any centre near Clayhidon. The matters that weighed were that my cousin Musgrove had his home there, which would afford to my wife pleasant and loving friendship should I be much from home. Then there were suitable schools for our daughter. And I was well-known at the Gospel Hall, which provided Christian fellowship. Also it was a good railway centre, for either Bristol and London, or the north and the south.

Our effects were therefore stored at Weston-super-Mare. In November we were distinctly guided to a flat at "Towerside", The Shrubbery, and in December 1915 we moved in; and this was our home for thirteen years. It consisted of a fair-sized sitting-room, with pleasant views over town and sea; a bijou kitchenette, and two small bedrooms, with the use of a bathroom. The rent was moderate and was restricted by the statute passed at the start of the war.

My cousin kindly gave me a second-hand cycle. It was a good make, a "Swift", and after thirty-five years was still running well. Many side lines of the railways having been sent to France, and trains in general being restricted, I journeyed by cycle all over England and in Scotland. This saved expense and also made possible visits to out-of-the-way houses and hamlets where the gospel seldom was taken.

In all these matters I had the advantage of a higher wisdom than mine.

Early in 1916 many soldiers were billeted in Weston-super-Mare, and a reading room, with refreshments, was opened at the Gospel Hall. As we did not allow smoking, dancing, cards, liquors or theatricals, men who wanted such entertainments went where they were provided, while the serious and more refined came to us. Not a few were led to Christ before they went to the slaughter-fields of France. One evening there came in a man dressed as a monk, in brown robe, rope girdle, and with tonsured head. He said he spent his time visiting such Rooms and talking to the men. His testimony showed that he knew and loved Christ. He commenced by saying that he had been at such a Room on Salisbury plain. The Army Scripture Reader introduced him by saying: "This friend wishes to speak to you. He looks like a priest, but he seems to be a Christian." The Lord still has those who love Him though in strange associations and strange attire.

Another line of service in these years was that of helping younger brethren to state before the Tribunals their objections to military service. At the Local Tribunals they were not seldom treated with scant justice or courtesy. Too many members of these Tribunals were men of small mind and great prejudice. At the Appeal Tribunals it was usually better, the members being more cultured and having a certain social dignity to maintain, and this obtained at the Central Tribunal in London. When the 1939 war broke out I thought of telling the authorities that I had had experience of Tribunals in 1916-1918, and that if they would make the first Tribunal to consist of two lawyers the former unfairness and troubles would be mostly avoided. I did not write, but when it was announced that the County Court judge in each district was to be chairman I saw that, in the good ordering of God, the end desired would be served, as was the case.

In the 1914-1918 War the Government had no easy task. A majority who applied for exemption had no real conscience in the matter, but were Socialists out to make trouble for the authorities. Those who failed to gain exemption and still would not serve in the army, were sent to prison, and shortly most of them were sent to the great prison buildings at Princetown on Dartmoor, used as a settlement. There they were unable publicly to spread their opinions.

Usually forty or fifty brethren from "Open" assemblies were there. I obtained a permit to visit them for religious purposes, and paid several visits of a week or a fortnight. I stayed at an hotel and went into the Settlement after the evening meal and all day on Sundays. They were picked men spiritually, and they valued the fellowship shown by one going to that inhospitable region and gloomy building. We had profitable Bible studies, seasons of prayer, and fine gospel meetings. One Sunday evening after I had spoken in the chapel a rabid Socialist simply rushed at me to attack what had been taught. Before the conversation ended he had turned to Christ, and he is following Him still after more than thirty years.

There were probably 2,000 men there most of the time. As far as I could tell, if 200 of them were true Christians it was a liberal estimate. The rest were there for political or personal reasons, and many were atheistic Socialists. They could not but respect the real Christians, for these had gone through the mill like themselves; but some of them said plainly to friends of mine, that when their time came it would be seen whether they could shed blood! It was this fact of the situation that compelled Government to make the conditions for exemption severe, or many more unworthy applicants would have attempted to evade service.

One evening on the way to my lodging I came upon a half-drunken soldier threatening and terrifying a young objector and his sweetheart. I drew off his attention and motioned to the pair to move off in the dusk, for they stood there helpless, much as birds frightened and fascinated by a snake. As we walked down the road the poor fellow stopped now and then, gazed at me, and said, "Ah, but you're an old man, and I wouldn't hit an old man." I was thankful for his chivalry, and did not undeceive him by saying that I was only forty-three and might myself have done some hitting had I too been tipsy. Perhaps my whiskers added to my age!

Of the hundreds of young brethren that went through that ordeal almost all returned after the war into fellowship and service in the assemblies. This, alas, is more than can be said of those who went into the Services. Some returned keener for the spiritual battles faced, but far more, I fear, lost their testimony to Christ; nor can he wonder or condemn who knows what soldiering means.

The first of the many cases I took before a Tribunal gave me a salutary warning. That morning I was struck with influenza. But unwilling to disappoint the young man I took the risk and nerved myself to the task. He gained complete exemption but proved most unsatisfactory and his exemption was cancelled. It would have been better in his case had he failed. It taught me the lesson to be learned from the words of king Saul: "I *forced myself*, therefore, and offered the burnt offering" (1 Sam. 13:12). It may occasionally be right to disregard the body, but I saw later that God had intervened to prevent me from a step I should later regret. I could never afterwards go before that Tribunal, having helped one found unworthy.

On another occasion I was privileged to be "counsel for the defence" at the court-martial of two earnest brethren, and was of service. Both the prosecuting adjutant and the officers who formed the Court were fair and courteous. Afterward I visited the brethren when serving their sentences in Taunton gaol.

This unforeseen fellowship with younger brethren in distress for Christ's sake was a service few others were ready to share. My early experience in matters legal and with Courts bore fruit now. I did not feel as strange or as awed in a Court as most would feel. God prepares His servants in advance. My kind friend Mr. W. R. Moore freely put at the disposal of his tried brethren his training as a barrister, and was a strength to their hearts. On the other hand, there were leaders in assemblies who opposed this testimony to separateness from the world and even asserted in the Press that it was not the recognized attitude of the "Brethren". This was contrary to history. For myself, to be intrusted with this work of supporting and comforting my brethren under these circumstances fully reconciled me to having been brought away from such happy service as Egypt had granted. Here, as there, I was doing what others would not have done. The joy is great of *adding* something to the cause of Christ, instead of duplicating work.

It is needful and good to walk and work in the communion of the Holy Spirit, for then what seems hopeless can be attained. On September 28, 1916, I visited at Southampton a man of sixty-eight years. He had been godless, but had a praying wife. He was in such extreme distress from what was diagnosed as the last stage of cancer that it appeared useless to talk with him. But I spoke to the effect that he had left his soul's affairs very late. If he had had property to leave he would have found it difficult to discuss business, but he could have said to his solicitor that he wished this and that done and would leave it to him to see to everything. Even so it was not possible to explain to him now the why and wherefore that the death of Christ avails to save sinners, but he could just tell the Lord Jesus that he would leave it to Him to be his Saviour. A few days later, being a little easier, he said that he had done this. It was not cancer, for six months later he was about again, and by then he had proved and shown that the Saviour had responded and had saved him from his sins.

There was another such case in Weston-super-Mare. A man sat in bed with heart disease, struggling for breath so desperately that it seemed idle to talk to him; but the few words spoken were applied by the Spirit, and a later visit revealed that he had understood and believed unto salvation.

In all experience, personal or with others, it is not firstly a question of what the Christian can be or can do, but of what the Spirit of truth and power can do in him and through him. "Your labour is not vain in the Lord."

In October 1916 I was in the north of Ireland. It was travelling thither that I had as companion Edmund Hamer Broadbent. Very much developed out of the friendship then formed, as will be related.

In November 1918 the path led to Ayrshire, and visits to many towns in that county extended to April 1919. On December 23,1918, at Irvine occurred one of the most decisive battles of my life. Late in the evening, walking towards my lodging, I passed the crossroads at the centre of the town. Cold sleet was falling, yet the hardy Scots were loitering and talking. It occurred to me that if they could stand about in such inclement weather a preacher ought to be ready to tell them the gospel. But I had never stood alone to preach and there rose in my heart a furious battle as to doing so there and then. Well I knew that were I to shirk this task it would involve a heavy defeat and serious setback. For twenty minutes I walked up and down that dark street, the conflict raging and surging. Suddenly the Voice spoke, and said, "Go ye and preach... and lo! *I am with you* all the days" (Matt. 28:19, 20). I was not alone. My mouth opened; with the first word the battle was won. Astonished at the sudden sound of an English voice, the chatting ceased, the people backed under doorways or against walls and listened. I went home more than conqueror through Him Who loved His foolish and feeble servant.

On New Year's Day 1919 friends took me to special meetings in the ancient town of Ayr. The hall was large and was well filled. The brethren asked if I could have a week of meetings there and we started on January 11, Saturday. That evening, the next day, and all the week numbers were good and the hearing excellent. It looked as if the assembly was healthy. But the skin may be pretty, yet the core unhealthy. In reality the condition was like that church the minister of which said that it was "looking up; because it was lying on its back, and all it could do was to look up." Visitation soon revealed that there was much strife, personal, family, and in the church, and consequently the Spirit was grieved. But it pleased the Lord to work salvation; healing set in. The leaders had the wisdom to see the hand of God and at their request we went on for over eight weeks. The Spirit of grace changed the whole situation, and the church is still vigorous after the intervening thirty years.

At the close I said to myself, that had I been booked up for meetings many months ahead, as usually was the case, I could not have had this privilege; and I resolved that, as the Lord was ready so to work when His servant was *really* at His ordering, there should be no further long-distance bookings for me, but I would follow guidance as it might be given, even were it from day to day. Since then my service has been one continuous experience of distinct guidance and perpetual working of the Holy Spirit. It had been thus in service in other lands; now it became so in England, as it ought always to have been.

The New Testament makes clear that this was the method by which the Head of the church then controlled His work and workers. The closer we work to His own revealed ways the more He can use us. The merely human system of arranging for preachers which is now the rule, is a chief cause of the little unction felt and the poor effects mourned. A convener of an annual Conference asked me in March if I would be one of the speakers for the following May twelvemonth. I answered that I would if he could tell me how to find out where my Master would wish me to be next May twelvemonth, for I did not know how to find out. As he could not help in this the matter dropped. On no account could I consent to turn back from the way of the Lord to the human method of service in the Word. It is borrowed from the world and bears no relation to that manifesting of the presence of the Spirit of God which is a chief reason for the presence on earth of the church of God (1 Cor. 12:7).

But it requires faith to walk in the ways of the Lord; faith in assemblies that the Lord will raise up or send in suitable ministers of the truth, and faith in the preacher that his Master will keep him busy and will support him and his family in things temporal. Decline of such faith is evidenced in every forsaking of the way of the Lord and in resort to the ways of the world. That faith should grow exceedingly is therefore the cure for every evil. And faith feeds on the faithfulness of God. "Have faith in God" may mean "Hold to God's faithfulness" (Mark 11:22).

The two months in question was one of the prominent occasions of spiritual advance on my part.

As there will not be occasion to speak again of Ayr I will bring forward here the mention of my next visit there. Twenty-three years passed before I felt any drawing to go again; but being in Cumberland in June 1942, and the cloud moving northward, I wrote to one of the brethren and said that, as I should be passing near, I would like to make a personal call by the way. Nothing was said as to meetings. The prompt reply was that the week proposed would be the Glasgow holiday week; their town would be crowded; they had arranged with one of the best known ministering brothers to give a series of Bible lectures; he had just then been obliged to cancel the visit, therefore my presence would be most welcome in his place. In the outcome this led to two and a half weeks of daily ministering, indoors and on the seafront. Christ's captive slave does not plan out his own service, but is "led about in triumph" (2 Cor. 2:14).

The first fortnight in April (1919) I spent cycling round the south-west coast of Scotland. I had a meeting in a different place almost every night, but the real object of the tour was to visit as many churchyards as I could find where Covenanters were buried. It included Anwoth, the place of Samuel Rutherford's ministry, and Wigtown, where the two Margarets are said to have been drowned rather than deny Christ. The tombstones bore regularly the like inscription, that the person was killed "for maintaining the crown rights of Christ as Head of His church!" That they fought with carnal weapons was wrong, but they did know for what they were fighting! How many (or how few) today will be prepared to die by violence rather than abate the rights of Christ at the dictate of rulers? Let us face it. The test will yet come in England: perhaps in subtle form first, so as to beguile the weak and unwary; then by violence to break down, or destroy, the valiant soldiers of Christ.

August (1919) was the month for meetings on the sands at Weston-super-Mare. On the 7th there sat next to me a man, well built and gentlemanly. On speaking to him I found he was a Christian. He desired conversation and we met in the afternoon, when it transpired that he was a major in the Indian army, but a slave to women. He had come away from his own town to where he was unknown, so as to escape the besetments of life. By the grace of God he came through into the liberty from the tyranny of the flesh which *death* grants, the death of Christ accepted by faith. And in this liberty he walked the many years we had contact.

On August 26, 1922, there came suddenly a call to wholly unexpected service. We went on a visit to Mr. E. H. Broadbent's hospitable home at Gislingham, Suffolk. The car had but left the station on the way to the house when the first word he spoke was, "I have wanted to see you, because I think you could help in the work in Europe." Instantly my heart knew that this was of God, which was duly confirmed abundantly. The preparations for this new and extended service must begin a new chapter, but from November 18 to 23 I attended my first conference in Berlin and commenced much happy fellowship with brethren of that land.

I returned to London for a few days and was at my father's house in Bowes Park on Sunday, November 26. The next day I was to leave for Norway, but it was clear that my father was dying. Being the eldest son I assured him that, if it would be any comfort to him that I should be at hand, I would willingly defer my departure. His reply was memorable, an evidence that Christ was, as ever, the major object of his heart. He replied: "Oh, no, my boy; the gospel needs you more than I do. You go, and may your work be blessed." And blessed it was, beyond most periods of my life.

The next night, or the Tuesday, my only brother was with him from south London. Presently Father said to him: "It is your care meeting at Lewisham tonight. I do not need you here. Go to the care meeting as usual."

Thus from his dying bed he sent one son to preach and the other to pray, and early the next morning, November 29, he went to give account of himself to the Lord of his heart and life. He was within sixteen days of his eighty-fourth birthday. He died as he had lived.

> *Teach me to live, that I may dread*
> *The grave as little as my bed;*
> *Teach me to die, that so I may*
> *Rise glorious in the awful day.*
>   *(Ken).*

Of my honoured father it was true that for him to live was Christ and to die was gain (Phil. 1:21).

> *Let me die the death of the righteous,*
> *And let my last end be like his.*
>   *(Num. 23:10).*

Europe

November 27, 1922, to July 28, 1923

Mr. Broadbent had suggested a visit to Norway to strengthen believers there. I wrote to Mr. McKinnon, a brother from Scotland, living at Skien, a town a fair journey south-west from Oslo. The immediate reply was a warm welcome from the assembly of believers there accompanied by £10 towards the journey. Thus encouraged I left England on Monday, November 27, 1922.

Mr. E. A. Toll, then of Kenilworth, thought it of God to accompany me on this tour. I had known him in adversity at Dartmoor. After conferring with the leaders of his assembly, who approved of his desire, we left together. We had five days with the Danish brethren in Copenhagen, and reached Skien on December 6. The weather was raw and searching and as I studied my companion on the long journeys I doubted if he were robust enough for the still longer journeys ahead to reach southeast Poland and the yet more severe weather expected. He felt the same and accepted the welcome of the friends in Norway to remain with them. Later his wife joined him, and he found help from God to render acceptable service for a few years, until Mrs. Toll's health brought them to England.

This going forth of a younger worker with an older followed the apostolic example of Timothy joining Paul (Acts 16:1-3). My brother was not a novice, but already a helpful teacher of the word; a very important point too often neglected in the going forth of young men to a foreign land. He was well spoken of by the local brethren where he lived, who, indeed, had expected that he would some day be called of God to devote his life to the ministry of the word.

But it is of the utmost possible importance to observe that the Derbe and Lystra brethren had nothing at all to say as to whether or not Timothy should join Paul. They commended him personally, and they joined with Paul in laying hands on him that he might be granted a special spiritual gift, which a prophetic message had intimated he should secure (1 Tim. 4:14; 2 Tim. 1:6); but whether he should go forth with Paul was not for them to say, but was entirely a matter for Paul and Timothy, subject to Divine guidance. It is clear that Paul had received in advance prophetic directions as to Timothy. He speaks to him of "the prophecies which led the way to thee" (1 Tim. 1:18). The guidance of the Lord having thus been given, of course the brethren at Lystra and Derbe could have no voice in determining the matter, though they had the privilege of concurring and supporting.

This is seen in other instances. The Spirit expressly directed that Paul and

Barnabas were to be separated for a certain forward movement. These also were not novices but experienced teachers. In view of the Spirit's direction it would have been impertinent for the brethren at Antioch to have consulted together as to whether they could commend the two brethren for foreign work. Their part was but to commend them *to the Lord*, and let them go, as "sent forth by the Holy Spirit" (Acts 13:1-4).

Later "Paul chose Silas" and the part of the brethren was simply to commend them" to the grace of the Lord" (Acts 15:40). Thus the decision to go, and to go together, was not taken by the elders or the church, though they showed their approval by prayer and support.

It was in connexion with E. A. Toll that the incident occurred given in my Memoir of E. H. Broadbent as follows:

In 1922 a young brother in Christ felt called to accompany me on a tour. The Passport Office delayed his passport and I went to inquire why. The official explained that so many persons had gone abroad whom they afterward wished had been kept in England, that they were becoming more cautious. In this I concurred from my own observation. He continued that this applicant seemed to be of no special status, merely a cabinet worker. He had no means, and no Church or Society behind him. He appeared to be intending a long journey, by the number of countries he wished endorsed on the passport, and he was leaving his wife behind. He concluded that he wanted to know how the wife was to be supported in his absence, and said frankly that he had sent the papers to the police in his town to report.

In reply, I pointed out that in religious work character was far more important than in any other sphere: that many of us felt that to guarantee a sufficient income to assure comfort was a most likely way to induce the wrong sort of person to offer for the work: that, on the contrary, it was likely to deter the unsuitable to say that they should show that they were convinced that it was God who was calling them by trusting Him to meet all needs for going forth, and by risking whatever trials and hardships might be met: that thus the very feature which made him hesitate, the lack of visible and guaranteed support, was the very thing that we thought of great value.

The official at once admitted the cogency of this, to him an entirely new aspect of the matter, and the passport came without delay.

At Skien I experienced a distinct working of God. I had arrived without money for getting further. On Monday, December 11, I spoke on Gal. 3:1-14. A lady said that night to a friend that she would not have missed that address for a thousand crowns. Her friend answered that therefore she ought to give that sum to the Lord! She was a milliner and had not so much, but the next day she brought me 300 crowns, equal then to £12. 10. 0. Other friends there and at Oslo gave sums totalling about £7. The Continental exchange was so heavily in favour of British money that this less than £20 took me from Norway through Sweden to Denmark; across the Baltic sea to Germany and Warsaw, and thence to the south-east province of Poland, where I was to stay. There it sufficed for expenses for two months and allowed me to help towards the cost of over fifty brethren and sisters gathered from the countryside for Bible study. Thus does the Owner of the silver and the gold transfer His ample resources from hand to hand.

The Berlin-Warsaw journey was made on Christmas Eve. The train was utterly congested with Poles going home for the festive season. I therefore took a first-class ticket. The cost for the perhaps 300 miles was six shillings. This proved of the Lord. My companion was a Polish lady, on the staff of the League of Nations. She spoke several languages, including good English. She travelled on a diplomatic pass, and when the passport and customs officers came at the frontier she made a brief remark, probably that I was a friend of hers, and they passed on without inquiry or searching my bags. We talked for hours about things spiritual and I afterward sent her literature. In her reply she said: "On the sea of life it's not smooth sailing now. I would give much to begin life over again—if I could begin again with the heart of a child." I pointed her to Ezekiel 36:26, where God promises: "A new heart also will I give you, and a new spirit will I put within you."[11]

Eastern and south-eastern Europe being now largely behind the Iron Curtain it will not be well to give particulars of places or persons. It being mid-winter life physically was hard. The land was under deep snow, the temperature around zero. The tiny houses were over-heated, food meagre, sanitation unpleasant or absent. The first sixteen days the sky was so leaden with snow clouds that I gained no idea of the position of the sun or of the points of the compass. When, however, the snow had fallen the short days were brilliant and the air invigorating. It was tiring to walk far in the heavy clothing necessitated by the cold. Pictures of life there are given in the Memoir of E. H. Broadbent.

The population was Ukrainian and Jewish, under Polish officials. In former days it had been part of Russia, and the Orthodox church, the religion of the State, had bitterly persecuted and suppressed evangelical Christians. When the region passed to Poland in 1919, and religious liberty came, sundry believers, humble of rank, commenced preaching the gospel in the villages.

---

[1] In *World Chaos* (111) I gave the sense from memory, not having her letter at hand.

The Lord responded, and, by the power of His Spirit, conversions multiplied until many thousands of peasants had turned to God. This went on for years, by their own testimony alone, and in spite of much family opposition which the converted had often to bear. They gathered every night, the meetings lasting for hours, and all being led by the Spirit of God.

The Polish authorities did not hinder this work of grace among Ukrainians. Themselves Roman Catholics, and having been formerly oppressed by the Russian rulers and the Russian church, they abhorred the latter and were pleased to see it weakened by these many defections. Thus does God turn the animosities of men to the furtherance of His purposes.

But the believers needed instructing more perfectly in the Word and ways of God, for which purpose the leaders gathered the fifty or so mentioned. They came from the very wide area where the work was in progress, and thus, though of humble status, were an influential company. We had three sessions daily. I explained the Scriptures for about four hours, my Russian-Jewish-Christian interpreter occupied the same time, and in the evening there was the usual public meeting. We took a general survey of the plans of God as revealed from Genesis to Revelation. These churches of believers had been incorporated by the leaders into a vast church organization. When we reached the Corinthian Letters it became evident to many that such an organization was not intended by the Head of the church.

The two months ended, and before leaving I pointed out to the leaders that many of their members now saw the real New Testament plan of each local assembly of Christians being administratively independent, bound to other believers by only spiritual ties of life, of faith, of love, and I suggested the probability that these would wish to adopt the Lord's ways in church life and worship. They themselves had confessed it to be according to Scripture; if therefore, I said, they would lead in the abandoning of human organization and adopting of the Lord's methods, then doubtless He would still use them as before; but if not, I thought it likely that they would lose the spiritually minded and be left with the rest.

The brethren thanked me, kissed me in Slav style, and I left on February 26, 1923. The forecast was soon fulfilled. The church in whose hall we had met asked to be put on the New Testament basis; but the leaders would not forgo their dominance and their salaries drawn from the Union, and told those who wished any changes they must leave if they would gain them. As the building was held in the name of the leaders they were in a position to assert their will. Some sixty of the ninety members formed an assembly in an adjacent village, and in due time some thirty other churches followed this lead.

The advantage of the Lord's ways was seen later when the region passed again under Soviet rule; for the Soviet rulers suppressed the Union and whatever had a Western appearance or connexion, but tolerated, at that time, what seemed to them purely Ukrainian.

The spiritual fervour of Christians in that period was highly exhilarating. Neither effort nor carnal devices were needed "to keep things moving." Because almost every convert had to face determined opposition few confessed Christ until the Spirit had made Him a reality to the heart. Devotion to Him being thus kindled they were actually anointed with the Spirit of witness and talked of the Lord to others. For them the personal indwelling of the Spirit was not merely a doctrine but a reality, an experience. Through this divinely energized witnessing the work spread from village to village, and was always ahead of every effort to help the churches formed. From up to seventy miles away they came begging for a visit and instruction. And those seventy miles had been tramped on foot through heavy snow and had to to be tramped back again.

One sister of seventy years walked over seven miles every Sunday to the Supper of the Lord, and back in the afternoon. It will be understood that when such effort was made, and made cheerfully and regularly, their hunger was not to be appeased by a meeting of only an hour and a quarter and a brief talk of fifteen minutes, such as is customary in many English churches. They expected from six to eight hours of fellowship, with exposition of the Word in proportion.

On one visit a peasant walked into a house where I sat. He told that sixteen miles away through the vast pine forests the Spirit had wrought and several churches had been formed totalling 500 members. They had no teachers as yet, but learning that forty miles away there were to be all-day meetings, he had walked those miles the day before, had gathered all the manna and honey he could during the ten hours of the meetings, so as to carry it back to his district, and this third day he was plodding the forty miles home. Hearing in the town that there were a few people who thought as he did, he had found us out to enlarge his store of spiritual food. Food for the body he declined, and a little before dark he started the remaining sixteen miles of his walk.

One who has ever shared in such apostolic conditions can only sorrow over the comparative dullness of spiritual life in England or other similar lands, and will pray and toil to strengthen the things that remain which are ready to die, in hope of a movement of the Spirit.

As the two months' Bible study drew to an end I was waiting upon God for His guidance elsewhere. I had met in Germany a business man who travelled widely and was zealous in the work of the Lord. He wrote to say that he was going into Roumania and would come out of his way to visit the work in Poland. He added that the visit to Roumania was in connexion with sorry conditions in a village church in Transylvania. As I read the letter my heart said that he would ask me to accompany him, though he had not hinted this. He had not been in my rooms five minutes before he inquired whither I was going next. I replied that it had not been made clear, to which he instantly answered, "Then you will come with me to Roumania." He explained that the Trustees of Stewards Company, Ltd., England, were involved in the trouble and had asked him and Mr. Johannes Warns to go down and deal with matters. Mr. Warns could not get away, so, said he, the £5 the Trustees had sent towards his fare was available for me.

In due time I returned to Warsaw to get the necessary visas, and took the morning train to Vienna. The journey took the whole day and I listened for hours to a flow of many languages. A Jew seemed able to chat with everyone and he tried me in vain in one tongue after another. Towards evening it occurred to him to try English. He was a God-sent aid, for the Polish and then the Czech customs had to be passed; I tacked myself on to his coat-tails, and he piloted me through smoothly.

The journey from Vienna was long and wearying. When we reached our railway station there remained a hard tramp of some miles, over snowy paths, to our village destination. My companion seemed never to tire, but on arrival I was all but exhausted. Yet there was a meeting to be addressed almost immediately. Of the local trouble I had learned little more than that the strife had been so bitter that for six months the church had refrained from breaking bread, a wise precaution in view of 1 Cor. 11:26-32, and one which other churches might well follow.

I learned later that the history was this. The village was in a lovely valley among the grand and delightful Carpathian mountains and was a holiday resort from the hot plains. A German brother, working in the gospel in the district, conceived the plan of putting up a good-sized house. The ground floor was to be a hall for the assembly, the first floor was to be rooms for the worker for the time being, that is, the "missionary". Above, there were to be two suites of rooms to be let to visitors on holiday, the rents to go to the maintenance of the premises and the work of God. A sister in the meeting advanced £500 and a wealthy brother in England found the rest, I think £1,500, and he stipulated that the property should be vested in Stewards Company, Ltd., a company formed to hold religious properties out of England.

In due time another German worker succeeded the one who put up the house, and presently he and the meeting quarrelled, and he would not come down to the gatherings beneath his rooms. It was a Saxon population, and the senior man in the church was a tough farmer. Greek had met Greek and the tug of war reached breaking point. The bad state of soul of them all was the *reason* for the strife, but the *casus belli* was paltry, as so often. The meeting said, "*We* represent Stewards Company in England and we are responsible to manage the house." The missionary said, "No, I live in the house and I am the one to manage it." But in reality it was that both parties wished to control the letting of the upper rooms and to enjoy what balance remained after meeting the upkeep of the property. The landlords could do little to help, being far away in England and the people on the spot using another language.

At the meeting that first evening I spoke on 1 John 2:28, "And now, little children, abide in Him; that, if He shall be manifested, we may have boldness, and not be ashamed from Him at His presence." The solemnity of the judgment seat of Christ for His own people was stressed heavily and the severity of the penalties that may then follow evil conduct by Christians. It was also pressed that if we do not cease from evil in this life, then must we meet again there the persons and wrongs outstanding and receive again the deeds done through the body. It was the solemn truth in the parables of the unforgiving and unfaithful servants (Matt. 18:21-35; 25:14-30) and of such passages as Ecc. 12:14 and 2 Cor. 5:9, 10).

The next day I left and ministered in other places for three weeks. Returning on March 30, 1923, teaching and visiting occupied three weeks. The Spirit strengthened for much of that conflict described in *Prayer Focused and Fighting*, without which the walls of Jericho do not fall but by which the giant sons of Anak are conquered. During this time the "missionary" fell ill, which gave opportunity to get near to his hard heart. Visits to the forests and fields with the farmer opened the way to his stubborn heart. At the end of the three weeks there was a perceptible softening of spirit in the community and in the meetings, and I proposed that on April 22 the holy table should again be spread.

It was a season never to be forgotten. The members were all present, some eighteen brethren and sisters, and the "missionary" had come down. I spoke awhile on 1 Cor. 11:26; Col. 3:17; 1 Cor. 10:31, and Zech. 7: 6, and sat down. There was a long silence in which I prayed and the Spirit wrought. The farmer rose and in direct and honest words expressed to the "missionary" his sincere regret that he had ever said or done anything to hurt him; then he offered his hand which the other shook in silence. One after the other each followed and offered the hand of fellowship, which was accepted. But the elderly sister who had helped to build the house did not move. I waited and prayed. Presently she said that Mr. H., the worker, had said in another place such and such wicked things about her daughter and she felt she could not forgive him. He said nothing, and I could do nothing but cry secretly to the Lord to act, and He did.

There had lately come to the house an elderly German lady who had retired from long years of devoted service in the capital as a deaconess. She was of social position and education. Though she had not been in England for forty years, one had only to shut one's eyes and listen to a cultured English lady speaking English perfect in language and accent. She was a charming Christian. The night before this meeting I had asked her if she had ever seen the Lord's Supper observed as we observed it, and had pointed her to 1 Cor. 14:26 as indicating the absence of formality in a Spirit-led assembly, where "each one" contributed a psalm, teaching, or revelation. She had never noticed the verse. I added that the Scripture demanded no other qualification for partaking of the Supper than that the partaker had been received by Christ (Rom. 15:7) and was walking with Him, so that if she wished to join us the next morning she would be most welcome. She came, and it proved that she was almost the only person in the whole land that could remove the block to which the meeting had come. When the mother had stated her difficulty, the lady intervened quietly and said: "I think I can help in this. I was present on the occasion, and what brother H. really said was so and so," which was entirely different to the false account which had reached the mother and contained nothing objectionable. Upon this the mother said: "Oh, that is quite another matter," she shook hands with Mr. H. and then we had such a melting, gracious season at the breaking of bread as I had never known before and have never known since.

Thus had the Lord ordered His own house. He had sent from a far-off land one whom He could use to serve His people, though he knew but very little of their language; and He had sent from a distant city one who could remove an unexpected hindrance to harmony. Later I learned that He had secretly begun the work of reconciling the two principal contestants by that first address on my arrival; for when the farmer learned of the serious prospect that lay ahead at the judgment seat of Christ he said to himself, "If this is how matters stand we'll have to get this trouble settled." Thus had his heart been given a new and right outlook and approach to the situation.

When the hearts of the community were thus softened towards each other it was simple to solve the matter of the house, by the suggestion that they should control it jointly. That solution would have occurred to men of ordinary sense. But often the sons of light are not so wise as the sons of this evil age, and these brethren missed the way because their souls were in a low condition and estranged. Sometime after Stewards Company, Ltd., sold the property and thus brought to an end the situation which was the occasion of the trouble.

For centuries before the 1914-1918 war the Orthodox Church had been the dominant church in Roumania and had resisted evangelical religion. Religious liberty was guaranteed in the new constitution of the enlarged kingdom which emerged from that war. A Department of Religion was created under a Minister of Religion. Let British and other Christians look this in the face, for they may need to understand the position.

Religion—the relation of a creature to the Creator, of man to God, and of the worship and duties involved—is a realm in which Governments have *no* authority from God to interfere. From the point of view of the Supreme Ruler their intruding into this realm and all their actions therein are *ultra vires,* beyond the powers possessed. Of old Israel was God's special people, where His rights and His laws were to be exhibited in national life. National and religious life was interwoven, the former to be pervaded and animated by the latter. Yet the secular rulers had no authority in affairs religious; they were as much bound by the laws of Moses regulating religion as were all their subjects.

In an hour of acute danger from invasion the first king of Israel presumed to act as a minister of religion and to offer a sacrifice reserved by law to the priest, and for this presumption he forfeited the permanence of his kingdom (1 Sam. 13:8-14). A later king presumed to enter the house of God and burn incense to Him, this also being a function of the priest only. The king was smitten with leprosy on the spot, and continued a leper to the day of his death (2 Chron. 26:16-21). Similarly in the Gentile world Nebuchadnezzar, emperor of Babylon, planned to rule religion, but God frustrated him (Dan. 3).

This principle obtains still. God now acknowledges no material temple, but He still claims sole authority over the love, worship, and spiritual service of men. Such of them as render this are His present kingdom on earth, the "house" in which He dwells by the Spirit. Of this sphere His Son, Jesus Christ, is the sole Head, and in this realm He has granted no authority whatever to secular rulers (Heb. 3:6). In things civil rulers have rights conferred by God (Rom. 13:1-7; 1 Pet. 2:13-17). In the religious life, the "house of God," His reserved realm, they, as rulers, are trespassers; and while every person, Christian or otherwise, is required by God to "render unto Caesar the things that are Caesar's" by the grant of God, no one is permitted to render unto Caesar the things that are God's (Matt. 22:15-22). These are reserved by Him for Himself and set by Him under the sole authority of His Son. A Minister of Religion is a personal affront to the Son of God.

The Roumanian authorities at that time did not violate the constitution by denying liberty of religion, but they largely nullified that liberty by seeking to impose regulations which it would have been very difficult, and sometimes impossible, to fulfil. Every community of Christians had to be registered and licensed or its meetings were illegal, and a first requirement was that fifty heads of houses must sign the application for a licence. In country districts this could easily preclude any application. Every preacher had to hold a licence, and to preach only in such place or places as the licence specified. Thus the spreading of the gospel and enlargement of the church of God by itineration were severely restricted. No preacher would be licensed who had ever been convicted of a crime, nor one who had not passed a certain standard of secular education. Thus could the supply of preachers be kept quite inadequate.

On May 5, 1923, I learned that there was to be the next day at a distant town a gathering of leading brethren to consider the above situation. Leaving at 3.30 a.m. I arrived with a friend at 7 o'clock. It transpired that an active evangelist had been in consultation with the Minister of Religion and had come with the draft of a Constitution which the Minister demanded should be adopted. All the assemblies of Brethren were required to federate into one Union, with President, Secretary, Treasurer, and Council, and to be governed by such regulations as have been outlined above. Failing acceptance, the meetings would be declared illegal.

Being asked my view, I showed that the New Testament knows of no visible organization of Christians whatever other than the local church gathered in each separate place. There was long and serious discussion, but the New Testament view was accepted by all but the evangelist in question. When he urged that, unless the demand of the Minister was granted, the work of the gospel would be stopped and persecution would follow, one of the others asked the simple fundamental question, *"But what has become of the cross?"*

By most of the believers the cross was shouldered. The battle went on for a long time, with considerable victory for the saints. Now the country is behind the Iron Curtain. At one time the Soviet rulers openly tolerated evangelical work, probably because it, like themselves, was adverse to the Orthodox Church. Recent news from Roumania is to the effect that sufficient religious liberty exists, even more than was the case under the Orthodox Church a generation ago.

The uncertainty of travel was illustrated on Sunday night May 13, 1923. The train left the northern town of Jassy at 7.35 p.m. After some time it stopped for several hours. Of this I thought little and did my best to sleep sitting on the narrow third-class boards. At length we started, but when day dawned, and we should have been near our destination, I fancied that the country looked unfamiliar. Presently we arrived back at Jassy. Heavy rain had washed away the line where we had stopped, so we were kept till morning to be the down train to Jassy.

After three weeks' service in various cities I left Roumania on May 25, 1923, crossing the frontier into Hungary the next morning with about 6s. in my pocket. After a few days in Budapest I came through to Wiedenest, in west Germany, expecting shortly to return to England. But a call from Poland prevented. The brethren at the centre where the New Testament assembly had been formed had decided to hold a three days' conference during a public holiday, and that the meetings should be entrusted to the rule of the Holy Spirit, instead of to human arrangement. But this was an untried venture. How could they risk it without one or more of their English brethren present who were experienced in such meetings? So they wrote urgent letters to Mr. Broadbent and myself to go to their help, and pending replies did not announce the conference. But they duly reflected that this dependence on man was a denial of reliance on the Holy Spirit, so they called the meetings without waiting for our replies. Mr. Broadbent could not go, but I went with the Johannes Warns mentioned above. The Spirit of God, of course, honoured their faith. The three days, with about ten hours of meetings each day, were a season of power, closing with the Lord's Supper. It was largely the influence of those days upon believers from far around which led to the many other churches adopting the New Testament ways of church life and ministry.

It was on this second visit to that part of Poland that the incident occurred narrated in the Memoir of Mr. Broadbent. At a question meeting it was asked whether it was right that a choirmaster should conduct the singing and beat time before the audience. The choirmaster of that church sat before me on the front seat. As I knew well how touchy such officials can be I sought grace to answer warily. I pointed out that they had suffered pain by the late separation from their former church and that the ground of their course had been that they had learned that the affairs of the house of God ought to be ordered by His word in the New Testament. If therefore they found in the New Testament that the early churches had choirs, very well, let them continue as before, and let the choirmaster continue to lead; but if they did not find it in the New Testament they would know what to do.

After the meeting I learned that it was the choirmaster who had put the question. The Ukrainians are intensely musical, and choirs were universal; but without ado or friction the choir was given up. The choirmaster grew in grace and became the pillar of that church. Some time later the whole village selected him to be their mayor. They knew that only under his administration would official corruption cease. Very reluctantly and only under great pressure he at last consented to act. The Polish police then asked him what their share of the "pickings" was to be.

He replied that there would be no "pickings". They therefore reported adversely to the authorities in Warsaw and the appointment was not confirmed.

After three weeks in that country and a week in Berlin I reached England on Saturday, July 28, 1923.

CHAPTER 12

Germany, Poland, Roumania

July 1923-December 1926

After several weeks visiting in England the path led to a fortnight of special ministry at Wiedenest in west Germany. On September 27, 1923, an unusual person travelled with me to England. She was a militant English suffragette, hatless, with shock hair, stocky and aggressive. Her special hobby was fostering international amity, and her important contribution just then to this excellent ideal was to bring some pet birds to England, which a Continental was sending to an Englishman. Our chat was friendly and interesting apart from religion. For this she had no use, professing to be an atheist. I pondered how to quicken in her some concern for the Christian faith. Standing on Ostend quay it suddenly came to me. "Did you ever know Christabel Pankhurst?" "Of course, I knew her well, and Sylvia." "Had you heard that Christabel has become a Christian?" "A Christian! Christabel Pankhurst a Christian!" It would scarcely have been surprising if she had toppled off the quay with astonishment. It opened the way to fuller statements concerning faith in Christ. She was not such an atheist as she professed to be, which is the case with many.

On October 26, 1923, I was again in Berlin and on the 30th in Warsaw, going thence to the country district where the Bible course had been held. The growth in believers was cheering. On November 8 nine sisters and four brethren, young men and women, were baptized in an open pond just ready to freeze for the winter. They were not prepared to defer obedience till the ice would melt in April. Clothed myself in heavy flannels, with leather coat and ulster, I shivered in the icy wind; but these warm hearts thus openly confessed their Lord.

On November 17, 1923, I returned to Berlin and ministered the word there until December 13, 1923. There was abundant scope for feeding the flock of God, and there was a warm welcome from believers in that land disordered by the late war. Apart from private ministrations, I gave fifty-one addresses in seventy days.

This was the period of the German currency inflation. As few readers will have had experience of such a time some details are now given. They may give pause to some who talk lightly of inflation. The German mark was nominally twenty to the £1. At one point during this time I received twenty *billions* of marks, almost worthless paper. I took a railway ticket costing nominally half a crown and ought to have received in change 235,000 marks. The booking clerk smiled and said, "I have no small change." I too smiled and went my way. That morning 235,000 marks were worth to me one thirtieth of a penny.

The inflation appeared to me to be a deliberate fraud by the then rulers. The French were in occupation of the Ruhr so as to draw reparation money from the mines and industries. They could not be driven out by the bayonet, so the money was debased, and the French had to bring in money to finance the district and it became a burden instead of a profit.

Further unjust ends were served. The country's internal debt was paid off in this worthless paper, and so the burden of interest on the loans accumulated was saved, but it robbed the investors. This bore most heavily on the great families and landowners who had lent large sums to the Imperial government, and thus was gained the end, dear to Socialists, of robbing and ruining the rich and aristocratic.

I visited a Christian of that class, running a family estate of 2,000 acres. There were sixty Dutch cows in his stalls, shut in because the land was under winter snow. I remarked that no doubt he could send much milk to Berlin. He replied that, being without money, he could not buy cake to feed them and they gave scarcely enough milk for his own village. The barns were packed with grains—wheat, oats, barley, rye—full to the roofs. I said that the city people were saying that it was the farmers who were depriving them of food by thus holding stocks. He answered: "But what else can we do? If I had sold all this grain two months ago, as usually I would have been glad to do, by now the money would be worthless and I would have nothing to carry us through the winter. The only way we can hope to get through is, that once a week I sell enough to pay the wages and get things indispensable. Directly my people get their money they buy at once food and necessaries, and spend all, because tomorrow the money may have lost half its purchasing power."

In due time estates had to be mortgaged or sold and so that class was undermined. It was the process that is going on in England by excessive taxation and confiscation by statute. Whether ultimately a large number of poor owners is better for a land than a smaller number of rich owners remains to be seen. But the process is heartless and dishonest.

Inflation has curious results. A German in the United States had left some dollars to his native town. The sum was not worth the trouble of transferring to Germany, so it lay in America. But now the town Treasurer bethought himself that dollars were of fabulous worth, so the money was claimed. The municipal debts were paid off, rates remitted for a year, and town improvements made. On the other hand, a manufacturer was fined eight gold marks (10s.) for breach of a factory regulation. He said to the magistrates that they

knew he could not find eight gold marks. "But you could sell your motor car!"
"Yes, I could sell my car, if anyone has money to buy it!"

The most skilled and best paid mechanic in a white metal factory I visited
was taking home half a crown a week to keep his family. I was living with
good middle-class friends, connected with one of the lesser nobility. They had
always received me as a friend, without question of payment. Now I gave my
hostess 10s. a week, which covered the expenses of the whole household. But
much money or little does not matter if there is nothing to buy. When money
is daily depreciating people hold on to articles that will keep their value and
sell only perishable goods. The markets were almost empty. Being mid-winter
vegetables and fruit were very scarce. For that eight weeks we lived on vegetables, poor bread, and a sweet mess called "jam". We had no meat, milk, butter,
cheese, or sugar. What did the families do who had only two and six a week?

A good friend in England, who had once visited the Sunday School at the
Hohenstaufenstrasse Hall, sent me £5 to help the scholars. They were a large
number, yet the sum provided the richest repast then possible, with a good
deal over to help in other ways.

Such a period of low diet leaves in the constitution a vacuum which it
takes a long while to refill. The Lord's people were touched that one from the
land that had lately been an enemy country was happy to share their trials
when he might have been in comfort at home, and this made the ministry
of the Word yet more acceptable and helpful to their hearts. The love of God
to His whole family annuls racial and national estrangements. The baneful
result when that love is absent is that natural and racial antagonism flourishes.
A French Christian was in Berlin. In England she had always broken bread
at our hall. When I inquired why I had not seen her at the hall in Berlin she
replied: "I feel I cannot take the Supper of the Lord with Germans." But the
Lord does not receive to His table Germans or Frenchmen but only children
of God, whether Jew or Greek (Gal. 3:26, 28).

Leaving on New Year's Day 1924 I should have reached Warsaw the next
morning, but that night, after crossing the Polish frontier the train ran into a
blizzard. Mercifully the driver got as far as Lodz, the second largest town in
Poland, the Manchester of that country. Had we been snow-bound in open
country, no food could have been obtained for the thirty-six hours we were
held up. A Polish officer courteously took money from me, walked into the
town a good distance from the station, did my shopping with his own, and
brought me bread and cheese. Face and hands were washed with frozen snow.
The engine was kept under steam and so the carriages were hot. In the train
the thermometer registered 82^0; when one stepped outside to wash or walk,
the temperature was 20^0 of frost.

By Thursday, January 3rd, 1924, the gale had dropped, the line was cleared, and we started from Lodz at 9.20 p.m., becoming the evening train to Warsaw and arriving at 12.45 a.m., instead of at breakfast time. My host lived three quarters of a mile away from the station, and at midnight the vast tenement house would be bolted fast, and as he lived on the third floor access was unlikely. I put my bags behind and under a chair in an open recess on the station and dropped off to sleep. After a time I became conscious of people being about. A small group were studying me, including a policeman and a droshky (open carriage) driver. In broken German the latter explained that at 2 o'clock the last train came, the station would be closed, and I must leave. He agreed to drive me to my friend. The bags were loaded to the carriage, when I took the precaution to ask the fare. "Twenty million zloty." equal to £1. Promptly I lifted out my bags. The policeman was watching. I asked him the fare. He said, five million zloty (5*s*.). The driver agreed and we went to the house. He shouted and banged until the porter opened the great outer door, and grumbled at being disturbed at that unseemly hour in the bitter cold. I gave the driver a ten million note. The darkness was lessened slightly by a feeble oil lamp far up near the high ceiling of the lobby. In the gloom he handed me the five notes of my change. As he had gone to the trouble of waking the porter I handed him back one note. He went off without the customary clamour for more, at which I wondered. In the morning my host asked if I would lend him three million zloty until he returned from his office. I handed him three of the notes. He remarked that these were not for one million but for only 100,000 zloty each. The rascal had taken advantage of the gloom to give me these, and departed with nearly ten shillings, instead of five, to him a goodly haul. Such is life; a good training in forbearance and forgiveness.

My host, with whom I had stayed on earlier visits, was able and learned. He had taken the full seven years' course in a Catholic Seminary and became a priest. He was highly trained in theology and philosophy. He knew Hebrew, Greek, and Latin, and was well read in the church Fathers. He spoke Polish, Russian, German, and English, and could interpret from anyone of these languages into any other of them. And he was a most lovable man, by far the most lovable of any Pole I knew. But it was Christ had made him this.

By some means he got into trouble with the Pope and was excommunicated. Nothing daunted, he persuaded some other priests to join him; they formed the Church of Mary, Catholic but minus the Pope, and built churches. But the 1914 war drifted him into Russia, where two godly women led him to the saving knowledge of Christ. Returning after the war he was as zealous as before, or more so, but as an evangelical. On my first visit, in 1923, he told me that he knew of at least two hundred persons whom he had been privileged to bring to the Lord.

Though the rest of his story will be out of date here, I will complete it at once. He took several journeys with me to other parts of Poland and was a true helper in the gospel. After some years he told me that he had somehow lost his joy, and really did not feel as happy as in his early years in the seminary. I warned him that this was dangerous, for the joy of the Lord is our strength, and pressed him to find out the cause of his loss and remedy it. But presently he lapsed from the faith into the pantheistic views of Spinoza, and his Christian witness ceased. Some years later business brought him to England, and he took a long week-end to visit me in Suffolk. In my sitting-room on Sunday morning he unburdened his heart, humbled his soul before the Lord for his failure, and was restored to fellowship with God his Father. For the first time for some years he came to the table of the Lord, and gave such a touching message as a restored and tender heart could give.

The history of his lapse was as follows. He had four fine boys and a daughter. Learned himself, he set his heart on each of these having a university education. To finance this plan he laboured inordinately at his insurance business and added the extra toil and anxiety of buying and selling houses. Thus he starved his soul of heavenly fellowship and food, became weak, and lost his joy and faith. He had ceased to seek *first* the kingdom of God and so he lost the power of that kingdom. And though restored by the Good Shepherd, who goes after the sheep that is lost until he find it, he had to reap what he had sown. He had exhausted his energies by excessive labours, and some months after his restoration his heart succumbed and he died suddenly.

But in January 1924 he was still full of unction, and we had a most happy fortnight of fellowship and service. On January 19, 1924, I returned to Berlin and enjoyed five and a half weeks of co-operation with the saints in the things of God, and reached England on February 28.

On Monday, November 10, 1924, I attended at Bethesda Chapel, Bristol, the funeral of one who, in one aspect of life in particular, is worthy to be mentioned, my friend H. W. Case. I was his best man at his second wedding, and it was he who sent the cheque which covered the fares of my honeymoon, as mentioned. As we were intimate friends, I learned these details of his life. As a young man he was worldly. At the time of his conversion he and his wife were selling dairy produce in their small shop. He asked the Lord to prosper the business enough to enable Him to give to His work £100 a year. God responded and this sum was soon trebled.

As his business enlarged so of course did his liabilities, and he felt it right to hold reserves enough to assure that, if necessary, say at death, his affairs would be solvent and all his creditors could be paid. Presently he found that the income from these reserve funds was enough for his personal and family needs, and, instead of enlarging his establishment, moving to a finer house and the like, from that time he gave to the work of God all the profits of the business. Whether he was able to continue this during the first great war I do not remember to have heard. He told me that he had said to his two sons that he would educate them for any profession they chose, or they could qualify for his business and take it over in due time; but they were to expect nothing more from him. They came into his business and followed in his steps, though one died early.

We were driving past a house to a brother whose will had been recently proved at £30,000. He shook his whip at the house and said: "I would think the Lord had a controversy with me were I going to leave £30,000." I suppose he might easily have done so, but his will was proved at £9,000 only, little more I should think than the value of premises, stock, and good-will.

"He that hath ears to hear, let him hear".

At the Keswick Convention, July 1925, I had the privilege to hear three of the leading speakers of that period—Graham Scroggie, Stuart Holden, and Charles Inwood. The last made a statement of profound spiritual importance: "God must set you free from the habit of testing His faithfulness by your consciousness."

At this Convention two friendships were formed which were to bear fruit. One was with Nicola Aboud from Egypt, the other with "Sister Eva", the baroness Eva von Tiele Winckler from Miechowitz, Upper Silesia, Germany. Of both more will be said. It was at this time that Sister Eva told me of the conversation with the last Kaiser, when she was able to set before him the return of Christ to the earth to establish here the visible kingdom of God. As an emperor he was arrested by this prospect, and she then pressed upon him that, according to the words of Christ, he must be born again or he could not see that kingdom. This stirred him deeply, and the next morning he sent for his court chaplain; but the Lutheran divine assured him that all that he needed in that matter took place at his baptism as an infant, and thus the impression made by the Spirit of truth seemed to be nullified by the soul-ruining teaching of baptismal regeneration. This was well before the 1914 war, and the mind cannot but speculate upon the possible world-wide benefit if that proud monarch had been brought under the personal influence of the Lord Jesus Christ.

On October 13, 1925, I was again in Berlin and on the 17th in Warsaw. On the 30th of that month I witnessed the baptism of a lawyer and his wife. In his boyhood his brother, a Catholic priest, had taken him to a "retreat" for priests. He learned nothing of the gospel, but there did come upon his heart a definite sense of the reality of God. In manhood he was passing a building in a suburb in Warsaw. Hearing singing, he entered what was a meeting of Baptist believers. Nothing that was said arrested him but again he felt the reality of

God and this time it produced a sense of his own unfitness for God. He came under conviction of sin and was sore troubled in conscience. After some time of distress, one day in his office there came into his thoughts the extraordinary intimation that if he would ring up a certain telephone number that was given he would get into contact with someone who could help. But he was not to do this until he should have returned from his annual holiday.

All the weeks he was away this singular idea persisted. On his return he hesitated to take so remarkable a step, for he had no idea whose number it was. But the distress and the urge drove him to the step, whereupon he was almost alarmed to learn that the number was that of the ex-priest whose story is given above. Would this aggressive man require him to take such an abnormal course as his own, and make himself ridiculous before the Church and society? Yet he went forward, and was soon rejoicing in peace with God through the Lord Jesus Christ. He developed into a faithful disciple and consistent witness whose testimony was blessed to souls.

If he had rung before he had returned from holiday it would have been in vain, for the other also was away. Let the sceptic toil as he will, he will not explain this series of steps that brought this boy and man from darkness to light. It is inexplicable save by the fact of a God of love who had from the beginning chosen this man unto salvation and took steps accordingly. This key fits the complicated lock.

> *There is a Providence that shapes our ends,*
> *Rough hew them how we will.*

Till January 18, 1926, was passed moving widely around the district in Poland first visited and beyond it. The next day took me to Warsaw until February 7, and on the 8th I crossed the south-west Polish-German frontier and reached "Friedenshort", at Miechowitz, Upper Silesia, the centre of the work founded and carried on by Sister Eva. This was one of the largest works of mercy conducted on the principle of trusting God for support. Including branches in different centres there were, as I remember, some 3,000 persons supported. They included aged and infants, healthy and sick, the destitute of every description. There was a branch for training deaconesses, who served in Europe and far beyond. It was a fine testimony to the wisdom of trusting the faithful God. Her noble relatives and friends had not greatly appreciated their humble, self-denying relative, who had put her fortune and life into service which brought little return such as the human heart seeks; but when, after the 1915 war ended, they could not keep up their castles but Eva in faith could ac-cept such places, and they saw in addition that she went on building premises, they could not but admit that she had the right view of life and could succeed when men without faith failed.

The 1914 war brought a signal instance of the preserving care of God. Sister Eva's personal and chief helper was English, Miss Annie Whisler. She was therefore liable to internment or expulsion. But the Kaiser had taken practical interest in the work ever since his first acquaintance with its founder, and the question of Miss Whisler was referred to him. He at once ordered that a permanent residential permit should be issued. But *this* "Most High" was *not* almighty, and found that not even he could grant a permanent permit. The limit of time was annual. But this was regularly renewed, and so one of an "enemy" country helped to conduct this great work of God without interference. From this I draw the practical lesson that if God wishes His servant to be at a certain spot He can keep him there; and conversely, that if He does *not* keep him there He does not wish him to be there.

The Hitler government, spreading out its tentacles to grasp everything, intimated to the Council that they proposed to appoint two representatives to sit with the managers. The reply sent was a mixture of due submission and God-given shrewdness. The Council said that they would accept the proposed representatives, but they thought it needful to point out that the conduct and financial maintenance of the Institution were carried on purely by faith in God and constant prayer to Him. They therefore hoped that the two representatives to be appointed would be such men as could co-operate with them in this vital matter. I understand they heard no more of the proposal.

When the 1945 war ended the Poles were allowed by God to seize Silesia. They drove from Friedenshort all Germans, and it ceased to answer to its name, Haven of Peace. As a centre of His work it had served His purpose, and He was glorified in the grace and patience with which His servants bowed to His permissive will and profited by the severe discipline. They had freely helped Poles; a branch home had been in Warsaw, which I visited. But the ferocity engendered by war failed to distinguish between Germans who had been kind and helpful and Germans who had been cruel and hurtful; the righteous suffered with the wicked, but they had God as their comfort and resource, a "very present help in trouble".

On February 16, 1926, I reached England but by June 17th I was again in Warsaw and went shortly through the south-east and south of Poland. On June 30 I visited the celebrated salt mines at Wielizka. My companion was a Welsh miner. He remarked that he had never seen such extensive and admirable scaffolding as there supported the high roofs and walls of the chambers.

After another visit to "Friedenshort" I penetrated to Ustron, a small town in the Teschen district against the borders of Czechoslovakia. The purpose was to visit a group of believers who had been drawn into the "Tongues" Movement. The leading local man was a gracious, gentle brother. But the dominant person was a domineering man who toured and ruled the district. After listening to my talk on self-control and divine orderliness he told me that he had from the first doubted if my coming was of the Lord and now he was sure it was not! I answered quietly; *"Der Tag wird alles klar machen"* ("The day will make all things plain").

He and others guided me to a spot where the depths of the soul were stirred. We tramped for hours up steep and lonely paths till we came, far up in the mountains, to a level place where was a large, flat, round stone, standing on a short pillar of stone. Beside it stood a larger upright stone on which were carved a book, a plate, a flagon, and a cup. In times not so very distant, well since the Reformation period, simple sincere believers had learned from the New Testament that formal organized Church systems were not the purpose of the Lord for His church. They therefore met in local congregations to worship by the Spirit, whereupon those usually bitter foes, the Catholic priests and the Reformed Church pastors, suspended their enmity and combined to persecute the common foe. So severe and sustained was the opposition, that these faithful sufferers for Christ were constrained to retire in secret to this remote mountain, and the table and the stone preseve the memory of their devotion and courage. Thus had Caiaphas and Pilate and Herod, haters each of the other, joined to destroy the Faithful and True Witness of their day.

The next three weeks were spent in Roumania, confirming the churches in Transylvania. At this time there was working in northern Roumania a man with a history. His father had been a British merchant of substance in Riga. When the son was sent to Rugby School he knew German as a native language, but could speak little English. He went to America to make his way, and eventually earned a comfortable income as a salesman. Leaving an hotel in Chicago he walked along a street, heard music in a hall, entered a Salvation Army meeting, and was forthwith turned from his worldly life to trust and serve Christ. So thoroughly did he respond to the claims of the Lord Jesus that after three weeks he gave up his post and took work in the old clothes store of the Army at extremely modest pay. His ability and value were soon recognized, he was made a Salvationist officer, and sent here and there to revive declining corps.

He married a lady who was in charge of the Salvation Army Maternity Hospital. Being desirous of evangelising in Russia when the First World War ended, the couple resigned from the Army. As it proved impossible to proceed beyond Constantinople, they were in the end led to work in Roumania, first in a former Russian province and then in two other regions. Many little churches arose as the result of their efforts.

While waiting for guidance at a Roumanian port, the brother in question rendered some temporary help to the American Red Cross, and witnessed much corruption in the country. Some experiences he narrated will illustrate the moral state of that land at that time. The Queen made a request for certain stores to be sent from his depot for soldiers at the capital. The station-master promptly asserted that the things simply could not be sent, not even for the Queen, for no railway trucks were available. But the present of a box of cigars promptly provided the trucks.

Sugar was very scarce. One night some bags of it vanished from the store. General X. in control of the district cast suspicion upon the Greek caretaker, but said inquiries should be made. These disclosed nothing. Soon after, the Head of the Red Cross was dining at a prominent house in the capital. The ladies deplored the lack of sugar, but one said that her friend General X. was very kind in sharing with his friends a supply he had secured.

After the work had been closed, the lieutenant in local charge demanded of the Greek caretaker a supply of shoes for his men. The Greek explained that distribution had ceased and he had no authority to hand over goods. The officer was abusive, but the other replied that were he to part with anything the lieutenant would be the first to deny that he had received the articles and would leave him (the caretaker) to face the charge of dishonesty. The lieutenant departed in anger, and that night the store was burnt to the ground.

It was among a people thus corrupt—more corrupt morally than can be put in black and white—that Mr. H. with his wife and boy decided to remain and evangelize. God blessed their testimony to very many. It was there that I heard a small group of young Christians sing a chorus, entitled "God is love," in ten languages, including Roumanian, Ukrainian, German, English, Russian, and Polish.

The place had been the county town of a district, where the courts sat and official business was transacted. The solicitor who arranged the purchase of a small house for Mr. H. told him that before long the town would lose these advantages and a town ten miles away would be made the county town. After this had taken place the lawyer explained the reason. It was that his town had made a present to the Minister of Justice (*sic!*) of only one and a half million lei (say £1,500), whereas the other town had sent to him twice that amount! In those days it was common knowledge that no Minister of State expected to hold office more than a few months, therefore constructive measures could not be put though, and Ministers used the opportunity each to fill his purse.

After a week in southern Roumania I took the river route to Hungary, profiting by the quiet days on the lovely Danube, spent a short time in Budapest, Bratislava, Freiburg-im-Breisgau, south Germany, visited other towns on the way to Wiedenest, and reached London on September 14, 1926.

The four following months were occupied with visits and ministry in different parts of England. In January a week was spent in Clayhidon, Devon, my wife's early home. There was to be sold a small house, which I thought to secure, considering that my wife would then be near her family during my long absences. The Lord graciously frustrated this purpose by the simple means of withholding money. It has long since been clear that my way would have been unwise and that His way was perfect. It is safer to be poor than rich; it is restful that one's matters and means be really and wholly at the ordering of Divine wisdom and power.

When the contents of this house were sold I attended. It was the only auction to which I ever went. For the first lot, twelve tumblers, no one would bid. Perplexed, the auctioneer looked around and said, "Will no one offer me a shilling?" I did so, and when I got the glasses home it was to find that six of them were cut glass. I bought also a few pounds' worth of odds and ends, such as garden tools, a garden seat, and such like. To be sure we had no garden, but my mind was ordered by higher wisdom than mine. I was secretly sure that one day we should need such things, which was presently the fact for over twenty years. How fatherly is the care of God for the small affairs of His children.

Chapter 13

Egypt, Palestine, Syria

1927, 1928

I would not have the restless will
That hurries to and fro,
That seeks for some great thing to do,
Or secret thing to know;
I would be humble as a child
And guided where I go.

IN the middle of December 1926 guidance came to fresh service in Egypt. Mr. and Mrs. W. L. McClenahan had continued their personal evangelizing in that land. They had formed and followed the plan of visiting every town and village at least once, preaching and leaving literature. With a houseboat as home they had commenced at the extreme south, in Upper Egypt, had persevered winter after winter and were now at Nag Hammadi in middle Egypt. They asked me to join them this season.

Leaving England on January 25, 1927, visits were paid in Paris, Lyons, Grenoble (where the Revolution started), Cannes, and Mentone. Marseilles was left on February 4 and I reached Nag Hammadi on the 11th, Here and in the adjacent village of Baghoura many openings came for ministry of the word. My interpreter was Nicola Aboud, before mentioned.

This faithful disciple was one of some young men who were associated with the McClenahans in the gospel effort mentioned and whom they entertained on the boat. It was a special privilege to influence these. Nikola was brought to Christ by the blesssing of God upon the perseverance of an American lady in Egypt. She almost persecuted him into the kingdom, a method not often advisable. He was in the Post Office service, but retired early, on a much reduced pension, so as to devote his life to the work of God.

His heart was open to the Spirit of truth and he grasped firmly what was shown him in Scripture, and acted upon it. I pointed out to him that, excellent as was the work of seeing that each village had at least one opportunity to hear the gospel, this did not reach the apostolic ideal, for the apostles had laboured to found a church in each place, that is, to establish a group of believers in Christ who should go forward to evangelize their own district. He saw also that the spiritual condition of membership in such a church was nothing more than a valid confession of Jesus as the Son of God, evidenced usually by immersion in water in His name; and that every person who could show that Christ had received him ought to be received by the church (Matt. 16:16-18; Rom. 15:7).

At that time there were no churches in Egypt gathered on this simple New Testament basis only. There were Church of England congregations, native Presbyterian Churches founded by the American Presbyterian Mission, various congregations established by others, such as Missions, "Pentecostal" and "Holiness" groups, and also perhaps 120 gatherings of Exclusive Brethren; but none of these met on the New Testament principle alone. With most of these Christians I had had happy fellowship during former visits to the land, as on the present occasion, but had always felt the barriers raised by unscriptural, human arrangements.

The history of the Exclusive Brethren meetings was noteworthy. Long years before, a gifted missionary with the American Mission had met with works of J. N. Darby. These enlightened him a good deal as to the mind of the Lord concerning His church and service. In faith he walked in this light from the Word of God, resigned his position and salary, and set out to act on the New Testament. God of course honoured this obedience and used him to many.

Presently, as I was told, a German colporteur from Syria visited Egypt and joined hands with the American brother. This colporteur was connected with the Exclusive Brethren of Germany. The present outcome of their labours is the large number of meetings mentioned. But they would not receive Christians solely as Christians. Thus I, for example, was not permitted to break bread with them.

They laboured only among Copts, the nominal Christian population. In 1910 or 1911 I visited Mr. Schlotthauer and found him a godly old man. He kindly gave me a fine piece of Sudanese ebony for a walking stick, but he would not have broken bread with me. When I inquired why they made no attempt to take the gospel to Moslems, who were eight or ten times as numerous as the Copts, he gave the amazing answer, that the Moslems had had their opportunities at the beginning of the history of Islam (that is in the seventh and eighth centuries of our era), and had rejected the gospel, and we Christians have no more responsibility for them.

Before long the seed rooted in the heart of Nikola Aboud sprang up and bore fruit. It pleased God to use him to build up assemblies gathered on the apostolic basis, and He gave him the heart of a true shepherd to tend His flock with toil and tears, in labours far beyond his natural strength, for he was feeble in body.

On Saturday, March 26, 1927, I left the boat and went to Luxor, further south. The immediate object was to visit again the ancient tombs and temples, but I took a letter of introduction to an Exclusive of that town. While seeking him I met Cook's representative, a leader of the Exclusive meeting. After some friendly chat he said suddenly: "Are you connected with us or with the Open Brethren?" I felt pained at being faced with this sad controversy in so remote a place and replied: "Dear brother, when we leave England we like to leave these unhappy differences behind us." But he pressed the question, and upon my acknowledging connexion with Open Brethren, like a pistol shot came his words: "Then you cannot break bread or minister among us."

Had I drawn the sword of controversy we should have spilled some bad blood and parted in ill will. But the Spirit of Jesus had taught me better. I replied gently: "Well, dear brother, I know your feelings, and I was not expecting to do either; but I suppose I may come to the meetings." This unexpected attitude confused and disarmed him. He replied slowly and quietly: "Oh yes, you may come to the meetings." I thanked him warmly and said I should be with them in the morning, which was Sunday.

Some seventy or eighty brethren were gathered and nearly as many sisters, the latter behind a latticed partition. Only a few years before this assembly had been very low and weak. Then the Lord worked in power. He saved a young Copt, gave him distinctly the gift of the evangelist, and shortly about forty young men were saved and added to the church. As worship and ministry went on it was plain that they were able to build up one another. All was led by the Holy Spirit.

When all had partaken of the cup this continued to be passed around until all the contents had been consumed. They explained this as being required by the Lord's direction "Drink ye all of it." It had not occurred to me that the English is ambiguous, as I suppose the Arabic must be. They were surprised to learn the real meaning, "All of you drink of it." This illustrates the need of accuracy in translation.

After the meeting they took me next door to the home of the interpreter. Some fifteen leaders gathered and desired to know more concerning the differences between the Exclusive and the Open Brethren. Here was seen the wisdom and ordering of the Lord. One was foreign correspondent in a bank and knew English well. Moreover, he had read my book, *Departure,* and so was already well acquainted with much that I had to say, and could state it readily in Arabic. They learned more in that hour-and-a-half than a lifetime had taught even the oldest of them.

They gave me sherbet and we parted in love. There was a meeting every night of the week, and always the Spirit was owned as Leader. The last evening I was to be there the interpreter whispered to one or two of his brethren and then whispered to me: "We think that if the Lord has given you anything for us, you ought to give it to us." Thus speedily had the Lord changed their spirits. I gave some exposition of 1 John 1:1-2:2, and departed the next morning. But more of this, which will be told in its place.

On March 31, 1927, I called on an Egyptian friend of 1910 and 1911. As he told me how to get to the great ruined temple at Denderah he said that at a certain point I must cross the "sea", meaning the river Nile. The usage has survived for millenniums. See Isa. 11:15: "the tongue of the Egyptian sea." The same day I returned to the boat which on April 4 was moved to Baliana, where we remained till April 25. It was now very hot, the Nile current was sluggish, by the bank where we were moored almost nil. We drank of the water, duly filtered through a large earthenware pot; but the refuse and sewage of the boat was only insufficiently carried away by the scarcely moving current. Shortly the boat work closed for that season.

On April 25 I went to Nekhaila, a town of some 20,000 people. The place had a bad reputation for crime. There had been six murders that year, in four months. No one was punished, for any one who gave evidence would be the next to die. On reaching Cairo I mentioned the report to an officer of the criminal investigation department. He replied: "I should be very much surprised if there have been only six murders in Nekhaila this year." Yet some say that Islamic religion is good enough for Moslems.

God was said to be working powerfully just then in that place and I went to observe and share His power. A Coptic brother had been with us on the boat and I became his guest for two nights.

We went first to the Exclusive meeting, lest they might not welcome me had I been elsewhere first. The room was the ground floor of an ordinary mud-built house. It was low pitched, and lit dimly by an oil lamp or two. We were the first arrivals, and we sat down on the mud floor against the wall. Two peasants joined us and I inquired whether they were believers. As they were not I went on to put Christ before them. Sundry folk began to gather in the dark lane and to peer in, but they did not enter.

Shortly there strode in a tall well-dressed, lordly man, and began a sharp discussion with my friend, who replied with heat. Divining the situation I asked what was the trouble. The reply was:

"He says there will be no meeting if you remain." At the same time the gentleman curtly ordered the attendant to put out the lights. We departed.

Thence we went to the hall of the Canadian Holiness Mission, and were welcomed warmly. They gave me a chair, that I might be spared sitting on the floor, and insisted that I should go to the little platform and address the meeting. It was evident that here the Spirit of God was working. The pastor, an Egyptian, was a true Christian. We could converse, for he knew English thoroughly. The contrast to the former treatment was complete.

Thence we looked in at the Presbyterian church, but the service was cold and formal. The wind of heaven was not breathing.

On the way to the house we encountered the lordly Exclusive. I said to him that by every law of Eastern and Christian courtesy he had treated me badly. I had come as a brother in Christ from a distant land and he had driven me out as a Moslem might drive a pig out of his house.

He replied sharply: "Then why did you not receive me when I called this afternoon?" Then first I learned that he had come; but Samuel, his cousin, knowing him well, feared he had come only to dispute and did not tell me he was there. I saw that I was seemingly in the wrong and could only assure him that had I known he had called I should most gladly have welcomed him. He was mollified but expressed no regret for his conduct.

The next morning I told my friend that now it was my duty to return his call. We went to his shop but he was not there.

The pastor of the "Tongues" meeting called to beg me to speak that evening to his company. We met in a small dark mud room; some twelve or so were present. I sat on a low mud bench (a *mastaba*) beside the wall. The group formed a circle, grasped hands, and commenced to jump up and down, getting more and more excited, repeating ever more rapidly the single word "Hallelujah". At length frenzy seized them, the word shot out with the speed and force of a motor-cycle explosion, and the dancing became furious and rotary. After perhaps an hour of this senseless and exhausting excitement the pastor succeeded in securing stillness that I might address them. I spoke on self-control in things human and things spiritual, and told them frankly that their doings that evening differed nothing from the Moslem *Zikr,* save that they used the word "Hallelujah" instead of "Mohammed" or some expression from the Koran. As soon as I had finished speaking one of the most energetic of the dancers sprang on to the bench, danced around, and shook his fist in my face wildly and often. And this is what many good people wish to call "Pentecostal".

The next morning I went to say farewell to the pastor of the Holiness Mission. While we were enjoying sweet fellowship, there was the sound of feet on the outside staircase, and the lordly Exclusive with two friends entered. Knowing he was in bad odour with all for his treatment of a visitor he would not let me depart without attempting to save his face. He talked much, trying to excuse himself. I contented myself by merely insisting upon the facts. It was a truly Oriental palaver, lasting an hour-and-a-half. But his Exclusive group, or some of them, had long groaned under his tyranny, and some half of the assembly broke away, using this as the occasion, and formed another group on more Scriptural lines as to reception of Christians. Yet commenced in no true spirit, with resentment of heart rather than from spiritual conviction, the new meeting did not prosper, and after some years most of them returned to their former associates, "Diotrephes" having died.

Moving northward to the large town of Minieh I visited my old friend the pastor of the Presbyterian Church. In a restaurant I saw my friend from Luxor. He introduced me to the person with whom he was sitting, a German Exclusive, who had taken up the reins of government of the Exclusive meetings. He courteously asked me to call at his hotel the next morning. I found him in semi-Egyptian dress, smoking a cigar. He said stiffly: "There has been a mistake. I did not know you were connected with Open Brethren, or I should not have asked you to call." "Dear brother," I replied, "I did not come to discuss our differences. Let us sit down and have a little fellowship concerning our Lord Jesus." "No," he answered, "I cannot receive you. It would be misunderstood. But I wish to say that our people are mostly uneducated. I hope you will not go among them and disturb them." "You must permit me to say," I replied, "that it is not we who so act, but yourselves." We were now at the door, and I added: "I would say one thing more: that if ever you are in England, and in Weston-super-Mare, and need fellowship, if you will come to the Gospel Hall, because I shall know you to be a child of God we shall readily receive you. I say this in the hope that you may feel that this bitterness and estrangement are on your side, not on ours." He said very stiffly, "I know those are your principles." He would not shake hands.

I went on to a chemist. As he did not know English and I did not know the Arabic for the article I wanted, a young Copt kindly told him. The young man was interested when I spoke of things spiritual and said, "I was just saying to my friend (another young Copt) that he ought to leave the Coptic Church." I replied that I could heartily endorse that. They were both much astonished when an English traveller brought forth a New Testament, and when shortly I produced a *Safety, Certainty, and Enjoyment* it became quite evident that I was one of the right brand. The first young man said: "You ought to come to our meeting and help us." I said that I should be happy to come; where did he attend? "The Exclusive Brethren," he replied. How singular, I thought, that within a few minutes of being rejected by the leader I should be invited by the follower. "Well," I added, "I shall be ready to come, only I should not like to get you into trouble. Your leader has just refused to shake hands with me because I meet with Christians he does not approve." He turned his nose to the ceiling and said, "He is not all the world!" I went to the hall at night. It was well-built and furnished, the gift of a wealthy Exclusive; and attached were rooms for the use of any travelling preacher, but the leader preferred an hotel. The meeting was an ice-well, as is too often the case in costly, handsome premises in all lands.

The remark of the young man was symptomatic. The Egyptian brethren were tired of foreign domination. The leader died shortly after and a younger man arrived from Germany thinking to take up the reins. But it was made very plain that he was *persona non grata,* and he returned whence he came. It is a lesson needed in very many mission spheres.

On May 4 I reached Cairo and the next day went to Port Said to see my wife's sister, Ada Brealey, on her way from India to England. There followed visits and meetings in Cairo, Bulkeley near Alexandria, Maadi, and Zeitoun.

On June 13, 1927, while walking in the centre of Cairo, a sudden failure of strength occurred. I was on my way to visit a Christian English dentist, Dr. Oswald Campion. As he was a medical man he kindly sounded my heart, gave the opinion that the general nervous energy was feeling the strain of years of labour and the heart was showing this. He advised me to leave the heat of Egypt and go to Palestine, as the nearest cooler region. This advice proved to be very distinctly of God. He added that he had taxed his own heart a week before while swimming and had seen his doctor, but that now he was quite fit again, and so I might expect to be with a little rest. In a few days, however, his servant found him dead in his bed. A young life cut short, while mine has been prolonged.

I wrote to Mrs. Shelley at Jerusalem and was assured of a warm welcome. But I was not immediately equal to the journey; and Miss Mitchell, who was in charge of the King George V Soldiers' Home in the Abbassia camp, kindly asked me to stay there. For a month I lay day and night under the mosquito net on a verandah, sweating at every pore. But each day enough strength was gathered to meet in the evening a group of nine British lads who were standing for Christ among the 3,000 godless men in the camp. This was about the average proportion of Christians in the army at that time. It is not higher since another demoralizing war. Such standard-bearers need the support of our prayers.

I mentioned to these lads that a doctor had told me that army medical statistics showed that in the 1914-1918 war about ninety per cent of British soldiers were immoral. They thought a little and said that that was about the proportion in that camp. At that time a renowned Christian general, Sir William Dobbie, was the G.O.C. in Egypt. His testimony was clean and steadfast. The humble manner in which on Sundays he took his place at the Lord's table among a group of Egyptians and others, including some of his own subordinates, was greatly appreciated by all. But the moral blight upon army life cannot be removed by the example of even such an excellent senior commander. Perhaps there has been one exception: the influence of Cromwell upon his Ironsides.

The nine lads proved eager students of the word. We went through *Ephesians* in detail. Their Christian experience advanced. Two of them were baptized on an early visit to Palestine. Three of them became evangelists after leaving the army. It is a light matter to be ill if one is thereby detained where the Lord has work to be done. "Ye know that because of an infirmity of the flesh I preached the gospel unto you" (Gal. 4:13). I still use a handbag they gave me as a love-gift when I left.

In an interval during the period at Abbassia (June 22-July 9) I stayed at Heliopolis with a son in the faith of 1914. He was then still a bachelor and had a Sudanese man-servant, black as coal. To honour the guest the servant adorned my bed with a fine red rug. Soon after getting into bed I discovered I was not the only occupant. The electric light revealed hundreds upon hundreds of bugs, from great-grandfathers to infants. Keating's powder worked powerfully, but a second onslaught was needful before the battle was won and I alone held the field. They bred in the fine rug while it was unused.

The black man's basement was infected with cockroaches, and at night they raided the whole house. To put Keating's on a cockroach is more hopeless than to put salt on a bird's tail. You see the creature in the middle of the room and then you don't see it. It has reached some hiding place with such incredible speed that the eye does not follow the movement, not once in twenty times. However, though I could not attack them neither did they attack me, so I slept. But it was a habit to have on a chair by the bed a pilule of Hyosyamus, in homoeopathic form, as a sedative when restless. One morning the pilule was gone and a dead cockroach lay on the chair. They devour the bindings of books, and seemed to have a preference for green cloth.

It was during this visit that my host told me the following mysterious incident, which I used in my edition of Pember's book *Earth's Earliest Ages:*

> Egypt is another land where the powers of darkness have been supreme for centuries, and can display their energies with impunity. In 1914 it was mine to lead to faith in Christ a young Copt, named Zaky Abdelmalik, serving in a Government department. On June 24, 1927, when staying with him in Heliopolis, he narrated the following circumstances from the experience of his own father, Abdelmalik Halil.
>
> Some thirty-four years earlier, his father, who was about forty-five years of age, was walking in a street in Ghizeh, near Cairo, and feeling anxious about the boy Zaky, then four years old, who was lying very ill in their village of Brombel, some forty-five miles south of Cairo. A sheikh he did not know spoke to him, and said: "Why are you troubled? Come with me, and I will tell you what is in mind." He led him to a darkened room in a house in a quiet side street, brushed the dust from a space of ground

and muttered some words which the other did not understand. He then told Halil to sit on the space of ground. The time was the middle of the day. There appeared suddenly a tiny man about four inches high. He disappeared and quickly returned with an equally tiny chair, and said: "The King is coming!" Immediately there appeared another such tiny man, but walking with pride and an air of importance. He set himself in the chair, and the former little man at once stood before him, as if he were a soldier-servant, standing to attention and waiting orders from his sovereign.

The King then said peremptorily: "Go to Brombel, to the house of Abdelmalik Halil, and see what each is doing there." The first little man disappeared, and was absent for perhaps three or four minutes. He then reappeared suddenly and told what each person in the house was doing, giving their names, and adding that the son who had been sick was playing. The sheikh then again spoke words which Halil did not understand, whereupon the two small men and the chair were gone.

Abdelmalik Halil gave to the sheikh a dollar and they walked away. Upon reaching the bank of the Nile, which was near, the sheikh formed a piece of paper into a small ship, and floated away on the water and was seen no more.

Halil had noted the hour when the tiny man gave the information about his house, and wrote to ask what they were doing on that day at that time. The information given had been correct.

Zaky had received the narration from his father. I wrote it down at the time, and he signed it as a true account. Ten days later his eldest brother arrived, and I got him to repeat the story as here given. He added that their father had told the man he was anxious to get news of his boy, which led to the incident.

The father was a Christian, and of what quality may be gauged from this following incident. Not very long after the former happening, a Moslem lay in their village paralyzed from his waist downwards. A sheikh from the great El Azhar University of Cairo was brought, who for three hours read over him portions of the Koran, but without effect. Halil then said that he would heal him by the name of Jesus. He prayed in the name and bade him rise, which he at once did, and walked here and there. The man was still alive in 1927, and active. That he had not become a Christian shows that miracles alone will not change the heart or produce saving faith. It is evident that the testimony of such a disciple can be trusted. He would not have deceived his own boys; and the fact that he wrote to his home to inquire of their doings would of itself require explanation on his return.

On August 10 I left Kantara, on the Suez Canal, by the 11.45 p.m. train.
On the train was a priest of the ancient Chaldean Church of Mesopotamia.
Beclouded on many matters, he had nevertheless a simple faith in Christ as
his Redeemer. Having passed Gaza, the dawn gave the first view of the hills of
Judea, a moving sight to the lover of Christ.

Jerusalem was reached at 9.17 on August 11, 1927. From Mr. and Mrs.
Shelley there was the warm welcome which hundreds have received. At that
time they kept seven beds for visitors. The spirit of their hospitality was well
illustrated when, later on, three of us men telegraphed from Haifa that we
would come the next day. Mrs. Shelley showed us to our rooms with the utmost cordiality, and only the arrival of our telegram after ourselves revealed
that our coming was unannounced. At that time the Lord's Supper was observed weekly in their house in its original simplicity, possibly the first such
renewal of the feast in Palestine since the early Christian days.

The house stood on the Hill of Evil Counsel, this forbidding name being
given because tradition has it that there was the house of Annas in which was
hatched the plot to kill Jesus. It commanded full views of the valley of Hinnom and of Zion. This is not a book of travel nor of archeology and I do not
give accounts of visits to interesting sites. It must suffice to offer the opinion
that very many of the "sacred" places are either bogus or at least insufficiently
verified. There are *two* Gardens of Gethsemane, one Roman, the other Greek
Orthodox, each with a large church, attended by monks. The famous Church
of the Holy Sepulchre has, I think, no claim to its title.

On the day of Pentecost the Orthodox Patriarch went early into a small
shrine within that church, waited till fire fell from heaven and then lighted
a lamp. He then passed the fire through a slit in the wall and lit the tapers
of the waiting throng. So fierce was the crush to get to the aperture that the
faithful trod one another under foot and every year some died. I was told that
when the British took over rule they determined to secure order and safety.
Of course the Patriarch could not control heaven and determine the hour at
which the holy flame should fall, and sometimes the packed and restless crowd
must remain all day, with consequently increased tension and commotion. But
the British seemed to have superior influence in heaven, and thenceforth by
their orders the fire fell at one o'clock.

The Via Dolorosa, with its "stations of the cross," was not there in the time
of our Lord. I am very doubtful as to Gordon's Calvary and the Garden. Scripture is silent as to a "green hill", or any hill at "the place of a skull". But some
spots are certain. Hinnom, Zion, the temple area, the valley of the Kidron,
Olivet, Bethlehem, Hebron, are doubtless those so named in the Scriptures.
But the grotto and manger at Bethlehem, and Abraham's tomb at Hebron, are
unverified, as I judge. The house in Jerusalem considered to have been Pilate's

Praetorium, may well be genuine. It is near the temple area. The basement of the house is flagged with great stones in Roman fashion. Upon one of these there is cut a dice board, and it is easy to imagine the soldiers sitting around on the ground gambling. This site was uncovered by a Catholic priest and that Church owns the premises.

These ten weeks in "the city of the great King" were deeply interesting and instructive, but I shall mention only one ramble, as illustrating the goodness of God. An archway in the Moslem quarter led into a courtyard. A stairway led up over the roof of a house, and a further stairway took one over another house built upon the one beneath. At one point there was a well by the side of the stairs allowing light to enter a window of a dwelling beside them. Looking down this opening one saw beneath the window a *tomb*. Following up a third flight I found I had reached the limit of the journey, and was about to retrace my steps when from the door of the top house a lad emerged and was astonished to find an Englishman there. He was Armenian. As he knew some English, I was able in that out-of-the-way spot to tell him something of Christ and to leave him some papers to read. God will watch over His word to make it fruitful.

Going on to the open space not far from the wailing wall, and passing near Robinson's Arch, it occurred to me to climb the staircase to the battlements of the ancient wall on the south of the city and walk around to the Jaffa gate, using the path on the inside of the wall provided for watchers and archers. After a while I was confronted by a huge dog of the wolf-hound type. We eyed each other suspiciously. For a short space he backed away and I advanced. He probably belonged to a camp of Bedawi whose tents were far below in the open space mentioned and who were watching us. But the dog was moving further from the steps which led to his home and shortly he stood at bay looking savage. He was so heavy and powerful that had he rushed and sprung I must almost certainly have been pitched off the three foot path and have fallen some twenty-five or more feet. He stood with his nose near the ground, glaring and alert, but as I studied his eye I saw that it was fixed not on my legs but upon the space between them and the edge of the path, as if he were considering whether he could get by. I backed up to the parapet, leaving the path clear, he shot past like a flash, and we went our ways mutually relieved, I thanking God.

Some way further the path was broken and recalled the exhortation "look therefore carefully how ye walk." On reaching the steps leading down to the city it was to find them barred by a high iron gate which would not open. It was now dusk and would be quickly dark. To go back the whole three-quarters of a mile would have been dangerous. But by the gate the path was confined by a parapet wall on the inside, presumably of a house. Getting on to the outside wall I was able to throw myself up on to this flat roof, and found, as I hoped, a door leading into the house. A loud knock brought quickly a splendidly built native gentleman who naturally was much surprised to find a stranger on his roof. I explained the reason, mentioned Mr. Shelley's name, which I saw acted as a password, and he courteously led me down the outside staircase of the house. As we descended I saw police drilling in the large courtyard below and realized that it was the head police station. To my guide I said pleasantly that it was the first time I had found myself in the hands of the police.

Mr. Shelley's comment on the ramble, especially that over the Moslem houses, was that he saw I meant to get into trouble. His special part of their hospitality was taking guests for outings. I shall mention two. He took Rev. W. W. Martin and myself by motor to Jericho. The route was the ancient and rough road and we bumped over huge stones which no Western motorist would negotiate. We passed the building considered to be the caravanserai where the Good Samaritan took his wounded "neighbour". The wild country on either side of the lonely road made it a suitable place for brigands to leave a wayfarer "half alive", as Wycliffe translated Luke 10:30. Surely this is an apt description of too many believers. There is a vast ravine down which the traveller gazes to sundry holes in the cliff where misguided monks, fleeing from the world, were immured never to leave. They were fed by food passed through a hole daily till they died. That some lost their reason from the horrible silence was but natural.

The name the Dead Sea has a forbidding sound, but it entirely belies the district. Looking from the north end and down the Sea the far-stretching vista is entrancing. The brilliant blue sky, the deep-blue water, the flanking mountains of Judea on the west and Moab on the east, 4,000 feet high, all toned that day in pale blue, made a prospect never to be forgotten. We paddled in the warm water.

Another afternoon we drove over the old road to Emmaus. It was deeply moving to stand looking down on the village and to see in thought the risen Lord walking and talking with the two disciples, they enthralled by His unfolding of the Old Testament, and then to follow them into the house where they saw Him one moment and the next moment saw Him not.

I must mention one other walk, that I took alone. On the east side of Hebron a long and steep path leads to the high plateau that stretches many miles to the Jordan valley. At risk of heart trouble I climbed that path till the undulating uplands came in view. Three thousand and eight hundred years before, the Son of God, in human guise, had walked across that plateau and talked with Abraham His friend (Gen. 18), which condescension emboldened Abraham to plead for the life of Lot, the real though unexpressed object of his intercession.

Such are the scenes which fill the believing heart with indefinable emotions and leave indelible impressions.

Haifa. On Wednesday, September 7, 1927, I went to Haifa. J. W. Clapham, of New Zealand, had been used by the Lord to commence an assembly on New Testament principles, the first such assembly in the Holy Land, as I suppose, since the first Christian church had been removed when Hadrian conquered the Jews in A.D. 135. The little group had spread the Lord's table the Sunday before I arrived. Mr. Clapham gave me a very warm welcome. My way had been prepared of the Lord by his having read my book, *Departure*, on gospel work and church life, with which he was in substantial agreement. We had much hearty fellowship, working together at intervals for between five and six months altogether. The Spirit worked very blessedly in saving sinners and building up the infant church.

Shemlan. On October 11, 1927, I travelled by car to Beirut. My companion was a commercial traveller, a Spanish Jew. He did not know that the region we were covering was part of the land promised by God to his people. He was very willing to give time that we might wander round the ancient town of Tyre. Shemlan is a village above Beirut, 3,000 feet up on the Lebanon mountains. An English brother I had led to Christ in Cairo in 1914 was there, with his wife, helping Miss Frearson in her Armenian orphanage. This was the English lady whom a Turkish-speaking man complimented by the remark in English that "Miss Frearson talks Turkish like a Turkey." She was a most devoted woman, who gave a long life to serving the Lord among Armenians, first in Armenia and later at Shemlan.

Climbing a steep path from a meeting my heart suffered. Miss Frearson lovingly insisted that I should stay on and rest, which I did until November 28. This gave me opportunities for opening the Word to her staff, some of whom knew English, as well as to the orphans and old people by interpretation. My interpreter was a very able and promising young Armenian school teacher. He made in English the finest summaries of addresses that I have ever seen.

One night there was a truly magnificent thunderstorm over the Mediterranean. Viewed from the mountains it was an awe-inspiring display of the majesty of the Creator, such a display as David describes in Ps. 29: "The voice of Jehovah is upon the waters: the God of glory thundereth. . . . The voice of Jehovah breaketh the cedars; yea, Jehovah breaketh the cedars of Lebanon." Alas, today there are very few cedars, but the voice of Jehovah is as grand as ever.

Aleppo. On November 28, 1927, I left for Baalbek and Aleppo, the visit described in *Anthony Norris Groves*. Aleppo lies high and in winter is cold. Influenza compelled me to return south on December 8. The Syrian car driver was reckless and the journey dangerous. But it gave opportunity for the care of God. As night fell we were by the shore under Mount Nebo, and the petrol ran out while we were twenty miles from the nearest town. A night by the sea in December would have been dangerous from cold and robbers. I lifted my heart to God. Cars on the road were now infrequent but the third sold a tin of petrol. As we neared Tripoli about 8 o'clock p.m. the French police post had to be passed, and the car lights were not working. The driver literally stroked the cheek of the officer and cajoled him into letting us pass. I was amused to imagine what would happen if a driver tried to stroke the cheek of a London constable; but it defies imagination.

We reached Beirut the next afternoon (December 9, 1927), and in the principal square we knocked a man over. The man was at fault. The near wing caught his heel and twisted him round. It was sickening to hear the crash of the back of his head on the pavement. Instead of stopping, the driver dashed into the traffic at the head of the square and twisted and doubled around several corners, but he had scarcely pulled up in a side street before a French police car stopped beside us. The officer took him away, leaving me and my bags in the car.

Where I now was in the city I had no idea; it was unlikely that any in the crowd that gathered would know English; I had to find another car to go up the mountains to Shemlan, and night was at hand. Again I lifted my heart to God for another proof that He is a "present help in trouble," and it at once occurred to me to utilize the situation by distributing gospel portions in the various languages of the people that chattered around me. After a few moments a Syrian gentleman, in European clothes, spoke to me in good English. Lifting up the tract he said: "I am glad to see these being distributed, because I am myself a preacher." Thus the Lord's angel of deliverance was at hand. He had come from his place far up the mountains, and was just about to start on his return when the incident occurred and curiosity led him to inquire. Two minutes later and he would have been gone. He kindly took me in hand, found a car going my way, and saw me off.

After ten days' happy fellowship at Shemlan I returned to Haifa on December 21, and continued there until April 19, 1928, with the exception of short visits to Tel Aviv and Jaffa, and three days in Galilee (April 5, 6, 7).

My companions in Galilee were Clapham, Rolls, and Woods, all of New Zealand. The route was across the plain of Esdraelon, then being rendered fertile by stern Jewish toil; up the mountain to Nazareth, back to Jezreel and the fountain of Harod, where Gideon's army camped (Josh. 7:1); and down the valley to Bethshan, where the bodies of Saul and Jonathan were nailed by the Philistines to the city walls. Excavations were then in progress. Thence we turned north up the Jordan valley to Tiberias.

The next day we skirted the lake northwards to Capernaum and visited the fine ruins of the synagogue of our Lord's time. It was a handsome building, and there is little doubt that it was the synagogue built by the centurion (Luke 7:4, 5), for on the lintel over the entrance the Roman eagles were carved. It must have been some irresistible influence that caused religious Jews to consent to the emblem of the hated heathen tyrants being on their synagogue. It was presumably in this synagogue that Christ taught that He Himself was the bread of life come down from heaven (John 6).

A solemn reflection presses upon the heart in that region. Around the lake there stood formerly several cities: Capernaum, Chorazin, Bethsaida, and Tiberias. Because of their unbelief and ingratitude, the Lord was obliged to denounce heavy judgment upon the first three of these (Matt. 11:20-24), and they are gone completely. The only ruin of any of them is the synagogue mentioned. But Tiberias was not condemned, nor is it said that Christ ever visited it; and Tiberias is there today, including some of the towers of His time. Truly His words never fail.

That evening at Tiberias we heard a lecture by the learned scholar, Dr. W. M. Christie, upon the geography of Palestine. He said that when he left his Scotch and Continental universities he went to Palestine a higher critic of the Bible, but that forty years in the land had completely changed his views. The Book was clearly written by men who knew the land intimately. If they said you go *up* to a certain place, or *down* to another place, you go *up* or *down* to those places; and there is not a geographical slip in the whole Bible. In this it carries its own testimony of accuracy and trustworthiness.

On Saturday we visited the caves at Hattin where Herod destroyed the robbers, as mentioned by Josephus. We were there at the exact time to enjoy the wondrous floral beauty of Gennesaret. For just those few weeks after the latter rains the whole land is thickly carpeted with lovely ground flowers of great beauty and variety.

As we climbed the slopes a group of Bedawi camel drivers were at the foot of the valley. They called and beckoned and we went down to them. A rough, cut-throat set they looked. They were baking their morning bread. In a pot was a sorry fluid of flour and water. Whence the water had come it would have been a pity to know. "Where ignorance is bliss, 'Twere folly to be wise." A thin, flat stone had been set on short upright stones. Brushwood kept burning under this had made it intensely hot. The thick fluid poured on to this hot plate was at once baked into a thin unleavened bread. Thus it was safe to eat it. The men gave us each a portion, which we ate. They ate of our sandwiches, a great novelty. We parted friends, having eaten of each other's bread, and we knew that for the rest of the day they would protect rather than injure us. Even to these hard sons of the desert it were the last step in iniquity to lift up the heel against him whose bread one had eaten (John 13:18).

Continuing northward we went as far as the waters of Merom. Returning via Safed and over the mountains of Naphtali we were glad to encounter a native, Moslem, wedding processsion, such as few travellers witness.

From April 19 to June 1, six weeks were spent in Jerusalem, visiting and speaking at various meetings. I am not sure whether it was on this visit or the former that, on the slope leading up from Hinnom to David's tower, I spoke to a Jewish lad. I meant to be friendly, but at being suddenly accosted by an Englishman, the poor boy's eyes dilated with a terror far beyond any natural fear of a stranger, and he fled fast down the path. Thus after more than 3,000 years was there still fulfilment of the words of Moses: "thou shalt fear night and day and shall have none assurance of thy life" (Deut. 28:66). Perhaps now, with Israel dominant in the land, this is changed.

A rich American gave money for building the palatial Y.M.C.A. premises just completed while I was in Jerusalem. On the voyage to share in the opening celebrations the donor died. The large notice board was covered with announcements of the very many meetings and events arranged to entertain young men and others, such as concerts, lectures, amusements, etc. By careful scrutiny I discovered a quite small card mentioning a Bible class. This was the one and only item of a spiritual character.

On motor journeys between Haifa and Jerusalem I sat twice by Jacob's well, and drank of its cold and clear water. The digging of this well was a notable work. It is perhaps 80 to 100 feet deep, correspondingly wide, and it is lined with stones. It is no wonder that sixteen centuries later people still spoke gratefully of "our father Jacob who gave us the well" (John 4:12). Yet it is still true that "everyone that drinketh of this water shall thirst again". The thermometer in Jerusalem, 2,300 feet above sea level, had stood at 102⁰ in the shade, and it was hotter at Sychar. But still more blessedly true are Christ's words: "whosoever drinketh of the water that I shall give him shall never thirst" (vv. 13,14).

Leaving Haifa on June 19, 1928, I spent one night at Hasbeya in the Lebanon, not far from Hermon, visiting Shuweifat and Shemian, and on the 22nd again reached Aleppo. Leaving by train at 7 p.m. the 25th, we passed within sight of Tarsus, reached Adana at 6 a.m. and climbed the steep track to the high tableland of Asia Minor. A Turkish officer, his two womenfolk, and a child, not to say their baggage, were my companions. The younger woman suffered badly from sickness, which was distressing for us all. But how easy was my journey, as compared with the toilsome ascent of that long and dangerous pass by Paul and his companions.

It was of interest to go over the high Galatian tableland where Paul laboured and suffered and the gospel wrought its earliest marvels beyond Syria. It was deeply affecting to stand awhile in Konya (Iconium, Acts 14:1-6).

Istanbul, Adrianople, Sofia, Belgrade were passed, and I was at Budapest on June 30. After a week there, Bad Homburg in Germany was gained on July 7 and London on the 10th, My wife and daughter joined me at the beloved Broadbents', Gislingham, Suffolk, until August 12. Ministry, in various parts of the south of England followed, and home was reached on September 12, 1928.

Thus was completed a journey of one year and nearly eight months which had been full of the loving-kindness of the Lord.

He gives the very best to those
Who leave the choice to Him—

which choice included for me ten months in the Holy Land, with ten weeks of this in the city of the great King. To be led about in triumph in Christ (2 Cor. 2:14) is in every way so very much better than to form and follow a self-devised programme.

CHAPTER 14

Walsham-le-Willows

1929-1945

Two and a half months were spent chiefly at home. Our small flat at Weston-super-Mare was pleasantly situated on the side of the hill under the woods and gave wide views of town, sea, and hills beyond. But the hill up to the house was steep and heart weakness forbade the climb. I had to go at least half a mile around to get easier gradients. And my head too was weary. It was evident I must move to level ground, but it was hard to know a suitable place.

On December 4, 1928, we went to Clayhidon, Devon, for the farewell of my wife's sister, returning to India. On the 7th I went on to Exeter to meet a worker from Africa. Having the afternoon of Tuesday, 11, free it came into my heart to spend it with my friend the late Arnold Robathan at Teignmouth. He mentioned his thought to return to Birmingham, which led me to remark that I also was looking for another home. He said: "I wish you would take a house I have to let." Instantly the Voice said in my heart: "Take note of what he will say: this is for you," and I knew that the needed leading had come.

He told me of the Elizabethan farmhouse where he had lived, near the village of Walsham-le-Willows, Suffolk, ten miles east of Bury St. Edmunds and four miles from the Broadbents at Gislingham. His son with his wife lived in one end of the house, but the larger part was empty. He said he could have let it lately to a clergyman, but must have spent £150 on repairs and alterations, which he did not wish to spend; and he added that he had said to his son that if they could find a tenant who would do his own repairs they would let it at £15 a year rent.

I knew I should take it, but deferred a decision till I should have seen it a few weeks later and be able to give account of the place to my wife and daughter. The rooms were of a good size, the views of meadows and cornfields pleasant, the country level, the air bracing. It would be the old-world country life. No water laid on, but a well next door. No gas or electricity, but oil lamps. But I saw the old house could be made a comfortable home, with the large garden, shrubbery, orchard, and vinery to add to the charm. It was a plain building, free from any grandeur, yet a sweet place to entertain the Lord's people needing rest. As to the repairs and the wild grounds, both had been neglected for years; but I had started life in the building trade and also had some knowledge of gardening, so that, by the help of God, this work I could do myself. In the issue it cost only some £20.

It is strengthening to faith to trace God at work in small items. When He has taken a matter in hand He provides for every detail. My dear friends the Mays of Bristol offered to send with me their eldest son, Geoffrey, to help with the repairs. We went in advance of the removal. He was handy with tools and was invaluable. Then again, in January (1929) I had occasion to visit my beloved friend Mr. Finnie at Olton, near Birmingham. He was the Birmingham agent of a large firm of manufacturers and dealers in metal goods. Hearing of my project he showed me drawers upon drawers of all varieties of screws, nails, door and window fastenings, and other metal oddments. They were old samples not further needed, and he sent a large case, including sundry tools, without charge, worth to me many pounds. And he supplied garden tools at wholesale rates.

And yet again, as soon as there were leisure and weather to deal with the garden, we were asked to entertain a Swiss youth, who wished to learn English. He was a son of a farmer, well trained in all out-of-door work, and helped greatly. The hedge by the road was very long, very high, and dreadfully overgrown. There came to stay with us a Christian from New Zealand, a stranger. In earlier years he had been a woodman, and was the very man for this job.

We moved in on March 30, 1929, and for sixteen years, until 1945, occupied "The Woodlands" at a cost of 10s. per week for rent and rates. Yes, in matters domestic, as in travel,

> He gives the very best to those
> Who leave the choice to Him.

It was our joy to welcome there, in the Lord's name and at His expense, over 600 guests, some 250 of these during the 1939-1945 war. Persons of small knowledge of God wondered how this could be done in war-time and with food-rationing; but such did not know the power of that promise, "Give and it shall be given unto you" (Luke 6:38).

From experience during the period of my return from Palestine in 1928 and onward I may be permitted to speak to my tired-out brethren in the ministry of the gospel. I was then fifty-four, and after some thirty-seven years of strenuous and unremitting effort in the work of the Lord, I was so exhausted in brain and heart that it seemed out of the question that I should ever again travel afar or do much preaching. Had I in that condition forced myself to keep on at public work, as many do, I must certainly have broken down completely and probably have died prematurely, as some fellow-workers dear to me have done. But my kind and thoughtful Master provided salvation by giving the house and gardens to be put in order, for Him to use to the comfort of His people. I did not refuse this withdrawal from "spiritual" work to "secular" occupation, but regarded it as His will and a means to the end desired. For two years I left my books on their shelves and gave rest to the brain. Both head and heart recovered tone, with the happy result of twenty further years of active labour in different countries.

Perhaps I shall put the finger upon the weak spot in some of my brethren if I point out that this withdrawal from constant public service demanded a working faith in God as to the supply of money for daily expenses. In this respect there were, of course, trials of faith sometimes long and severe; but, equally of course, God proved His faithfulness. He that abounds unto every good work shall find that God will make all grace abound unto this end; and he who scatters abroad shall find that he is enriched in everything unto all liberality (2 Cor. 9:8-11). The trials are essential, not incidental, and of incalculable benefit to the soul.

As the days went by some souls were saved at "The Woodlands", some of these in the garden. As mentioned above, one beloved friend from eastern Europe, who had departed from the Lord, returned to Him in our sitting-room, an untold joy to my heart, for we had had much fellowship in his land.

There was in the village an assembly formerly well attended, but some sixteen or eighteen in number when we arrived. These had clung together around a small farmer, a brother of little gift but rich in grace. Apart from the breaking of bread and occasionally preaching on Sunday evening, the one meeting I allowed myself was the prayer meeting. This was attended by the farmer and a Christian tradesman who had been baptized and came regularly to the gospel service also, but took no part in church life and never opened his mouth at the prayer meeting. I joined these two and we prayed on for some few years, not yielding to the common temptation to plan and arrange some effort of our own to "stir things up".

Then God Himself began to work. There called on us an evangelist from Scotland, William Steedman. He was working in Suffolk with his tent, and came without invitation, nor had I heard of him. His broad Lowland accent sounded unpromising, but I thought him sent of God, and, with the fellowship of the assembly, he brought his tent to the village for a fortnight. There was not much stir, but after the last meeting, and outside the tent, I had the joy of hearing a confession of Christ from a dear girl whose family were with us at the hall.

This was the commencement. Without further special efforts, quietly and steadily young people were converted. Two sisters of the girl mentioned had been converted previously, now two brothers and a sister of another family, three brothers in a third family, a grandson of beloved friends who were with the meeting when we went but who had died, and a workmate of his, one of the naughtiest lads in the village—these and others were saved and baptized. Thus in a comparatively short time, in place of a handful of adults, the assembly was largely composed of young believers. These were given nothing but the regular meetings of the church, and they needed nothing more. They came steadily to the weekly gathering for prayer and Bible study, now attended by eighteen or twenty instead of but three. They grew in grace, presently took over the Sunday school, and, after some fifteen and more years, I believe all of them are going on with the Lord, and others have been added.

As I was now often away the work ran no risk of depending upon me, and still, several years after we left the district, the Spirit of the Lord has worked yet more effectively and the assembly has grown, though the farmer mentioned has departed this life.

For a few winters I gathered in my study on Thursday evenings three or four of the young men, to study the Word. They brought out their problems, gained confidence to hear their own voices in prayer, and presently began to take part in the Bible and prayer gathering and at the Lord's table. In due time these and another older brother began to preach, and in that small country assembly there were five preachers, in addition to myself.

This substantial and enduring growth went on without "campaigns", "rallies", "classes", or "societies", without clubs, tennis, or other human schemes. In a movement born in prayer and initiated by God, the Spirit was free to work after His own manner, and built up souls. They were nourished upon the "healthful words of our Lord Jesus" (1 Tim. 6:3), and neither needed nor desired other food or other occupation or recreations than worship and witness in the Spirit.

For God is waiting to do His own blessed work in His own simple way, yet we turn to ways of our own which hinder Him. When Evan Roberts was asked the secret of the Welsh revival of 1904, he replied, "There is no secret. It is only, Ask and ye shall receive." On the other hand, very many churches, though they abjure worldly ways, are dead because they have no zeal in that type of "asking" which prevails with God and man and defeats the Devil.

During the war we were in a danger area. All around were vast airfields. By day and by night bombers, German, American, British, passed in streams over the house. The airfields were attacked frequently: American bombers often crashed around. The defence guns of East London kept our windows shivering, though forty miles away. But the village was not damaged. One night a German blew up a Stirling bomber, which exploded like a terrific thunderclap. The Stirling drifted ablaze over us and landed in its own airfield. Had it burst a couple of miles further off it could have landed in our village. The vicar proposed a thank-offering to God for His mercy, which met with a better response than might have been expected from a community in which not more than one in eight or ten ever attended public worship. The money was sent to a philanthropic agency.

As our village was near the east coast the authorities were naturally watchful against possible secret contacts with the national enemy. George Fenn, evangelist, worked with a tent in Norfolk and lived in a caravan. The local police inspector fulfilled his instructions by searching the caravan lest there should be a wireless transmitter. Taking up my friend's black Bible wallet he asked what it contained, and was told that it held a sword! It was only natural that I should be similarly considered, seeing the considerable number of guests from Europe that had visited us steadily over several years. After the war had closed I learned that an army officer of rank had inquired about me. In the good providence of God he approached a leading resident who had always been friendly and who kindly disarmed his mind, so that no difficulties followed. "The hand of our God is upon all them that seek him, for good" (Ezra 8:22).

> *How blessed are they who still abide*
> *Close sheltered by Thy watchful side;*
> *Who life and strength from Thee receive,*
> *And with Thee move and in Thee live.*

Chapter 15

England, Europe, Egypt, Palestine
1932-1950

The last chapter is a summary of sixteen years, of which period the more part was used in frequent visits and ministry in England, Scotland, and Wales. This need not be detailed, though the many journeys proved convincingly the feasibility of moving from place to place by present leading, without long prearrangement. It is a fallacy that New Testament methods are not suitable to modern life, nor apostolic ways to western lands. They are entirely suitable, and eminently superior.

But faith is indispensable, and today it has declined lamentably in two directions.

First, Christian churches cannot trust the Head of the church to raise up spiritual ministry in their own midst or Himself to send it to them when needful and best; and so they follow the world and arrange for themselves. This suits especially leaders who love power, for they soon quietly exclude heart-searching ministry such as awakens and humbles and which they do not relish.

In one large centre over a good period I gave such teaching. A younger brother said to me: "We never get such ministry here, and I am sorry to say our leading brethren are not entitled to give it." Some while after Handley Bird wrote from there: "I meet many here who thank God for your ministry but the chief priests were offended." The plea they made was that my views of prophecy were wrong, though these I had not pressed among them. The judgment of the Lord may be that the plea was insincere, the real ground having been that they disliked ministry that searched the conscience.

Such brethren seem to think that the house of God can be run by the spirit and methods of their houses of commerce. But it is merely the shell of the house that can be so maintained: the family spirit of the heavenly household succumbs to the spirit of the world, and that word is fulfilled, "thou hast a name that thou livest, and thou art dead" (Rev. 3:1).

The second phase of the lack of faith is that preachers fear to face trials through lack of funds if they are not well booked up. But Paul knew how to be abased and hungry as well as how to be filled and abound (Phil. 4:11-13). When he says "I have *learned the secret*" he uses a single word *memuēmai,* found here only in the New Testament. It means "I have been *initiated*" and refers to the process, often long and strict, by which applicants were keenly tested before admission to a secret society. Its root *muo* means to *shut the mouth*. The applicant was tested to prove that he could be trusted not to betray secrets. Paul had gone through a long and severe discipline of trial, of various kinds and degrees, and had learned not to open his mouth, either in complaint against God or in appeals to his brethren for help.

The novice in this particular class of the school of faith is shocked when churches or individual Christians fail to minister to his needs. And it is sadly true that both may be forgetful or stingy, a severe reproach to them. But the servant who aspires to the highest intimacy with his Lord, perseveres in this painful process of initiation into the poverty of Christ, into true dependence upon the Father of mercies.

The spiritual novice feels it needful to have his name appear on a list of workers and his letters in a magazine; or he sends around circular letters, in which he asks for prayer but is careful to mention his wife and family, some even giving particulars of a newborn babe, the date of its birth and its weight when born. Such items may be in order in private letters to intimate friends, but in general letters they create the impression of an ulterior motive. It is the same with some books narrating travels or service, especially when written by younger men or women.

Even in the last century Spurgeon mourned the frequent lack in preachers of a lowly mind that walked before God only, and said that there were too many who could not kill a mouse without announcing it in the *Gospel Magazine*, whereas Samson killed a lion and said nothing about it.

But the initiate has the stopped mouth and the weaned heart. With the ancient and much-exercised psalmist he says to himself when tried:

> *My soul, wait thou in silence for God only;*
> *For my expectation is from Him. . .*
> *He only is my rock and my salvation.*
> *(Ps. 62:5, 6)*

And if saints of old could advance to such undivided reliance upon God, knowing Him only as *El* and *Adonai,* how much more may the Father now look for a yet fuller trust from His children in Christ, and be rightly pained when it is withheld? The Lord did not ask that Peter might escape the Devil's sieve, but that his faith might not fail under the tossing (Luke 22:31-34). Paul was deeply thankful when the faith of his converts was growing exceedingly (2 Thes. 1:3). Striking are the words of Belcher, quoted by Upham (*The Hidden Life*, 97): "I find that, while faith is steady, nothing can disquiet me; and when faith totters, nothing can establish me." Faith is born, nourished, and protected by the promises of God (Rom. 4: 19-21). They are its proper food, upon which it thrives, without which it dies. Nor will faith flourish if that food be mixed with husks that swine do eat.

After three and a half years the goodness of God had rebuked my fear that long-distance travel was no more to be possible. I found myself guided to the Continent and equal to the demand. On November 8, 1932, I left for Germany, and went to Wiedenest and Berlin. On November 17 I visited the celebrated scholar Dr. Adolf Deissmann. His learning was prodigious. Among other topics we discussed the phrase "in Christ Jesus". At parting I said, "Doctor, it is a blessed thing, is it not, to be in Christ Jesus?" The ony response was a curt "Yes".

November 22 to 27 I was at Chemnitz, Saxony, the Manchester of Germany, to visit a young man who had spent a summer vacation at our home. On the 28th I went to Leipzig, specially to visit W. J. Martin, now of Liverpool University, then studying for the Doctorate in Semitic languages. Visits to Hof and Triebes took me through the pine forests of Thuringia to Bad Homburg, the beautiful inland watering place where kings used to meet to take the waters and discuss high politics. The Kaiser had there a palace and a finely decorated Lutheran church. I went through these, but my concern was with the true church of God in the town.

December 5 to 11 were passed at the once royal city of Stuttgart, where lived one I had known and helped as a Christian girl at Haifa. The weekend I was lovingly welcomed by an elderly lady, widow of a former general of high social rank. She and her daughters lived in a third floor flat, with the relics of former grandeur in the shape of fine and large furniture and family portraits. Thus fades worldly glory; but the old-world courtesy and Christian hospitality had well survived the decay of fortune. Grace *reigns* (Rom. 5:21).

December 12, 1932 to January 3, 1933, were passed in Switzerland, at Basle, Neuchâtel, Berne, Baden, Zürich, and Küssnacht, of which last lovely spot more will be said later. For two weeks the land was swathed in thick mist and neither lake nor mountain was visible. I said to friends that it was a good illustration of faith, for it was a matter of faith that there were lakes and mountains in their country. But on December 26, I went to the Bernnese Oberland to visit Hans Lehmann, the young man who had helped in our garden. There, thousands of feet up, the sun shone so gloriously at Christmas time, that one sat outside with comfort, on snow-carpeted ground, enjoying the far-stretching views of vast snow mountains sparkling in the sunlight. It was a natural parallel to the elevated spiritual experience

There, there on eagle wings we soar,
And time and sense seem all no more;

And heaven comes down our souls to greet,
And glory crowns the mercy seat.

After brief visits to Lausanne, Geneva, Monnetier-Mornex in Upper Savoy, France, I visited Paris on January 5, 1933, and till the 17th enjoyed the society and fellowship of my beloved friends Commander E. A. Salwey and his wife and daughter. When he saw me off to London he lovingly bought the ticket, not knowing that I had not the money to take it.

There followed another spell of journeys all over England, lasting till June 22, 1934. I think it was in this period that a rather unusual incident occurred at the annual gatherings at Teignmouth, probably on September 1, 1933. During the morning session Commander Salwey referred to me by name very affectionately. That does not often happen at a public conference, but in the afternoon another good brother repeated it. He was urging that the "wicked" servant, who had not used the money his lord had intrusted to him (Luke 19:22), must represent an unbeliever, for, said he, Christ could not possibly apply the word "wicked" to one of His own blood-bought people. As he closed his remarks he looked down at me and said: "And dear brother Lang, if you were to tell me anything different I wouldn't believe you." I had only just time to glance at my Greek Testament and then said: "I earnestly hope that neither our dear brother, nor anyone else, will ever believe anything merely because I say it. Let us have the word of God for what we believe. But as to this word 'wicked', on an earlier occasion (Matt. 18:32) our Lord had applied it to a servant whose debt had been all forgiven but who would not forgive a fellow-servant, which shows that one whose sins as a servant had been freely forgiven may be 'wicked'."

My dear friend W. G. Walters, of Balham, had printed in German large numbers of R. Laidlaw's booklet *The Reason Why* and they had been distributed on the Continent. He used to send to me letters in German to be translated. One such arrived towards the end of May 1934. It was from a lady in west Poland. She told of having distributed the booklet, among other literature; of the readiness to receive these; and ended by asking Mr. Walters to send some one to teach them more of the truth of God in Holy Scripture. As I read this at the breakfast table the Voice said in my heart: "You will be the one to fulfil this desire." I gave the gist of the letter to my wife and daughter and said that I should be the one to go.

Preparations were in progress to leave at the end of June, when on the 21st a telegram came from my former host at Küssnacht, on the Lake of Zürich, Switzerland, saying that his wife (who was English) had died, and asking me to give an address in English at her funeral on the 23rd. Could I have had even one more day, preparations for the other journey could have been completed and I could have gone direct from Switzerland to the north, but this was not possible and I was obliged to return to England first.

For this hurried trip my kind friend R. C. Thomson, then of the Foreign Office, gave efficient help, as he has done to very many of the Lord's servants. I sent him my passport, he obtained necessary *visas,* met me at Liverpool Street station the next day, took me to the proper offices for tickets, and saw me off at Victoria station in the afternoon. Without this brotherly and expert aid the journey would not have been possible in the limited time. I stayed with my bereaved friend till Tuesday, 26, and returned home. Distinctly more arose from this visit, as will be related presently.

My first objective in the north was to visit my friends the Sauers, of Wiedenest, who were resting on the coast of Denmark. The spot was remote, a good distance by rail from Esbjerg, the port, and some miles from the nearest station. These miles had to be covered on foot. There came a gracious provision of God. The road was lonely, through uninhabited sand hills. But a lorryman pulled up and kindly asked if he could take me with him. We could not converse, but I showed him the address, and he put me down not far from the bungalow. Apart from this saving of time I would have been just too late and should have been left in the dunes in perplexity: for the Sauers were leaving sooner than I knew, had already packed, and we departed immediately.

There followed some days of meetings at Haderslev, Denmark. Leaving at 3 a.m. on Thursday, July 5, I crossed Berlin that morning. During the night there had taken place the dread bloodbath, when more than a hundred men of position, who were plotting to overthrow Hitler, were murdered by his orders. Outwardly the city was quiet. That evening at 9.30 p.m. I reached my destination.

This was the first town bombed by the Germans in the 1939 war. It was then a fine city. The lady was keeping house for her widowed father, a lecturer in engineering; she was a converted and keen Protestant, he a Roman Catholic. But he entertained me courteously for six weeks, during which we had serious talks upon salvation. The daughter was a very capable woman who made great efforts to induce people to foregather. Every night except Saturdays she brought together a very varied company—spiritists, Catholics, Lutherans, theosophists, Reformed Seventh Day Adventists, atheists, etc., and interpreted my poor German into Polish.

The leader of the Reformed Adventists was a doctor. He corresponded in thirteen languages and edited a magazine in Polish, German, French, and English. He spoke the last language fluently. This body had broken from the main Adventists, and were to be found in various lands. They had renounced the fundamental errors of the older body. The magazine had an article on the Holy Spirit entirely Scriptural and very able. They still adhered to the observance of the seventh day of the week as the day of rest, to tithing their incomes, and to an ordinance of feet washing, but were very clear and firm that these observances were only for true believers on Christ and played no part whatever in salvation. With this dear man of God I had real heart fellowship, and have often wondered how he and his fared in the war.

The remainder of 1934 was spent in deeply interesting labours in Poland, Roumania, and Bulgaria.

By the end of the year I felt sure I was to go into Palestine. Financial conditions in the Balkans were difficult. The traveller was allowed to take out of Roumania only some 15s.: with this he was sent over the frontier into Bulgaria. No more money could be taken out of Bulgaria than the sum brought in. It was necessary therefore to buy in the land tickets for the next stage of the journey, and I had nothing towards this. The friends I was with were poor, but God arranged and provided. When leaving my bereaved brother in Switzerland on June 26 he had lovingly given me a cheque for £15 to meet the cost of going to him. But I was doubtful whether at that time of expense he could easily give this sum, and asked him to allow me the privilege of attending his wife's funeral at my own charges. He assented, but reluctantly. Now, six months later, as I was purposing this further long journey, of which he knew nothing, on January 2, 1935, I received a letter in which he said that he had never felt happy about that £15 and therefore sent it for my use. This met the need.

Sunday, January 13, 1935, was passed with a group of eighteen believers in southern Bulgaria who were being bitterly persecuted by the police officer of the village, at the instigation of the priest of the Orthodox Church. Their leader said that their neighbours were inquiring why the sergeant was treating thus such good-living, pious people, which gave them excellent opportunities of explaining the truths they held, "and this", said he, "is all we care about". Thus does the Spirit of truth fire believers today with the same courageous spirit as in the first days, of which we read that persecuted and scattered Christians "went about preaching the word" (Acts 8:4).

That night I crossed into Turkey. On the train I gave to a few persons some Scripture portions. The passport officers had seen my papers, but presently they returned and asked if I would give copies to them, which I did, being unaware that Turkish law did not allow distribution of literature without licence. Were a British official to find a foreigner breaking a regulation he would politely inform and warn him. Not so in Turkey. These officials collected what papers they could and took them straight to the secret police in Istanbul, who at once sent a detective to fetch me. But God had provided a British friend who knew intimately both Turkish and Turks, and, after a warm and long discussion, during which I stood by praying, the officer reluctantly agreed to take no action.

Leaving Istanbul on January 15, 1935, it was deeply interesting to sail down the Dardanelles and over waters that Paul often crossed. The next day gave opportunity for a few hours in Athens, visiting the Acropolis and Mars Hill. In Paul's day a heathen temple stood on Mars Hill, and thither Paul went with the philosophers and expounded truth as it is in Jesus (Acts 17:22-31). Ponder this: the apostle preaching in a heathen temple! Yet there are sincere but narrow-hearted brethren who complain if a preacher ministers in a Christian church, chapel, or hall outside of their own particular circle of buildings.

The next day we passed Rhodes and Cyprus and on the 19th reached Haifa. It was a joy after seven years to be again with saints there and to mark growth and extension. But by the middle of February the latter rains had set in and the climate was damp and cold. The past six months I had been moving ever southward and had enjoyed unbroken sunshine. The change felt severe, and, as I had been ill twice on late journeys, I decided to go to Egypt, where I wished to renew contacts, and where the weather would not mean risk of influenza.

I went by rail on February 14, 1935. At Lydd the train was flooded with Moslem pilgrims going to Mecca. I was in the third class, sitting next to the window on a two-seater bench. A mountain of human flesh, wearing clothes in proportion, sat herself on the narrow space beside me. I was squeezed against the wall and wholly eclipsed, though five feet nine inches in height. It being impossible to travel thus all the afternoon and all night I emerged from beneath the mountain and sought the second class, the third being flooded with pilgrims. Lo, this also worked together for good, for I travelled in comfort and was not charged extra. No doubt the Amazon felt pleased at my departure.

As I neared Cairo the next day I remembered that one of my spiritual sons, because he was a Christian, had been banished by his Moslem superiors to Aswan, the southernmost town in Upper Egypt. Though it would be a 500 mile journey I felt I must go and see as to his spiritual state. Two years before he had married an American missionary, and after this long interval she had at last written to introduce herself to me. Her letter had been to England and had come back to Cairo the very morning I arrived! She expressed their hope that, if ever the Lord should send me again to Egypt, I would be their guest, and she put in enough money for the journey. Truly, I thought, one need not belong to the Oxford Groups to get guidance.

After various visits I reached Aswan on February 26. My host had scarcely met me when he asked if I remembered George Effendi. I replied that I did; he was Cook's interpreter in Luxor in 1927. He said they had moved him to Aswan, that he was overjoyed when he heard I was coming and begged me to give them all the help I could at the Exclusive meeting, held in his house. I broke bread with them for six Sundays. Thus happily had the grace shown at Luxor worked gracious fruit in his heart. And the Lord had wrought further to grant me acceptance. In 1914 a young Egyptian, already converted, had been greatly blessed by my English meetings in the tent in Cairo. He was now a leading evangelist among the Exclusive Brethren, and was truly delighted that we met again. During the days of this visit he interpreted for me into Arabic. Thus I was doubly endorsed.

The German Lutheran pastor was a godly man and welcomed ministry, nor was he stumbled when he learned that I was by no means Lutheran, nor a "pastor". The native Presbyterian minister also begged that his flock might be given food. So in that remote town God opened three spheres for service.

The winter climate of Aswan is delightful and the colourings of land, river, and sky are very lovely, so that it has been one of the most desirable of tourist centres and therefore most expensive. I, who have often left my own house for the gospel's sake, have indeed had a hundred, yes, hundreds of houses opened to me (Mark 10:29). The Lord grants the sweetness of His company when one of His servants wanders without a home, and also shows His presence and control and care by opening many homes.

Zaky decided that his Egyptian tailor must make me a suit. Silently wondering what the fit would be like I pointed out that the one I had was quite good and that I had another for use in England. But he was not to be turned aside. When the book of patterns came, it was interesting that it was from Huddersfield. I looked through it without giving special attention to the qualities, and selected a cloth merely because of its colour. The tailor smiled and remarked it was the most expensive cloth in the book. When I showed the suit to a tailor in England he commended the work, turned back the collar, pointed out the machining that had been done, and said, "You won't get a collar made like that in England." That suit was made fifteen years ago and is still (1950) being worn. It is mentioned below.

It was now very hot and I left Aswan on Saturday, April 6, 1935, visited several places on the way north, and reached Haifa on the 18th. The work had developed. Formerly ministry in the assemblies had perforce been interpreted twice, for English, Arabic, and Turkish were required that all might profit. Thus a talk lasting fifteen minutes occupied another half hour for interpretation, with the consequence that very little food and instruction could be imparted. But now a separate meeting of Armenians had come into being.

In May I visited Tel Aviv, Jaffa, and Jerusalem. In the last place contact was renewed with a young Egyptian who had been with us on the boat in 1927. Able and earnest, he gave his life to the gospel, but his faith did not rise to walking with the Lord in direct dependence upon Him for guidance and supplies. He had therefore moved from Mission to Mission. The subject came up again, and to encourage him in God I said: "You see this suit I am wearing." "Yes; I said to my wife, 'There's Mr. Lang dressed like a king'." This made me glad that I had mentioned the matter, so that a misconception could be removed which could have injured him in soul and also have left in his heart a barrier against me. I added: "It was given to me by an Egyptian brother." He was amazed; almost incredulous: and I pressed upon him that God has altogether unlikely servants and measures for helping those who trust in Him.

May 14, 1935, to June 4 was spent in Haifa. On the last date I left by sea and on the 6th reached Piraeus, the port for Athens, and had four happy days with Mr. and Mrs. Willey at Old Phaleron. This gave more time for seeing Athens. The night of the 10th was spent at Salonica (Thessalonica). The journey the next day gave sight of the upper country of Greece, with Mount Olympus in the distance. Five days were spent at Belgrade with Mr. and Mrs. J. W. Wiles.

June 17 to 27 were passed at Budapest, and from the 28th to July 8, I was with my kind friend near Zürich. On the last date I travelled from Zürich, via Basle and Cologne to Wiedenest in Germany. At the German frontier the money control officer asked if I wished a declaration of what money I was bringing in. It was only the same amount that I should be permitted to take out. I said it was not necessary. His voice betrayed slight surprise, but he passed on. He might have been suspicious had a British traveller told him he was carrying only two shillings and sixpence. My wife and daughter were awaiting me at Wiedenest. After a happy week together with our dear friends there we left on July 17, 1935, and were at Walsham-le-Willows on the 19th.

The next two and three quarter years were spent travelling about England, with periods at home. On April 25, 1938, I left for some days in Holland and some weeks in Germany, including a brief visit in north Switzerland. There was a specific purpose for this tour of nine weeks.

In 1937 the Nazi rulers had suppressed the meetings of the Exclusive Brethren and had intimated that they would suppress the Open Brethren unless the two sections agreed to combine and to form such an Association as the police authorities would sanction. This compelled the Exclusives to face the question whether the opposition of ninety years to Open Brethren was warranted by the Word of God. After much heart-searching and conference the great majority decided that the separation ought never to have existed, and perhaps 30,000 joined the Open Brethren in Christian fellowship.

The object of my visit in 1938 was to form an opinion as to how far the Exclusives had changed their opinion and practice with intelligence and conviction, or was it only under State pressure and threat? Visits were paid to many centres and I formed the judgment that in general their change was one of mind and heart. This was confirmed by the fact that, after the Nazi rule was past, and full freedom of action returned, it was only a minority who went back to the Exclusive position, perhaps twenty-five per cent, as I was told in 1950. In view of the tenacity and long period of the Exclusive rejection of Open Brethren we could but exclaim: "What hath God wrought!" For this enlargement of heart and testimony one could give thanks, but I was and am wholly opposed to the organized union which was formed to satisfy the police. In principle and detail it is contrary to the New Testament and a denial of the sole right of the Son of God to order the house of God. His Word sanctions no visible association of Christians other than the local church in each separate place.

By a law of our mind if truth is faced and refused we become the more fixed in any error that holds us. On my former visit to Zürich the large Exclusive meeting allowed me to partake at the Lord's table. They were then accustomed to permit this to a visiting Open Brother as to any other accredited Christian not in their immediate circle. But the defection of the majority of the German Exclusives alarmed and hardened their former associates in adjacent lands, and in 1938 I was denied fellowship at Zürich. If their former practice was godly their latter refusal was ungodly. Let the love of God decide the issue.

In 1939 the flood of Satanic malice and human folly burst all bounds in the war. When the raging tide subsided in 1945 a British official in Germany paid an early visit to our friends in Wiedenest. The message they sent by him was that all through the war their *love had never wavered!* Thus does the love of God triumph in human hearts over the devilish national hatreds of men. Nor is such divine love the exceptional attainment of a few advanced saints. It was early in His ministry that the Lord said to His yet immature followers: "Love your enemies. . . that ye may be sons of your Father who is in heaven" (Matt. 5:43-48). One who does not love his enemy (yes, really *love* him, "not in word, neither with the tongue, but in deed and in truth" 1 John 3:18) may conceivably be a *child* of God by new birth, but he is not yet a *son* of the Father in heaven, for He, just because He is of heaven, is far above the racial and national animosities of earth and loves all men alike, including His enemies. "God commendeth His own love towards us, in that, while we were yet sinners, Christ died for us" (Rom. 5:8). He whose heart knows the power of that heavenly love is moved no more by the national distinctions of earth: he loves all his fellow-men, and most especially all fellowmembers of the heavenly family whatever their race or nation. Since he is of heaven, earth's distinctions cease to move him.

From about the year 1940 it became clear to me that "The Woodlands" was proving too great a tax upon us each, especially its gardens. For five years I prayed and inquired, but nowhere in extensive travel did even the slightest sign of a place come before me. But when God's time comes God's hand works. When I was in Bournemouth for meetings in November 1944 a friend telephoned to me, saying that his mother and he were about to sell the house at Wimborne where she had lived, but that, if it would suit me, they would like to rent it to me. To rent a house at all was almost unheard of, and the rent proposed was not half the sum that could be reasonably charged. So in pure Christian affection, as a service to the Lord we all loved, they forwent an advantageous sale at a high price and gave us the benefit of a small modern house, very pleasantly placed, where these pages are being penned. It would be too long a story to narrate the ordering by God of the many details of the removal. He saw to it all, giving full proof that the change was of Him. While the house was still empty I worked there for some six weeks (passing the nights with friends a few miles off), doing repairs indoors and getting the garden into order. This was in January and February 1945. Once again the absence of brain tax, with the manual labour, mostly out of doors, and the entire freedom from conversation all day long, greatly renewed my energies of mind and body. We moved in on March 29, 1945.

In 1947 access was gained to a camp of German prisoners about half a mile away. I paid a weekly visit; some came to our house, some to the hall. A few were converted to God.

In this year a notable event occurred, illustrating how God loves to do the unlikely. Money was beginning to get scarcer in England, while prices had commenced to rise. Twenty years earlier I had become intimate with a Christian (not British) in the Near East. He was then not too well off and was glad that I paid for my board when his guest. In July 1947 he wrote that he and his wife had money of the Lord on hand and they wished me to distribute it for them. The sum sent was £1,000. Very shortly afterwards his land left the sterling area, and the sum could not have been sent. Thus it came to pass in the good ordering of God that when, in the usual course, less money would have been in my hands I, a poor man, had the joy of helping the needy, as well as fellow-workers in many lands, more liberally than ever in my life.

This offers occasion to consider Psalm 118:8,9:

> *It is better to trust in Jehovah*
> *Than to put confidence in man,*
> *It is better to trust in Jehovah*
> *Than to put confidence in princes.*

Few question this as to things eternal; few accept it as to things temporal. Few will credit that it is actually *better* to trust God as to daily supplies than to have a regular income from man. Yet George Müller, with no visible or humanly guaranteed resources, and with his immense burden of feeding, clothing, and otherwise caring for 2,000 orphans, could say, "I am a happy old man, a very happy old man!" And when he was asked if he had ever thought of creating a reserve fund to meet possible emergencies, he replied that it would be the greatest possible folly, for his heavenly Father would say, "George Müller, you bring out those reserves before I give you anything more." How, then, is it that a Christian father or mother can feel overwhelmed by the burden of a few children?

With the rest of folk I have passed through two World Wars and their economic conditions, and have been able to entertain some thousand or so guests, as well as to travel in many lands, and to publish many books. Had I been dependent on man for a fixed salary or a retiring pension, or upon income from small investments, expansion of income would have been unlikely, or at least inadequate to meet rising costs, and thus curtailment of outlay probable. But being called to rely literally on the promises of God, and accepting increased responsibilities as and when given by Him, I could undertake increased expense without sense of risk or burden, the Lord of all being responsible to honour His guarantees. Therefore it is *better* to trust in the Lord than in man when one is honoured by the call to this line of life, or whenever in ordinary walks the alternative offers.

It is to their own loss that children of God prefer to depend upon "princes", as upon an insurance company, or upon State insurance, or Government education grants or old age pensions, rather than to trust the living God, as did their Christian forbears before these sources of supply existed. It is to their own loss that believers who have it in their power to help fellow-believers, even if to only a small degree, will suffer their brethren and sisters in Christ to go to the world for help, fearing that they themselves may suffer hardship by helping them. It is a sorry state of heart when a member of the family of God feels secretly thankful that the State should take off him the privilege of succouring the needy. It is to the Christian's real loss when he lays up treasure on earth thinking thus to safeguard the future. Christ distinctly forbade His followers to do this, because He wished them to learn the blessed fact that it is *better* to trust in God their Father (Matt. 6:19). The magnificent promises and prospects that follow this verse to the end of the chapter, can be enjoyed by those only who obey the introductory injunction quoted.

Long before I was called out of secular business, and separated unto the gospel, I had been taught by the love of God to find happiness in keeping my personal expenditure low and using for others the whole surplus. For thirty years I have not issued circular letters as to journeys or other undertakings, and I have thus proved the thorough soundness of George Müller's resolve that he would not knock at man's door until he should find his heavenly Father's door locked against him. That was a valid and prevailing argument by Catherine of Siena, that she was prepared to be the second to whom God should fail to keep His word but she was not willing to be the first.

I know not what severe tests of faith, or real hardships, the good will of God my Father may have in store for me ere life shall close; it is simple to leave this to His love: but it is fact that, throughout these later years, in which those who have to trust in men or in princes find life more and more difficult, my own income has expanded beyond the increasing needs. The Lord has said, "Give and it shall be given unto you... for with what measure ye mete it shall be measured to you again" (Luke 6:38); and "seek ye first the kingdom of God and His righteousness, and all these [earthly] things shall be added unto you" (Mat. 6:33). Whoso will follow these directions shall find that it is indeed *better* to trust in the Lord than in men or princes; whereas whoever will live on worldly principles must carry the same strain and care as does the man of the world.

It is, therefore, a mistake to suppose that this path of dependence and subjection is always attended with more troubles than those of a self-ordered life. It is true that in seasons of general persecution the church of God is to expect exceptional difficulties and hardships, and the aggressive evangelist also may meet Pauline trials, such as a soldier on service expects; but I am persuaded that in general faithful children of God do not have heavier burdens than others. But even when they do have that experience they secure the comfortable assurance that, for those who love God and therefore keep His commandments, all things work together for good (Rom. 8: 28). This enables them to endure patiently and in hope, until trial has wrought out its certain and intended benefits.

CHAPTER 16

Conclusion

A life so long and varied would yield more that would be interesting and instructive, but enough has been written to illustrate and enforce the one theme of this book, that God does really order human life, as really now as in ancient times, and with the same unique advantages this ensures.

This Divine ordering begins before one's birth, and covers ancestry, home life, and business as certainly as what we regard as more distinctly spiritual affairs. It begins betimes to use parental or other instruction of children in the truth; it effects the new birth; produces personal sanctification; engages the heart's affections with the Son of God; incites to service to Him and equips and empowers for the same.

This care and control by God extends to all times and places, so that "if I take the wings of the morning and dwell in the uttermost parts of the sea, even there shall Thy hand lead me and Thy right hand shall hold me" (Ps. 139:9, 10). Hence arises the safety of going to remote places in unknown lands, so long as this is done at the command and leading of God. No such guarantee attends a man's own schemes or the plans of human organizations.

Nor is God's sovereignty exercised over His own servants only; but rather in their interest He makes all persons, creatures, and events to serve their good and His purposes. For the Father has appointed the Son to be Head over all things for the welfare of the church, because it is the members of this community that are to Him a body, through which He, being in heaven, operates on earth (Eph. 1:22, 23).

But this relationship of Head and members necessarily creates conditions for the exercise of the control and energy of the Head. All *wisdom* is found in the Head; no member has any in itself. All *right* and all *skill* to direct are in the Head; no member has any; the foot does not plan its course nor the hand its work. All *energy* is generated in and distributed from the Head: "apart from Me ye can do *nothing*" (John 15:5). Failure to own this truth in practice and in detail is a chief cause why many Christians experience so little of the control and care of God, and why so very much of their religious activity, though sincere and often feverish, is fruitless.

The only right relation between the Lord and His people was declared by Peter when he described the three years of intercourse between Christ and the apostles in the words, "the Lord Jesus went in and went out *over* us" (Acts 1:21;

R.V. mgn. *eph' hemas*). The Gospels illustrate this fully. The Lord was Teacher,[1] the apostles were learners, disciples: He was Leader, they were followers: He commanded, they obeyed: He ever took the initiative, they co-operated.

This is all-important. On the occasions when the disciples took the initiative they blundered. For example:

Luke 9:49, 50: "we forbade him... Jesus said, Forbid not."

Luke 9:54, 55: "wilt Thou that we bid fire to come down from heaven and consume them? But He rebuked them."

Mark 8:32, 33: "Peter began to rebuke Him.... But He rebuked Peter."

Mark 9:5-8: "let us make three tabernacles... he knew not what to answer. .. they saw no one any more, save Jesus."

Luke 22:50, 51: "one of them smote the servant of the high priest... Jesus healed him."

Too little Christian living and far too little Christian service are ordered with due regard to this principle of discipleship, with the painful consequence of much disorder in life and little unction on vast efforts. In the home, the business, the church, and the gospel it is dreadfully usual for Christians to make their own arrangements on their own initiative and by their own wisdom, and then they ask the Lord to add His blessing. But the Lord of glory is not our lackey to further our plan but our LORD to command us for the furtherance of His plan, and for this we must wait His initiative, His directions, His prior activity: "when thou hearest the sound of marching in the tops of the mulberry trees, *then* thou shalt bestir thyself, for *then* is Jehovah gone out *before* thee" (2 Sam. 5:24). We may bestir ourselves vigorously before God has gone forth, but defeat will attend.

He who is ready to follow this path resolutely, and so to secure the perfect ordering of his affairs by God, will say at last with David (the soldier who was thus ready to wait for Divine guidance, and not to act on his own experience as a trained commander), "As for God, His way is perfect.... And He maketh my way perfect" (Ps. 18:30-32). Let the serious of heart study the matter in the Acts of the Apostles and their Epistles, where is exhibited the blessed activity of God in human lives, together with the readiness of believers to be guided. The former book would be more accurately entitled "The Acts of the Holy Spirit."

It is my especial wish and prayer that this account of the Lord's gracious ways with myself may encourage my brothers and sisters in Christ to give to God their Father His full rightful place as the sole Orderer of life, to His praise and their own good. And in particular I long that my fellow-preachers of the Word should commit their service to His direct ordering, and abandon

---

[1] In nearly every place where English Versions have "Master" the right translation is "Teacher."

the injurious practice of regularly mortgaging the future by booking ahead, unless, of course, by unmistakable Divine guidance. How can one be a *messenger* unless he waits every time for both the message and the time and the persons to whom to deliver it? The general habit of taking time and gifts out of the actual control of the Head of the church has plainly forfeited His unction to a lamentable degree. In this churches and preachers have concurred, incurring general loss and weakness.

In periods of public disorder, or of persecution, man's schemes break down and the Lord recovers His rights; therefore such periods prove times of spiritual enrichment. Or in seasons of exceptional activity by the Spirit of God, which we term Revivals, He sets human routine on one side, reasserts the sovereignty of the Head, and grants corresponding blessing. Presently His servants (!) reassert their own ideas and preferences, the Spirit is grieved, formality is resumed and deadness returns.

But any individual servant who will allow his Lord to control will be guided and used continuously in that line of service, and to that degree which the Lord sees fit. God has not allowed me to have to mourn any period of ineffective service. I would, indeed, that I had been such as He could have used a hundredfold more, but He graciously cheers my closing days by news of blessing given on His truth twenty, thirty, even forty years ago, as well as recently. And the harvest will certainly be vaster than the first-fruits. It is glorious to serve in the only kingdom that cannot be shaken. Nor have I been one of those rare workers who have lived in the limelight, moving vast crowds. My life is an example of an encouragement to the large number who serve Christ in quieter ways, unnoticed by the world or the church, not talked about in religious journals, but recorded in heaven.

The mightiest movement of God the earth will ever see lies in the future. The Spirit will be poured out upon the Jewish people, and then upon all flesh. But this will be contingent upon the Lord Jesus, at His return to the earth, being accorded His rightful place as Lord of all. The principles of this gracious visitation are set before Israel in Isaiah 58, for their humble reception.

This chapter pictures a national condition marked by religious zeal and formality, all secretly directed by self-pleasing. They seek God daily, maintain the forms of worship, and delight to know God's ways and ordinances (ver. 2). They fast, walk with downcast mien, and sit in sackcloth and ashes. Yet to all this serious external piety God makes no response, but sternly reproves their transgressions and sins which wholly vitiate their professions and ceremonies.

But when they shall have put away unrighteous conduct, and shall, in particular, have reinstated the sabbath as the day for a joyful honouring of the rights of God, instead of its being a day of leisure for their own pleasures, then light shall disperse their darkness, as morning dispels the night; their healing shall spring forth speedily; and "thou shalt be like a watered garden, and like a spring of water, whose waters fail not" (ver. 8, 11). Prayer will be answered (ver. 9), continual guidance will be given (ver. 11), ruins will be restored (ver. 12), God will be their joy, victory and authority will be secured, and the rich portion guaranteed by oath to Jacob will be assured (ver. 14).

Now it is to be observed that it was from verse 11 above quoted, that the Lord drew His promise that "He that believeth in Me, as the scripture hath said, out of his innermost being shall flow rivers of living water. But this spake He of the Spirit, which they that believed on Him were to receive" (John 7:38, 39). Thus the *spiritual* element of the promised reviving and restoration is already available to faith, though the external earthly privileges are deferred until the return of the Lord to the earth. He is already here in the Spirit, and the blessings in the spirit may be now enjoyed: He will later return to the earth in visible glory, and then the visible and earthly prosperity will become available to faith and obedience.

But now, as then, the conditions are the same and are inexorable. "Believing in Christ" is simply the New Testament expression to cover all that which will be involved for Israel in that coming day. They will acknowledge Him as their Lord and God, will therefore cease from every act or course which does not accord with His sovereign rights, and will study in all things to please Him. Thus they will become morally fitted for the high privileges they will then enjoy and the noble service they will render to God and the nations.

It is thus with us today. Believing in Christ means that we sincerely own that He is what He is, the Son of God, and therefore sanctify Him in the heart as LORD (1 Pet. 3:15). This produces deep heart-searching, a sensitive conscience, a putting away of all known sin, a humble, resolute carrying out of His commands, a trembling at His word, a genuine and detailed testing of all acts and practices so as to secure conformity to His will. It is in the measure that the believer is sincere and practical and thorough in this that light is granted, the heart is filled with the Spirit, and the living waters overflow to the refreshment of others. For God gives His Spirit to them that obey Him (Acts 5:32); that is, to those who do truly purpose to give to Christ the position which God has given Him, those who in reality "crown Him LORD of *all.*"

What has been narrated from my own experience of God's grace and guidance will serve its intended purposes only if it stimulate and strengthen others to the Caleb life of following the Lord wholly. Not, indeed, that I have attained or am already made perfect in this life. I am deeply conscious of the imperfection that has retarded progress and usefulness.

I stand upon His merit,
I know no other stand,
And least *where glory dwelleth,*
In Immanuel's land.

Yet I know well that in my teens God showed me His Son as the only worthy Object for whom to live. He thus caused me to loathe myself and my sins, and count Christ alone as my legal righteousness and actual holiness.

By this vision of Christ I was granted the further mighty, saving favour of regarding the present world system of human life, from which Christ is excluded and over which Satan is Prince, as being wholly without God, as having been sentenced to destruction, as a bankrupt business is sentenced by the court to be wound up, and as being therefore thoroughly unworthy that one should sink in it time, powers, and possessions (1 John 2:15-17). Thus, by the will of God the Father, the Son "rescued me out of this present evil age" (Gal. 1:4), since when Christ, as the Centre and Sovereign of the eternal kingdom, has been ever the Object of my devotion, the all-embracing, all-satisfying Saviour and Lord. To have personal acquaintance with Him, and with His Father revealed in Him, is the only true life, the eternal life, for "he that doeth the will of God abideth for ever," because that holy and perfect will abideth for ever (1 John 2:17). Only that which is ordered by God can fit into the order of His eternal kingdom. All else is death, not life.

As I review the way the Lord has led—a way of grace to one wholly unworthy, marked on His side by the faithful fulfilment of every good thing He has promised, what can I say? My narrative commenced with the opening verses of Addison's well-known hymn, it shall close with the last verse:

Through all eternity to Thee
A joyful song I'll raise;
But, oh, eternity's too short
To utter all Thy praise.

Thus has begun in the shadows of time the song of praise which shall never cease in the glories of eternity:
TO THE ONLY WISE GOD, THROUGH JESUS CHRIST, BE THE GLORY FOR EVER (Rom. 16:27).

Epilogue

Mr. Lang spent October, 1948, at Wiedenest, with a few days in Holland. July and August, 1950, were also spent at Wiedenest; during these two months he was busily engaged in revising with Mr. and Mrs. Erich Sauer the whole English translation of Mr. Sauer's *The Dawn of World Redemption* and *The Triumph of the Crucified*, and in discussing the many points of theological interpretation raised in these two volumes. Mr. Lang's courage in undertaking to translate German theological works is the more noteworthy in a man who left school before his fourteenth birthday and had no formal linguistic training.

In the summer and autumn of 1953 he made his last extended journey through various parts of Great Britain, going as far north as Aberdeen, where he attended the wedding of George Patterson of Tibet and Dr. Margaret Ingram of India. On his return from this journey his medical advisers warned him that for the future he must be very careful, and the last five years of his life were years of increasing weakness and pain. His eightieth birthday (November 20, 1954) was an occasion of much joy to him as he received tributes of love and esteem from a host of friends, including not a few who in earlier days had engaged in controversy with him.

His intellectual powers remained unabated throughout these years, and as far as strength permitted he gave himself assiduously to written ministry. Perhaps his finest expository work, *Pictures and Parables*, appeared in 1955, and it was through his initiative that Johannes Warns' great work on *Baptism* was published in its English version in 1957. In May 1953 there was issued under his editorship the first number of *The Disciple*, "a periodical for the Lord's people, designed to promote intelligent devotion to Him and His interests." Twenty-two numbers in all appeared, the publication of the last number coinciding with his death. The regular production of this periodical was no mean achievement for a man of his years, and the quality of his own contributions to it gives ample proof that his spiritual bow abode in strength to the end. These contributions illustrate his aptitude for historical research, his skill as an accurate expositor of Holy Writ, and his passion for the promotion of holy living, first in himself and then in his fellow-Christians. At the same time he maintained a worldwide correspondence, of great spiritual profit to those who kept in touch with him thus. His personal influence on many who occupy a strategic position in evangelical life today, especially in the assemblies of Open

Brethren, has been greater than is commonly realized, for it was exercised mainly through private correspondence and conversation.

Towards the end of 1957 his frail health was gravely weakened by pulmonary thrombosis; although he recovered in measure from this, he knew that his days on earth were numbered. "Remember me still," he wrote in December of that year, "a frail old warrior, ready to fold his cloak around him and go to sleep." And then a characteristic exhortation: "The Lord make you as bold as you are discreet."

He died peacefully at his home in Wimborne on October 20, 1958, and his mortal remains were laid to rest four days later. At the memorial service in Mount Hall, Poole, were sung by his own choice some of Mrs. Cousins' well-known stanzas, including the lines which he so repeatedly emphasized:

> *I stand upon His merit,*
> *I know no other stand,*
> And least *where glory dwelleth,*
> *In Immanuel's land.*

So he takes his secure place in the ranks of those whom we are bidden to bear in mind: "Remember your guides, who spoke to you the word of God; consider the outcome of their life, and imitate their faith" (Heb. 13: 7).

F. F. B.

Principal Writings of G. H. Lang

Unanimity : The Divine Method of Church Government (Bristol, 1900).

The Sinner's Future (Bristol, 1902.).

Prayer Focused and Fighting (Ootacamund, India, 1909; latest edition, 1948).

Controlling the Situation (London, 1910; later incorporated in *Prayer Focused and Fighting*).

The Modern Gift of Tongues: Whence is it? (London, 1913).

God's Plan, Christ's Sufferings and the Spirit's Power (Birmingham, 1917).

Praying is Working (Birmingham, 1918; 5th edition, 1949)

The Raptures and the Tribulation (Weston-super-Mare, 1918).

Affiliation: A Study in Church Life and Order, with Special Reference to Denominational Federating (London, 1921).

Departure: A Warning and an Appeal addressed by one of themselves mainly to Christians known as Open Brethren (London, 192.5).

The Churches of God (London, 1928; new, revised and enlarged edition, 1959).

The Local Assembly: Some Essential Differences between Open and Exclusive Brethren considered Scripturally and Historically (Walsham-le-Willows, 1929; 5th edition, 1955).

The First Resurrection (Walsham-le-Willows, 1931).

The Gospel of the Kingdom: The Message of its Five Chief Preachers (London, 1933; 3rd edition, 1957).

Ideals and Realities (London, 1934).

The Clean Heart (London, 1935).

The Christian Relation to the State and to War (Walsham-le-Willows, 1936; 2nd edition, 1937; 3rd edition, Wimborne, 1955.)

Firstborn Sons: Their Rights and Risks (London, 1936; znd edition, 1943)

The Rights of the Holy Spirit in the House of God (Walsham-le-Willows, 1938).

Anthony Norris Groves (London, 1939; znd edition, 1949).

The History and Diaries of an Indian Christian (London, 1939).

The New Birth (Birmingham, 1918; 3rd edition, 1946).

The Histories and Prophecies of Daniel (London, 1940; 4th edition, 1950).

Firstfrsits and Harvest (London, 1940).

Church Federation (London, 1942.; 2nd edition, 1955. Replacing *Affiliation*, 1921).

Past, Present and Future: Guidance and Warnings for Followers of the Lamb (Walsham-le-Willows, 1943).

The King and Other Verses (Walsham-le-Willows, 1943).

The Revelation of Jesus Christ: Select Studies (London, 1945).
Balanced Christianity (Wimborne, 1946).
Edmund Hamer Broadbent: Saint and Pioneer (London, 1946).
The Unequal Yoke: Divine Directions for Difficult Situations (Wimborne, 1947)'
Divine Guidance (Wimborne, 1947).
World Chaos: Its Root and Remedy (London, 1948).
Coming Events: An Outline of Bible Prophecy (Wimborne, 1949).
The Epistle to the Hebrews (London, 1951).
Israel's National Future: The Testimony of the Word of God (London, 1951).
God at Work on His Own Lines (Wimborne, 1952.).
Pictures and Parables: Studies in the Parabolic Teaching of Holy Scripture (London, 1955).
The Earlier Years of the Modern Tongues Movement (London, 1958).
The Last Assize (London, 1958).
Contributions to *The Disciple* (edited by G. H. Lang):
"Inquire of the Former Age", May 1953, pp. 13-22.; Oct. 1953, pp. 13-2.2.; Jan. 1954, pp. 51-66.
"Baptism", May 1953, pp. 23-29.
"The Lord's Supper", Oct. 1953, pp. 23-36.
"Selective Rapture and Resurrection in Relation to the Eternal Security of the Regenerate", Jan. 1954, pp. 73-80.
"Important Texts", April 1954, pp. 92-100; June 1954, pp. 151-153; Oct. 1954, pp. 188-190; Jan. 1955, pp. 3-4; April 1955, pp. 73-76; July 1955, pp. 117-119; Oct. 1955, pp. 155-158; Jan. 1956, pp. 34-37; April 1956, pp. 76-83; July 1956, pp. 122.-125; Jan. 1957, pp. 191-205; April 1957, pp. 239-243; July 1957, pp. 294-299; Oct. 1957, pp. 333-339; Jan. 1958, pp. 21-24; April 1958, pp. 85-93.
"Bible Schools", April 1954, pp. 101-103.
"George Müller and R. C. Chapman", April 1954, pp. 112.-122.
"The Personal Indwelling of the Holy Spirit", June 1954, pp. 123-138.
"Pages from an Ordered Life", June 1954, pp. 158-163; Oct. 1954, pp. 190-197; Jan. 1955, pp. 17-24; April 1955, pp. 78-84; July 1955, pp. 121-127; Oct. 1955, pp. 158-167; Jan. 1956, pp. 38-44; April 1956, pp. 84-95; July 1956, pp. 125-135; Oct. 1956, pp. 171-178; Jan. 1957, pp. 217-222.; April 1957, pp. 250-262.; July 1957, pp. 299-306; Oct. 1957, pp. 345-351; Jan. 1958, pp. 43-54; April 1958, pp. 93-102; July 1958, pp. 140-147; Oct. 1958, pp. 189-201.
"Divorce and Re-marriage", Oct. 1954, pp. 174-186.
"Atoning Blood: What it does and what it does not do", Jan. 1955, pp. 24-42; April 1955, pp. 47-67; July 1955, pp. 93-111.
"What Took Place at the Lord's Supper", Oct. 1955, pp. 140-148.

"The Sabbath", Jan. 1956, pp. 5-2.1; April 1956, pp. 47-61.

"Walking by Faith", April 1956, pp. 66-69.

"The Danger of the Subjective Test", July 1956, pp. 99-115; Oct. 1956, pp. 139-157.

"Wandering Thoughts", Oct. 1956, pp. 165-170.

" The Self-Limitation of Jesus Christ, the Son of God", Jan. 1957, pp. 181-191.

"Solitude", April 1957, pp. 225-235.

"Mysterious Ways", April 1957, pp. 245-250.

"Egypt in Prophecy", July 1957, pp. 265-282.

"British-Israelism", July 1957, pp. 2.82.-2.93; Oct. 1957, pp. 319-327.

"George Bowen of Bombay", Oct. 1957, pp. 327-333.

"Abiathar, High Priest", Oct. 1957, pp. 343-345.

"John Wooldridge, Evangelist", Jan. 1958, pp. 30-43.

"Take Heed: Care Needed in Applying Prophetic Scripture", April 1958, pp. 76-84; July 1958, pp. 121-133.

"Death in the Pot", Oct. 1958, pp. 169-178 .

Contributions to *The Evangelical Quarterly* (edited by F. F. Bruce):

"An Ancient Egyptian Prayer", July 1950, pp. 188-204.

"An Ancient Egyptian Queen", Oct.-Dec. 1957. pp. 206-217.

"God's Covenants are Conditional", April-June 1958, pp. 86-97.

"Melchizedek", Jan.-March 1959, pp. 21-31.

The Patient to be Treated: What is he? (The Fellowship Chronicle of the Missionary School of Medicine, 1938).

Unpublished MS: Prevailing to Escape.

Edited by G. H. Lang:

G. H. Pember, *The Great Prophecies of the Centuries concerning Israel, the Gentiles and the Church of God* (London, 1941).

G. H. Pember, *Mystery Babylon the Great and the Mysteries and Catholicism* (London, 1941).

G. H. Pember, *Earth's Earliest Ages* (15th edition, Walsham-le-Willows, 1942.).

Translated by G. H. Lang:

E. Sauer, *The Dawn of World Redemption* (London, 1951).

E. Sauer, *The Triumph of the Crucified* (London, 1951).

E. Sauer, *From Eterniry to Eternity* (London, 1954).

E. Sauer, *In The Arena of Faith* (in collaboration with Dr. and Mrs. Wilder Smith, London, 1955).

J. Warns, *Baptism* (London, 1957).

Index

10089230R00133

Made in the USA
San Bernardino, CA
04 April 2014